MELODY AND THE LYRIC

MANUSCRIPT OF SONG BY NATHANIEL GILES, MASTER OF CHAPEL ROYAL, IN THE LIBRARY OF CHRIST CHURCH, OXFORD. (See p. 130.)

MELODY AND THE LYRIC

FROM CHAUCER TO THE CAVALIERS

By

JOHN MURRAY GIBBON

WITH 200
MUSICAL ILLUSTRATIONS

HASKELL HOUSE
Publishers of Scholarly Books
NEW YORK
1964

published by

HASKELL HOUSE

Publishers of Scholarly Books

30 East 10th Street • New York, N. Y. 10003

Library of Congress Catalog Card Number: 65-15882

DEDICATED
TO THE MEMORY OF
WILLIAM CHAPPELL

INTRODUCTION

We are the music makers,
And we are the dreamers of dreams,
Wandering by lone sea-breakers
And sitting by desolate streams,
World-losers and world-forsakers
On whom the pale moon gleams:
Yet we are the movers and shakers
Of the world for ever, it seems.

ARTHUR W. O'SHAUGHNESSY.

THE identification of poetry with music is so much an axiom with the literary critic that he interchanges the words "poem" and "song," and "poet" and "singer" as if they were synonyms. The modern poet himself does not object. He rather likes to be thought of as a sort of troubadour, wandering in spirit, if not in body, through romantic landscapes, rivalling the lark, the thrush, and the nightingale, in his melodious raptures, and eventually being buried to Chopin's "Funeral March" in the most desirable, though somewhat overcrowded, corner of Westminster Abbey. Although as a rule he confesses to ignorance of anything but verbal music, he considers himself certainly in the Meistersinger class.

There is a certain looseness in this use of language, for the musical synonym for "poet" should not be "singer," but "composer"; but then the word "composer" has a prosaic sound, suggesting midnight oil, not the spontaneous inspiration which the poet likes to have associated with his lyrics.

When one investigates this claim of the modern poet to be a "maker of music," one finds it too seldom justified. Poetry and music, so far as English literature is concerned, more or less parted company at the end of the seventeenth century, and if any connection remains, that is due rather to the English musician than to the English poet.

Between the poetry of Chaucer and the lyrics of the Elizabethans there has been thought to be a lyrical desert of a century and a half, in the sands of which only the scholar has been inclined to linger. The printed poems of Gower, Lydgate, and the other northern followers of Chaucer need a vast amount of culling to yield an adequate bouquet. In deference to the standard histories, a certain homage is customary to the memory of Sir Thomas Wyatt and the Earl of Surrey; but lyric poetry

vii

for most of us began with Sir Philip Sidney and John Lyly, followed immediately by the almost tropic luxuriance of Shakespeare and his contemporaries. Does the English lyric, as one might think from Palgrave's *Golden Treasury*, begin with the sixteenth century?

The reason for the neglect of so much pre-Elizabethan poetry lies in the very nature of the lyric, which might be called amphibious—living half in words and half in music. Music is an element in which the literary critic can seldom swim, and therefore he notices the amphibian only when he finds it high and dry in a book. And printed books were comparatively rare before Elizabeth's reign.

Considered without relations to the music of its time, the lyric of Medieval and Tudor England can be but half understood. Indeed, until the carols and songs of that time had been deciphered from neglected manuscripts, the richness of that lyrical output would have been entirely forgotten.

Until the execution of Charles I, it was the recognized qualification for any man of breeding to be able to sing his part in a madrigal or trio at sight. Music, moreover, was an art to which poetry was a willing handmaid. The foremost Tudor and Stuart poets were willing to write verses for a ditty and make no complaint if their names were not published with the music. Milton, Herrick, Suckling, Carew, and Waller seem to have worked in ready and yet anonymous partnership with the composer Henry Lawes. In certain cases the tunes with which they were familiar were tunes to which they wrote their verse.

To bring this home, I have endeavoured to trace the musical knowledge and musical acquaintances of the poets from the time of Chaucer to the time of the Cavaliers, and to discover where possible the melodies they knew and may have had in mind when writing their lyrics. This field of research has been little exploited except in the case of Shakespeare, but the prospects surely deserve more thorough development. It has surprised me to find myself apparently a pioneer in suggesting a musical background for *Piers Plowman*, and in tracing the influence of Huguenot psalm-tunes on the metres of Sir Philip Sidney and Ben Jonson. The influence of dance tunes on English lyrical metres is apparently unknown to most of the authors of the innumerable volumes on English metrics. The tunes running in Herrick's head when he wrote his *Ceremonies for Christmas* or *The Cobbler's Catch* do not seem to have interested the annotators, and the lovely melody to which George Wither wrote his equally lovely "Sleep, baby, sleep, what ails my dear?" is here, apparently, for the first time identified. A small library of music books and anthologies has had to be collated to illustrate the extent to which Henry Lawes collaborated with the poets of King Charles's time.

For the convenience of those who desire to pursue this line of study, the first known records of the melodies are supplemented with references to recent reprints more readily accessible. Through the convenient invention of the photostat, it is possible nowadays for those who live even in so new a country as Canada to peruse in facsimile medieval scripts— otherwise the present volume would never have seen the light.

In conclusion, the author wishes to pay tribute to the scholarship of that priceless history of early English melodies, William Chappell's *Popular Music of the Olden Time*. He also desires to make special acknowledgment to Fortunat Champagne, master of the choir in the Basilica at Ottawa, for his advice on the Gregorian melodies referred to in the earlier chapters, and for his drawing of the music which adorns these pages.

J. M. G.

1930.

CONTENTS

PAGE

INTRODUCTION vii

CHAPTER I I
Influence of Guillaume de Machault—Chaucer and his knowledge of music—The White Paternoster.

CHAPTER II 10
Langland, the chanting priest—Psalter tunes—St. Francis—The Franciscan poet friars—Early English carols written by both monks and minstrels—Old ballads: "Robin Hood," "Chevy Chase."

CHAPTER III 25
Tudor Period—Skelton—Henry VIII—William Cornysshe—Gray—"Pastime with Good Company"—Anne Boleyn—Wyatt—Surrey.

CHAPTER IV 38
Edward VI—Translations of the Psalms by Clément Marot, and Sternhold and Hopkins—Sidney—Wedderburn—Martin Luther's hymns—Day's psalter—Este's psalter—William Byrd.

CHAPTER V 44
Ballads and ballad tunes—Anthony Munday—Thomas Deloney—Ballad tunes arranged for virginals by Byrd and Bull—"Fortune My Foe"—Robin Hood ballads.

CHAPTER VI 52
Ballads sung to dance tunes ("Sellinger's Round" and "Green Sleeves")—Dances mentioned in Shakespeare—Words of lyrics fitted to dance rhythms—Popularity of dancing in Tudor times—Dance songs in masques—A Saraband rhythm—Dance tunes—"Robin lend to me thy bow."

CHAPTER VII 68
Queen Elizabeth and music—Sir Philip Sidney—Sidney and the Huguenot Psalter compared—William Byrd.

CHAPTER VIII 75
Musical education under Elizabeth at school and college—The Children of Paul's—Lyrics—Lyly—Peele—Greene.

CHAPTER IX 84
Italian influence on Elizabethan literature and music—The madrigal and canzonet—Nicholas Yonge—Thomas Watson—Yonge's *Musica Trans-Alpina*—Thomas Lodge—Importance of madrigal music in relation to poetry—Madrigal texts by Sidney, Spenser, Raleigh—Lute songs.

CHAPTER X 91
Lutenist poets and composers — Thomas Campian — Measured music — John Dowland—Captain Tobias Hume.

CHAPTER XI 99
Shakespeare and music—Widespread knowledge of vocal and instrumental music in Elizabethan times—Shakespeare's use of old ballads—Mad songs—Scotch ballads and tunes introduced with James I — French influence on Scottish music — Collections of drinking songs, rounds, and catches accessible to Shakespeare—Shakespeare songs set by Morley, Robert Jones, Ford.

PAGE

CHAPTER XII 118
    Shakespeare and music (*continued*)—Robert Johnson—Music in *The Tempest*,
    The Winter's Tale — John Wilson — Ballads and songs in Fletcher's and
    Middleton's plays.

CHAPTER XIII 129
    Use of boy-actor's voices in Elizabethan plays—Plays produced by children's
    companies—Collections of popular songs, *Pammelia* and *Deuteromelia*.

CHAPTER XIV 139
    Masques under the Stuarts — Ben Jonson—Alfonso Ferrabosco — Music and
    masques—Nicholas Laniere—Traditional tunes—Ballad and dance tunes—"Joan's
    Ale is New."

CHAPTER XV 152
    John Donne — Donne and Dowland — George Wither — Wither and music —
    Orlando Gibbons—"Sleep, Baby, Sleep."

CHAPTER XVI 165
    Robert Herrick—Nicholas Laniere—Henry and William Lawes—"To Anthea"
    —Herrick and country dance tunes.

CHAPTER XVII 176
    William and Henry Lawes—Settings by Henry Lawes of songs by Milton, Waller,
    Carew—Lovelace—Cavalier poets—Sir John Suckling—Cromwell and music—
    Martin Parker, "the Prelates' poet"—Francis Quarles—Marquis of Montrose.

CHAPTER XVIII 194
    Purcell—Dryden—Summing up.

NOTE.—The song versions of many of the lyrics dating from the period covered by this book
contain variations from the literary versions which are naturally more familiar to the
average reader. This should be kept in mind when comparing the words printed under
the music and the words printed alongside. The differences are particularly noticeable
in the Stuart period, cf. p. 170.

CHAPTER I

Influence of Guillaume de Machault—Chaucer and his knowledge of music—
The White Paternoster

GEOFFREY CHAUCER was essentially a Londoner, and the London of his day was still one of the largest French-speaking cities in Europe. The French there spoken was not the French of Paris, but the French of Stratford-atte-bow, in which lisped the Prioress of the *Canterbury Tales*. Most of those who spoke it spoke also English, some with an accent echoing Anglo-Saxon, others with the Norman inflections which one hears to-day in the English spoken by the French Canadians. Latin was still the tongue of the universities and of the clergy, and, therefore, a living language—the churches and monasteries between them contributing one-fifth of the thirty-five thousand inhabitants of London—not all monks and friars, to be sure, for a cathedral such as St. Paul's had a vast personnel of secular servants.

The Medieval Church was the keeper and maker of books, and was also the keeper and teacher of music. In the *scriptoria* of the monasteries were written the innumerable manuscripts and copies which filled the libraries of the well-to-do, or passed from hand to hand until the welcome invention of printing enabled the supply of reading-matter to keep pace with the demand. Many tales had been kept alive from generation to generation, not by written records, but in the mouths of minstrels, who would sing them to the harp as an entertainment in great houses, or in taverns or at fairs.

Chaucer landmarks a period of transition. Troubadours and trouvères were passing out of fashion even in their native France. The minstrels were becoming too frequently a nuisance, although as Piers Plowman says: "It is the way of the rich to keep all manner of minstrels for the lords' and ladies' sake in whose house they stay."

Chaucer's patron, John of Gaunt, had to bring at least some of them under discipline by forming a court at Tutbury with an appointed *Roy des Ministraux* to maintain due standards and rules of conduct. In London itself the choristers of St. Paul's had to petition Richard II against the competition of "ignorant and uninformed persons," no doubt minstrels, in the performance of Christmas plays. The singing school at St. Paul's dated from the year 1042, twenty-four years before the Norman Conquest, and by Chaucer's time had traditions to respect. "The Rime of Sir

Topas" indicates that Chaucer knew the minstrels, and thought little of their ballad singing, although some of the ballads they sang provided him with stories he was glad enough to use.   Chaucer's pilgrims do not seem to have included in their company any minstrel, although this professional musician, with his shaven face, close-clipped hair, flat shoes, and parti-coloured coat, was a familiar figure on the road to Canterbury, or indeed anywhere in medieval England.   The description given by Rutebeuf in the thirteenth century still held good in fourteenth-century Europe:

> When a man makes a marriage or a feast, whereunto well-nurtured folk come, the minstrels sure get wind of this; for they ask for nothing better.   Then they flock to his house, up hill, and down dale, some on foot and others on horseback.

As a valet and esquire of the King's Household, Chaucer's youth was spent in chambers where much of the time was spent in "piping or harping and singing lays."   King Edward the Third had nineteen players of instruments on his household staff, and himself loved a good song. Music was in favour at the English court.   Of Edward the Second, Marlowe makes Gaveston say:

> I must have wanton poets, pleasant wits,
> Musicians that with touching of a string
> May draw the pliant king which way I please.
> Music and poetry is his delight.

Some of this Edward's Latin verses were known to Joshua Barnes in the late seventeenth century, and by him translated.   While he was still Prince of Wales, Edward wrote to the Abbot of Shrewsbury asking that his rhymer might be taught the minstrelsy of the crowd,[1] and be housed at the convent the while.   Edward the Third was more of a fighter, but we have that vivid picture drawn by Froissart of this monarch on board ship waiting for the Spaniards to attack:

> The King posted himself in the forepart of his own ship; he was dressed in a black velvet jacket, and wore on his head a small hat of beaver, which became him much. He was that day, as I was told by those who were present, as joyous as he ever was in his life, and ordered his minstrels to play before him a German dance which Sir John Chandos had lately introduced.   For his amusement he made the same knight sing with his minstrels, which delighted him greatly.

Sir John Chandos took part in the expedition to France in which Chaucer also served attendance, only to be taken prisoner.

Prisoners of station at that time were well treated, and this confinement may well have given Chaucer better opportunity of making acquaintance with the song-poems of Guillaume de Machault, last of the trouveres,

---

[1] Harp.

who became his spiritual master.   He may well have whiled away the time in writing the "many a song and many a lecherous lay," for which he ultimately begs forgiveness at the close of the Parson's Tale.   The music composed by de Machault for some of his ballades and roundels must have been known to Chaucer—for instance the tune of

Qui bien aimé a tard oublié

cited in *The Parliament of Foules*, of which he says:

The note, I trowë, makëd was in France.

The music of one of Guillaume de Machault's ballades fits so perfectly the words of Chaucer's ballade in *The Legend of Good Women*, that it needs no stretch of the imagination to fancy that the tune was running in Chaucer's head at the time he wrote his English verse.   This ballade was clearly intended for the women in the train of the God of Love, who,

wenten in compass
Dancing about this flower an easy pace
And songen, as it were, in carol wise.

Chaucer adds, as if for emphasis, "When that this balade all y-songen was."

Hide, Absalon, thy giltë tresses clear;
Esther, lay thou thy meekness all a-down,
Hide, Jonathas, all thy friendly manere;
Penalopë and Marcia Catoun,
Make of your wifehood no comparison:
Hide ye your beauties, Iseult and Elaine,
My lady cometh, that all that may desteyne.[1]

Thy fairë body, let it not appear,
Lavine; and thou Lucrece of Romë town,
And Polixene that boughten love so dear,
And Cleopatrë, with all thy passion,
Hide ye your truth of love and your renown;
And thou, Thisbe, that hast of love such pain,
My lady cometh that all that may desteyne.

Hero, Dido, Laudomia, all y-fere,
And Phyllis, hanging for thy Demophon,
And Canacë, espyëd by thy cheer,
Ysiphilë, betrayëd with Jason,
Make of your truthë neither boast ne sound;
Nor Ypermistre or Adriane, ye twain;
My lady cometh, that all that may desteyne.

[1] Bedim. *(Collated from Texts A and B.)*

The "balade notée" of Guillaume de Machault, the melody of which in rhythm and accent so exactly fits this lyric of Chaucer, is printed here for comparison, although that can only properly be made by reference to the "balade" as printed with the music in Wolf's *Geschichte der Mensural Notation*.

S'amours ne fait par grace adoucir
Vostre franceur, dame, a qui sui donnes;
Je suis certains qu'il mi convient morir
De ma dolour ou d'estre refuses.
Ce m'est avis qu'il me vaut miex asses
Par vo refus tost morir sans deport
Qu'en ma dolour languir jusqu'a la mort.

Music was so much in the air in that day that Chaucer could not but be influenced by it. Judging by his portraits of the Canterbury pilgrims, music must have entered into every walk of life. The Young Squire "sang or fluted all day." The Pardoner "sung so merrily and loud." Well could the Friar "sing and pleyen on a rote"—

And in his harping, when that he had sung,
His eyen twinkled in his head aright.

The Summoner sang a burden to the Pardoner, of whom it is said:

Full loud he sang, "Come hither love to me."

It was to the tune of the bagpipes that the Miller brought the company out of town. The Prioress, when she sang divine service,

Entunëd in her nose full seemëly.

Tune from Johannes Wolf, *Geschichte der Mensural Notation*, Vol. III, p. 66. (Breitkopf & Härtel, Leipzig).

Chaucer tells no more moving story than the Prioress's Tale of the little choir-boy singing his *Alma Redemptoris* as he passed through the Jewish quarter to be thrown, with his throat cut, into a pit where, still singing, he was heard and found by the searchers, and so brought to the altar.

"My throat is cut unto my neckë bone,"
Saidë this child, "and as by way of kind
I should have died, yea, longë time agone,
But Jesu Christ, as ye in bookës find,
Will that his glory last and be in mind,
And, for the worship of his mother dear,
Yet may I sing 'O Alma' loud and clear."

Melody from *Vesperal pour tous*, published by Bureau des Œuvres liturgiques,
Abbaye du Mont-César, Louvain.

The melody he sang was that here printed and written in the eleventh century by Herman Contract, a monk of the Abbey of Reichenau. This melody Chaucer must many a time have heard at Advent.

The Prioress's Tale is the tale of the ballad of Hugh of Lincoln, a contemporary version of which in Anglo-French is cited by Child. There are various tunes to which this ballad was traditionally sung, the oldest of which appears in connection with Ophelia's song in *Hamlet*:

Good morrow, 'tis Saint Valentine's Day,

and is known also as

Who list to lead a soldier's life.

This is simple enough to be quite an old ballad air, and may have been one known to Chaucer, though of course he would not have known the northern version of the ballad with which it came to be associated, and which for convenience' sake is here printed:

SIR HUGH, OR THE JEW'S DAUGHTER

The rain rins down through Mirry-land
    town
  Sae does it down the Pa;
Sae does the lads of Mirry-land town
  When they play at the ba'.

Then out and came the Jew's dochter,
  Said, "Will ye come in and dine?"
"I winna come in, I canna come in
  Without my play-feres nine."

She powd an apple red and white
  To intice the young thing in;
She powd an apple red and white,
  And that the sweet bairn did win.

Percy's Reliques, I. 32.

Tune, "Who list to lead a soldier's life," in Chappell's *Popular Music of the Olden Time.*

The "Mirry-land town" of Percy's version is an apparent corruption of "Merry Lincoln," cf. Child's *English and Scottish Popular Ballads,* and is printed accordingly with the music.

Absalon in the Miller's Tale, sings a descant to a tune he plays on the fiddle.[1]

Rivalling the Young Squire as a songster is Nicholas, the clerk in the Miller's Tale:

And all above there lay a gay sautrie,
On which he made a nightës melodie
So sweetëly, that all the chamber rang;
The Angelus ad Virginem he sang;
And after that he sang the "kingës note";
Full often blessed was his merry throat.

[1] Rubible.

Angelus ad Virginem
Subintrans in conclave
Virginis formidinem
Demulcens inquit "Ave,"
Ave Regina Virginum,
Coeli terraeque Dominum
Concipies
Et paries
Intacta
Salutem hominum;
Tu coeli porta facta
Medela criminum.

Quomodo conciperem
Quae virum non cognovi?
Qualiter infringerem
Quae firma mente vovi?
Spiritus sancti gratia
Perficiet haec omnia.
Ne timeas
Sed gaudeas
Secura
Quod castimonia
Manebit in te pura
Dei potentia.

British Museum, Arundel Collection, 248.
Cf. *The Story of British Music* (Kegan Paul).

As to the "kingës note," Warton suggests this is a translation of "chant royale," but it is more likely that a "clerk" would sing another Latin hymn, and this might very well be the beautiful sixth-century "Rex gloriose," still to be found in *The English Hymnal* (No. 183), and in the antiphonaries of the Roman Catholic Church.

Rex gloriose Martyrum
Corona confitentium
Qui respuentes terrea
Perducis ad caelestia,

Aurem benignam protinus
Intende nostris vocibus;
Trophaea sacra pangimus,
Ignosce quod deliquimus.

Tu vinces inter Martyres
Parcisque Confessoribus;
Tu vince nostra crimina,
Largitor indulgentiae.

It is, of course, possible that there is reference here to some lost song written by or for Edward III. If so, one may surmise that it carried as refrain the joyous couplet used as his motto at the institution of the Order of the Garter:

> Hey, hey, the white swan!
> By God's soul, I am thy man.

Following this same flight of fancy, the tune of this would certainly have given an edge to the later rhyme of John Ball:

> When Adam delved and Eve span,
> Who was then the gentleman?

The tunes of the songs that Chaucer refers to are now hard to trace, but one mentioned in the Miller's Tale as "The White Paternoster" has been claimed by the Rev. S. Baring-Gould as the possible source of a folk-song still sung in England to a very old tune with words of an antique turn:

MATTHEW, MARK, LUKE, AND JOHN

Matthew, Mark, and Luke, and John,
Bless the bed that I lie on,
Four angels to my bed,
Two to bottom, two to head,
Two to hear me when I pray,
Two to bear my soul away.

Monday morn the week begin,
Christ deliver our souls from sin.
Tuesday morn, nor curse nor swear,
Christës body that will tear.
Wednesday, middle of the week,
Woe to the soul Christ does not seek.

Thursday morn, Saint Peter wrote
Joy to the soul that heaven hath bote,
Friday Christ died on the tree
To save other men as well as me.
Saturday, sure, the evening dead,
Sunday morn the book's outspread.

God is the branch and I the flower,
Pray God send me a blessed hour.
I go to bed, some sleep to take,
The Lord, he knows if I shall wake.
Sleep I ever, sleep I never,
God receive my soul for ever.

The White Paternoster

Traditional melody, quoted in *Songs of the West*, Rev. S. Baring-Gould (By permission of Methuen & Co. Ltd.).

A fascinating chapter on "The White Paternoster" may be found in *Essays in the Study of Folk Songs* by the Countess Martinengo-Cesaresco (Everyman's Library).

Apart from the Prologue to the *Canterbury Tales*, so much of Chaucer's verse is now known to be translated that quotations referring to music may be misleading, but there are lines inserted into his translation of *The Romaunt of the Rose* which are personal. Speaking of his minstrels, he says:

> Some songë songës of Lorraine,
> For in Lorraine their notës be
> Full sweeter than in this country.

Although thus acquainted with music, as indeed every man of breeding in his period must be, Chaucer was a translator and narrator rather than a lyric poet, and too much stress should not be laid on the line which says that his *Troilus and Cresseid* was "to be read or sung to the harp." Like his Clerk of Oxenford he was more concerned with words than melody —a bookish man, revealed in the fifteenth-century illustration which shows him reading his poems in the wooded castle grounds to a courtly audience, mostly of women. The music that interested him was the word-music with which he resolved the uncouth harshness of Anglo-Norman speech into something that came in tripping verses from the tongue.

CHAPTER II

Langland, the chanting priest—Psalter tunes—St. Francis—The Franciscan poet friars—Early English carols written by both monks and minstrels—Old ballads: "Robin Hood, "Chevy Chase."

VERY different from Chaucer, the literary courtier, is William Langland, chanter of masses, who in *Piers Plowman* sang his alliterative allegory of the Field Full of Folk, of Lady Meed tried before the King, and of the Search for Truth.

Of himself he says:

And I live in London	and on London bothë
The looms that I labour with	and livelihood deserve
Is *pater noster* and my primer	*placebo* and *dirige*
And my psalter some time	and my seven psalmës
Thus I sing for their soulës	of such as me helpen.

Passus VI, lines 44–48, C text.

To this professional singer of masses, the Latin lines so liberally interwoven would have been familiar as chanted, not as something read:

There is another Medë measureless	that masters desireth
To maintain misdoers	Medë they takë
And thereof saith the psalter	in a psalmë's endë
In quorum manibus iniquitates sunt	dextera eorum repleta muneribus.

In quorum manibus in i qui ta tes sunt dextera e o rum reple la mu ne ri bus —

So when one chants the English lines, broken with the cæsura just like the Latin, and finds them slide so easily into any of the eight tones specified for the psalter, one feels that they may well have been so composed to this music. One can imagine Langland in the quiet of the Malvern Hills, or later in the throng of London life, chanting to himself:

A thousand of men tho thrungen together
Cried upward to Christ and to his cleane mother
To have grace to go with them truthe to seeke.

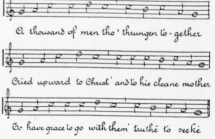

A thousand of men tho' thrungen to-gether

Cried upward to Christ and to his cleane mother

To have grace to go with them' truthë to seekë

The rhythm of the old alliterative Anglo-Saxon metre came naturally to one who was steeped in the rhythm of Church Latin—he passes in the same breath from one to the other:

And said, "Si ambulavero in medio umbrae mortis, non timebo mala quoniam tu
    mecum es
I shall cessen of my sowing," quod Pieres, "and swynk not so hardë."

Langland's temperament was in any case alien to the French jingle of the court poet. It was not a desire for popularity that drew him to select this metre. As Skeat indicates, the success of his first edition (the A text), came as a surprise to the poet. He was no cithern singer, and had small sympathy for the music of minstrels, or even for the "hey trolly lolly" of the peasant folk-song. Though he satirized his own profession of singing priest, he was saturated with the music by which he gained his livelihood.

The musical quality of *Piers Plowman* has been obscured by modernized versions which should be taken only as a bridge to the original. One of these versions, issued with the imprimatur of two learned scholars, one a Professor of Poetry, excuses its translation of *Piers Plowman* into prose on the ground that, "the poet was not a great artist in metre." Of course, if poetry is to be confined to the straitjacket of symmetrical rhyme, this may be so. But there are some who think that King David, who did not rhyme, was a better artist in metre than Nahum Tate.

One must also remember that the English of all classes in Langland's day were familiar with this church music—the nobles heard it daily in their private chapels, the lesser folk in the churches which were their common meeting-place. They learned this music in their childhood, for, as Cardinal Gasquet points out in his *Parish Life in Medieval England*, in these days "every little boy either sang or served about the altar in church." These were tunes that did not need to be set down in notes— they were better known even than the ballad tunes which the later printers merely named on the broadsides.

While Langland wrote his visions with the psalter tunes running in his head, his verses may indeed have been recited rather than chanted by those who quoted or read them in the written copies, just as the lyrics written by Robert Burns to definite melodies have still their independent charm for the mere reader.   It may be also that Langland framed his verses as much to an inner as to a sounded music.   Such was the case with those other mystics, Heinrich Suso and Richard Rolle, the hermit of Hampole, who tells how

> While my whole heart and all my desires were engrossed in prayer and heavenly things, suddenly, I know not how, I felt in me within a symphony of song, and I over-heard a most delightful heavenly harmony which remained in my mind.   For, straight-way, while I meditated, my thoughts were turned into melody of song, and for meditation I, as it were, sang songs.   And that music voiced itself even in my prayers, and psalmody; and by reason of the interior sweetness which was outpoured upon me, I was impelled to sing what before I had only said.
>
> *From the translation by* FRANCES M. M. COMPER.

Somewhere about the time of Chaucer, a Franciscan friar of Norwich, John Brackley by name, wrote a carol of the Virgin Mary, "I saw a sweet, seely sight."

I SAW A SWEET, SEELY SIGHT

I saw a sweet, seely sight,
A blissful bird,[1]
A blossom bright,
That moaning made
And mirth of manger.
A maiden mother so mild,
A knavë child
In cradle keep
That softly sleep;
She sat and sang.

[1] Maid.

From a MS. in the British Museum tran-scribed in *The Story of the Carol*, Edmonstoune Duncan (Walter Scott Publishing Co.).

The Gospel according to St. Francis of Assissi was a gospel of happiness. He had learnt the gay songs of the jongleurs from his mother, who was a native of musical Provence, and, both before and after his renunciation of the world, was forever singing. He would have his followers called "joculatores Dei," or "minstrels of the Lord," the "merry singers, heaven's minstrels" of Piers Plowman, for his gospel was a gospel of song. St. Francis also made popular the old custom of celebrating Christmas in church with the visible manger. St. Bonaventura, his biographer, says that "he prepared a manger and brought hay, an ox and an ass to the place appointed. The brethren were summoned, the people ran together, the forest resounded with their voices, and that august night was made radiant and solemn with many bright lights, and with tuneful and sonorous psalms."

Many of the early English carols undoubtedly came from Franciscan poets. One gets a glimpse of the spirit of these singing friars from an incident narrated in the chronicle of Lanercost, in which we are told of two Franciscan missionaries who had recently arrived in England, approaching Oxford on a cold Christmas day.

Going into a neighbouring wood, they picked their way along a rugged path over the frozen mud and hard snow, whilst blood stained the track of their naked feet without their perceiving it. The younger friar said to the elder, "Father, shall I sing and lighten our journey?" and on receiving permission, he sang with a loud voice a *Salve Regina Misericordiae*.

The spirit of joyousness that one finds in so many early English carols seems to carry one back to Assisi. Here, for instance, is one taken from a manuscript dating from the year 1400, the date of the death of Chaucer.

Now well may we merthës make,
For us Jesus mankind doth take
Only for our sinnës sake,
Alleluia, Alleluia, Alleluia, Alleluia.

A King of Kings now forth is brought
Of a maid that sinnëd not,
Neither in deed neither in thought,
Res miranda.

An angel of counsel this day is born
Of a maid I said beforn
For to save that was forlorn,
So de Stella.

That sun hath never down going
Neither his light to time losing,
The star is evermore shining
Semper clara.

MS. Selden, B 36 f. 10. From *Early Bodleian Music*, facsimile 51. Transcription, Vol. II. J. F. R. Stainer, B.C.L., M.A., and C. Stainer. Edited by Sir John Stainer, M.A., Mus.Doc. (Novello & Co. Ltd.).

Right as the star bringeth forth a beam
Of whom there cometh a marvellous stream,
So childeth the maid withouten womb
Pari forma.

It would be wrong, however, to ascribe all these early carols to the friars. Most of these followers of St. Francis lived in houses among the people, and the people of the fifteenth century were in a perpetual tumult of civil war. The serenity one finds in some of these carols suggests rather the quiet cloisters of a monastery, nor should we forget that the keepers and teachers of music in these days were the monks. One carol of especial loveliness breathes the essential fragrance of such cloistered serenity. It seems to date between the years 1450 and 1460, when England was being rent by the Wars of the Roses. Who can forget those matchless lines of Shakespeare?

This brawl to-day,
Grown to this faction in the Temple Garden,
Shall send between the red rose and the white
A thousand souls to death and deadly night.

Thinking then of this conflict between York and Lancaster, and remembering the sweet hymn "Laetabundus" of St. Bernard, some English monk wrote this carol of another rose:

There is no rose of such virtue,
As is the rose that bare Jesu,
Alleluia!

For in this rose contained was
Heaven and earth in little space,
Res miranda!

By that rose we well may see,
There be one God in persons three,
Pares forma.

The angels sungen the shepherds to,
Gloria in excelsis Deo,
Gaudeamus!

Leave we all this worldly mirth,
And follow we this joyful birth,
Transeamus.

Cambridge MS. T.C.C.O. 3, 58. Transcribed in *English Carols of the Fifteenth Century*, J. A. Fuller Maitland (Leadenhall Press).

The celebration of Christmas Day in a monastery of the fifteenth century is described by Sir Walter Besant from the records of Father Ambrosius (Hugh de Steyninge) who entered the Abbey of St. Peter, Westminster, about the year 1472.

On Christmas day they celebrated the Office of the Shepherds, acted by boys for the angels and the Brethren for the Shepherds. They also enacted a Feast of Asses, for which there was to be prepared a furnace made of cotton and linen ready to be fired; there was a procession of prophets including Balaam on his ass. . . . On the Epiphany they performed another miracle play called the Office of the Three Kings. Another Feast of Asses represented the Flight into Egypt.

After witnessing such miracle plays, one can fancy some monk composing the carol:

This endernight
I saw a sight,
A star as bright as day,
And ever among
A maiden sang—
Lullay, by-by, lullay.

This lovely lady
Sat and sang,
And to her child gan say,
"My Son, my Lord,
My Father dear,
Why liest Thou in hay?

"Mine own dear Son,
How art Thou come,
Art Thou not God veray?
But nevertheless
I will not cease
To sing by-by, lullay."

British Museum, Royal App. 58, fol. 526.
Transcribed in *The Story of the Carol*, Edmonstoune Duncan (Walter Scott Publishing Co.).

The Child then spake
In His talking,
And to His mother said:
"I called am
A heaven-king,
In crib though I be laid.

"Now, sweet Son
Since Thou art King,
Why art Thou laid in stall?
Why hast Thou
No rich bedding
In some great kingës hall?

"But angels bright
Down to me light,
Thou knowest it is no nay;
And of that sight
Thou mayest delight
To sing by-by, lullay."

"Ye shall well see
That kingës three
Shall come the twelfth day:
For this behest
Give me thy breast
And sing by-by, lullay."

The familiarity with the drama of a miracle play no doubt helps to account for the dialogue character of some of these early English carols, such as:

What tidings bringest thou, messenger,
Of Christës birth this yearës day?

A Babe is born of high nature
Is Prince of Peace and ever shall be.
Of heav'n and earth He hath the cure,
His lordship is eternity.
Such wonder tidings ye may hear,
That man is now made Godës fere
Whom sin had made but fiendës prey.

A seemly sight it is to see
The bird that hath this Babe y-born,
Conceived a Lord of High Degree,
And maiden as she was beforn.
Such wonder tidings ye may hear,
That maid and mother is one y-fere,
And always lady of high array.

This maid began to greet her Child
And said, "Hail Son, hail Father dear!"
He said, "Hail mother, hail maid mild!"
His greeting was in quaint mannere.
Such wonder tidings ye may hear,
Her greeting was in such mannere,
It turnëd mannës pains to play.

A wonder thing is now befall,
That Lord that formëd star and sun,
Heaven and earth and angels all,
Now in mankindë is begun.
Such wonder tidings ye may hear,
An Infant that is not of one year
Ever hath y-been and shall be ay.

Selden MS, B 26, f. 15. Transcribed in *Early Bodleian Music*, by J. F. R. Stainer, B.C.L., M.A. and C. Stainer. Edited by Sir John Stainer, M.A., Mus.Doc. (Novello & Co. Ltd.).

The Trinity College, Cambridge MS. with slightly different words is transcribed in *English Carols of the Fifteenth Century*. J. A. Fuller Maitland (Leadenhall Press).

While the monks lived, on the whole, cloistered lives, this did not mean that they were quite out of touch with the people. The monasteries offered hospitality to travellers, and minstrels were not unwelcome. In the old ballad of "Robin Hood and Allan-a-Dale," we read:

"What dost thou do here?" the bishop said,
"I prithee now tell to me."
"I am a bold harper," quoth Robin Hood,
"And the best in the north country."

"O welcome, O welcome," the bishop he said,
"That music best pleaseth me."
"You shall have no music," quoth Robin Hood,
"Till the bride and the bridegroom I see."

Bishop Grosteste, when he asked why he kept a harper in the chamber next his own, replied:

> The virtue of the harp through skill and right
> Will destroy the fiendës might.

As the monks were the keepers of music, the tunes sung by the minstrels might well sometimes be tamed to the service of the Church. And sometimes a monkish hymn in turn might be sung outside by a minstrel to more secular words. There is one tune recorded as serving such a double purpose, as a Nativity Carol, and as a Drinking Song:

> Nowell, Nowell, Nowell,
> This is the Salutation
> Of the Angel Gabriel.

and also:

> Bring us in good ale, good ale,
> For our Blessed Lady's sake, bring us in good ale.

Nowell, Nowell, Nowell,
This is the Salutation
Of the Angel Gabriel.

Tidings true there be come new
Sent from the Trinity
By Gabriel to Nazareth,
City of Galilee.
A clean maiden and pure Virgin
Through her humility
Hath conceived the person
Second in deity.

DRINKING SONG

Bring us in good ale, good ale,
For our Blessed Lady's sake
Bring us in good ale.

Bring us in no brown bread
For that is made of bran,
Nor bring us in no white bread
For therein is no gain,
But bring us in good ale, good ale,
And bring us in good ale,
For our Blessed Lady's sake
Bring us in good ale.

Bodleian MS. Eng. Poet. E 1 ff. 41, 42. Facsimile 100. Transcription in Vol. II of *Early Bodleian Music*, J. F. R. Stainer, B.C.L., M.A., and C. Stainer. Edited by Sir John Stainer, M.A., Mus.Doc. (Novello & Co. Ltd.).

C

At one time there was an old tavern in Barton Street, Westminster, called "The Salutation" with a sign on which were painted an angel and the Virgin Mary. The monks of the abbey were accused of frequenting the taverns of their neighbourhood, and it is just possible that one of these bibulous brethren made this parody for the edification of his fellow ale-bibbers.

A very beautiful love-song of this period shows that the Church had not a monopoly of either poetry or music:

Now would I fain some merthës make
All only for my lady's sake,
When I her see;
But now I am so far from her
It will not be.

Tho' I be far out of her sight
I am her man both day and night,
And so will be;
There would I as I love her
She loved me.

When she is merry then am I glad,
When she is sorry then am I sad,
And cause is why;
For he liveth not that loved
So well as I.

She saith that she hath seen it writ
That seldom seen is soon forget,
It is not so;
For in good faith, save only her,
I love and no mo!

MS. Ashmole, 191, f. 191. Transcribed in *Early Bodleian Music*, J. F. R. Stainer, B.C.L., M.A., and C. Stainer. Edited by Sir John Stainer, M.A., Mus.Doc. (Novello & Co. Ltd.).

Wherefore I pray both night and day
That she may cast all care away
And live in rest,
And evermore, wherever she be,
To love me best.

And I to her to be so true
And never to change for no new
Unto my end;
And that I may in her service
Ever to amend.

The minstrels helped in the singing of carols interspersed between acts in the mystery plays, and the influence of balladry may be traced in certain of the carols which have come down to us as folk-songs. In one very early manuscript there is a carol of Corpus Christi Day, written evidently by some mystic to be sung to a tune of which there is no record. To this carol there is a metrical parallel in a ballad, also very old, with an equally old tune which has been preserved. When one remembers how readily tunes were bandied about from ballad to ballad, one wonders whether this melody did not serve the carol as well.

The ballad is " There were three ravens sat on a tree ":

There were three ravens sat on a tree,
Down a down hey down, hey down,
There were three ravens sat on a tree,
With a down.
There were three ravens sat on a tree,
They were as black as they might be,
With a down derry, derry, derry down, down.

The one of them said to his mate,
"Where shall we our breakfast take?"

"Down in yonder greenë field
There lies a knight slain under his shield.

"His hounds they lie down at his feet,
So well they can their master keep.

"His hawks they fly so eagerly,
There 's no fowlë dare him come nigh."

Down there comes a fallow doe,
As great with young as she might go.

She lift up his bloody head,
And kissed his wounds that were so red.

She got him up upon her back,
And carried him to earthen lake.

She buried him before the prime,
She was dead herself ere evensong time.

God send every gentleman
Such hawks, such hounds, and such a leman.

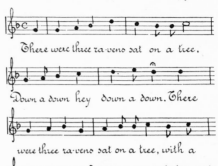

Ravenscroft's *Melismata* (1611).
Cf. *English Melodies* (J. M. Dent & Sons Ltd.).

The carol to which this melody so admirably fits is

THE FALCON HATH BORNE MY MATE AWAY

Lulley, lulley, lulley, lulley,
The falcon hath borne my mate away.

He bare him up, he bare him down,
He bare him into an orchard brown.

In that orchard there was an hall,
That was hanged with purple and pall.

And in that hall there was a bed,
It was hanged with gold so red.

And in that bed there lieth a knight,
His woundës bleeding, day and night.

By that bedside kneeleth a may,
And she weepeth both night and day.

And by that bedside there standeth a stone,
Corpus Christi written thereon.

Chaucer's influence dominated English secular verse for a century after his death, and as his genius found expression in narrative, one has to delve in musical manuscripts or in early ballads handed down by tradition to recover lyrical treasure from that period.   While the destruction of so many musical manuscripts by the Reformers has sadly diminished this field, there are still enough left to prove the lyrical muse still alive in these distracted years of struggle with France and of the Wars of the Roses. Music was preserved by the Church and in the universities where the clergy were trained.   The Oxford statutes of 1431 stipulated that music be studied for one year for the degree of M.A.   All clerks were expected to

bene con—construe well
bene can—sing well
bene le — read well.

Instruction in singing was provided, and examinations on song and writing were held.

The musicians themselves were concerned more with experiments in harmony than with delight in melody, for this was Dunstable's century, and the lyrics we find are written to arrangements in two, three, or more parts, a concord less likely to survive in tradition than the simple folk-song melody.   There were undoubtedly such folk-songs, as there were May-days and wassailings, and all the country dance songs that went therewith.   The ploughman, the shepherd, the milkmaid sang, the carmen whistled at their work, and on the Thames the London watermen sang to a fifteenth-century Mayor a rhyme with the oft-quoted refrain:

Heave and ho, rumbelow,
Row the boat, Norman row,
Row to thy leman.

Pammelia (1609), and Chappell's *Popular Music of the Olden Time.*

The people, says one writer of the day, would rather go to the tavern than to Holy church—"to hear a song of Robin Hood, or of some ribaldry than to hear mass or matins."   One such song of ribaldry might have been:

Welcome be ye when ye go
And farewell when ye come;
So fair as ye there be no mo'
As bright as berry brown.
I love you verily at my toe,
None so much in all the town.
I am right glad when ye will go,
And sorry when ye will come.

And when ye be out far,
I pray for you certain
That never man, horse nor mare
Bring you to town again.
To praise your beauty I ne dare
For dread that man will sayn—
Farewell, no more for you I care,
But pray you of my song have no disdain.

As for the songs of Robin Hood, these vigorous ballads have more lyrical ring than one can find in the literary poets of the century. The ballads were without question sung, but whether the tunes recorded with them in the seventeenth and eighteenth centuries are the old tunes is less certain. In any case, the following traditional melody can readily be sung to several of the oldest known versions of "A Geste of Robin Hood."

Two-part song, transcribed in *Early Bodleian Music*, J. F. R. Stainer, B.C.L., M.A., and C. Stainer. Edited by Sir John Stainer, M.A., Mus.Doc. (Novello & Co. Ltd.).

A Geste of Robin Hood

Lythe and listen, gentlemen,
That be of freeborn blood;
I shall tell you of a good yeoman,
His name was Robin Hood.

Robin was a proud outlaw,
(Whiles he walked on ground,
So courteous an outlaw as he was one
Was never none found.)

Robin stood in Bernesdale,
And leaned him to a tree;
And by him stoodë Little John,
A good yeoman was he.

Chappell's *Popular Music of the Olden Time.*

Robin loved Our dearë Lady
For doubt of deadly sin,
Would he never do company harm
That any woman was in.

"Master," then said Little John
"And we our board shall spread,
Tell us whither that we shall go,
And what life that we shall lead.

"Where we shall take, where we shall
    leave,
Where we shall abide behind;
Where we shall rob, where we shall
    reive,
Where we shall beat and bind."

"Thereof no force," then said Robin;
"We shall do well enow;
But look ye do no husbandë harm
That tilleth with the plough.

"No more ye shall no good yeoman
That walketh by greene-wood shaw;
Ne no knight ne no squire
That will be a good fellow."

Child's *English and Scottish Popular
    Ballads*, 117—before 1450.

ROBIN HOOD AND THE MONK

In summer when the shawes be sheen
And leaves be large and long,
It is full merry in fair forést
To hear the fowlës song.

To see the deer draw to the dale,
And leave the hillës high,
And shadow them in the leavës green,
Under the greenwood tree.

Child, 119, *circ.* 1450. (*For another possible
    melody cf. pp.* 55–6.)

ROBIN HOOD AND QUEEN KATHERINE

In summer time when leaves grow green
And flowers are fresh and gay
Then Robin Hood he deck'd his men
Each one in brave array.

He deck'd his men in Lincoln green,
Himself in scarlet red;
Fair of their breast was then it seen
When his silver arms were spread.

With hattës white and feathers black,
And bows and arrows keen,
And thus he yetted towards lovely London,
To present Queen Katherine.

Child, 145, later than 1500.

To the middle of the fifteenth century is ascribed one version of "The Hunting of the Cheviot," referred to by Sidney as "the old song of *Percy and Douglas*," a ballad sung to many tunes. According to Chappell, the oldest tune identified with this ballad is that known as "In Peascod Time":

In peascod time, when hound to horn
Gives ear till buck be kill'd,
And little lads with pipes of corn
Sat keeping beasts a-field,

I went to gather strawberries tho'
By woods and groves full fair;
And parched my face with Phœbus so
In walking in the air,

That down I laid me by a stream,
With boughs all overclad:
And there I met the strangest dream
That ever shepherd had.

Methought I saw each Christmas game,
Each revel all and some,
And everything that I can name,
Or may in fancy come.

Chappell's *Popular Music of the Olden Time*.

Sidney's often - quoted reference to this ballad will well bear once more repeating:

Certainly, I must confess my own barbarousness. I never heard the old song of *Percy and Douglas* that I found not my heart moved more than with a trumpet: and yet is it sung by some blind crowder, with no rougher voice than rude style.

Bishop Percy, in his *Reliques of Ancient Poetry*, claims to have discovered the version of this ballad which Sidney may have heard. This was in a manuscript on which appears the name of Richard Sheale, a minstrel who was in the service of Edward, Earl of Derby, in Sidney's day. This minstrel was something of a poet himself, and has left a rhymed account of how he once was robbed on Dunsmore Heath, upbraiding himself for thinking that his harp and the reputed poverty of minstrels would save him from such misadventure.

THE HUNTING OF THE CHEVIOT

The Percy out of Northumberland
And a vow to God made he,
That he would hunt in the mountains
Of Cheviot within days three
In the magger of doughty Douglas
And all that ever with him be.

The fattest harts in all Cheviot
He said he would kill and carry them away:
"By my faith," said the doughty Douglas
again,
"I will let that hunting if that I may."

· · · · · · ·

The doughty Douglas on a steed
He rode all his men beforn;
His armour glittered as did a glede;
A bolder baron was never born.

· · · · · ·

"Yield thee, Percy," said the Douglas,
"And, i' faith, I shall thee bring

Where thou shalt have a yarl's wages
Of Jamie, our Scottish king."

· · · · · ·

The Percy leaned on his brand
And saw the Douglas die;
He took the dead man by the hand,
And said, "Woe is me for thee."

Five out of sixty-eight verses, Child, No. 168A. MS. Ashmole 48, Bodleian Library.
Cf. Percy's *Reliques*, Vol. I. (Everyman's Library.)

A popular tune might be used for many ballads, and sometimes indeed was called by another name if a later ballad written to it became so popular that it superseded the original words. As the ballads themselves were modernized, they might become identified with new tunes. Thus, when "The Hunting of the Cheviot" was transformed by Henry Jones, a sixteenth-century balladmonger of Oxford, into "Chevy Chase," it became identified with the tune of "Flying Fame."

God prosper long our noble king,
Our lives and safeties all,
A woeful hunting once there did
In Chevy Chase befall.

To drive the deer with hound and horn
Earl Percy took the way;
The child may rue that is unborn
The hunting of that day.

The stout Earl of Northumberland
A vow to God did make
His pleasure in the Scottish woods
Three summer days to take.

.   .   .   .   .

The gallant greyhounds swiftly ran
To chase the fallow deer:
On Monday they began to hunt
Ere daylight did appear.

.   .   .   .   .

Lord Percy to the quarry went
To view the tender deer;
Quoth he, "Earl Douglas promised once
This day to meet me here."

.   .   .   .   .

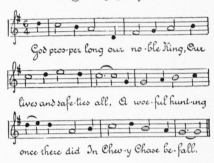

Chevy Chase.

Tune from *Pills to Purge Melancholy.*
Cf. *English Melodies* (J. M. Dent & Sons Ltd.).

"Lo, yonder doth Earl Douglas come,
His men in armour bright;
Full twenty hundred Scottish spears
All marching in our sight."

.   .   .   .   .

"Show me," said he, "whose men you be
That hunt so boldly here,
That without my consent do chase
And kill my fallow deer."

.   .   .   .   .

CHAPTER III

Tudor Period—Skelton—Henry VIII—William Cornysshe—Gray—"Pastime with Good Company"—Anne Boleyn—Wyatt—Surrey

THE English in Tudor days were undoubtedly a musical race. Writing in 1509, the date of the accession of Henry VIII, Erasmus calls them "the most accomplished in the skill of music of any people." Sagudino, Venetian ambassador to Henry's court, says of the Chapel Royal, "Their voices are really divine, and as for the deep basses, I do not believe they are equalled in the world." Henry's tutor, John Skelton, loved the clavichord, and Henry himself, according to Hollinshed, "exercised himself daily in shooting, singing, dancing, wrestling, casting of the bar, playing at the recorders, flute, virginals, in setting of songs, and making of ballads." Lutenists were encouraged to come from Italy, and with the lute flowers the lyric. The statutes of Trinity College, Cambridge, founded by Henry VIII, enjoined that the candidates for fellowship should show what skill they had in singing. All members were supposed to be capable of singing a part in choir service.

John Skelton wrote jingles and sometimes lyrics which came as a relief from the formality of Chaucer's successors. Take, for instance:

> Star of the morrow gray,
> The blossom on the spray,
> The freshest flower of May;
>
> Maidenly demure,
> Of womanhood the lure,
> Wherefore I make you sure.
>
> It were a heavenly health,
> It were an endless wealth,
> A life for God Himself;
>
> To hear this nightingale,
> Among the birdës small,
> Warbling in the vale:
>
> Dug, dug,
> Jug, jug,
> Good year and good luck,
> With chuk, chuk, chuk, chuk.

Sir John Hawkins, in his *History of Music,* shows from the poem "Against a Comely Coystrowne" how intimate was Skelton's knowledge of music, and Dr. E. W. Naylor finds twenty-six musical allusions within twenty-eight lines. In his *Book of Philip Sparrow,* Skelton parodies the Office for the Dead (which, of course, was sung), introducing sections of his poems with the opening phrases of antiphons and psalms. Dr. Naylor illustrates the poem with the music of the Office, but with all due deference to this musical scholar, I venture to submit a different rendering which I think gives a more correct and complete interpretation of the parody. It is not impossible that Skelton intended the whole poem to be sung to the various tunes of the Office which are indicated from time to time. The English lines which follow the opening notes of an antiphon should be considered a rhyming echo of those notes, and should not be fitted to the continuing notes. As the poem is too long to be quoted in full, selections have been made which include the verses that unquestionably were meant to be sung.

Pla ce bo
Who is there? Who?
Di le xi
Dame Margery
Fa re mi mi
Wherefore? and why? why?
For the soul of Philip Sparrow,
That was late slain at Carrow,
Among the Nuns Black.
For that sweet soul's sake
And for all sparrows' souls
Set in our bead rolls,
Pater noster qui
With an *Ave Mari*
And with the corner of a Creed;
The more shall be your need!

Heu! Heu! me!
That I am woe for thee!
Ad Dominum cum tribularer clamavi.
Of God nothing else crave I
But Philip's soul to keep
From the marees deep
Of Acherontes' Well
That is a flood of Hell.

Do mi nus!
Help now sweet Jesus!
Levavi oculos meos in montes
Would God! I had Zenophontes,
Or Socrates the wise,
To show me their device,

Tunes from the Office for the Dead transcribed by Fortunat Champagne, Choirmaster of the Basilica, Ottawa.

Moderately to take
This sorrow that I make
For Philip Sparrow's sake.

Si in i qui ta tes.
Alas! I was evil at ease!
De pro fun dis cla ma vi,
When I saw my Sparrow die!
Now, after my doom,
Dame Sulpicia, at Rome,
Though she would pretend
My Sparrow to commend,
I trow she could not amend
Reporting the virtues all
Of my Sparrow small.

O pe ra
La Sol Fa Fa
Confitebor tibi Domine! in toto corde meo!
Alas! I would ride and go
A thousand miles of ground!
If any such might be found,
It were worth a hundred pound
Of King Crœsus' gold
Or of Attalus the old.

A porta inferi
Good Lord! have mercy
Upon my Sparrow's soul!
Written in my bead roll.

Au di vi vo cem!
Japhet! Cam! and Shem!
Mag ni fi cat.
Show me the right path
To the hills of Armony!
Wherefore the birds yet cry
Of your father's boat.
That was sometime afloat.

Kyrie eleison! Christe eleison!
Kyrie eleison!
For Philip Sparrow's soul,
Set in our bead roll,
Let us now whisper
A *Paternoster!*
Lauda, anima mea, Dominum!
To weep with me, look that ye come,
All manner of birds in your kind!
See none be left behind!
To mourning look that ye fall
With dolorous Songs Funeral!
Some to sing, and some to say;
Some to weep and some to pray;
Every bird in his Lay!

Ne quando
Male cantando
The best that we can,
To make him our Bell-man;
And let him ring the bells.
He can do nothing else.

While he censeth
He shall sing the verse
Libera me!

And now the dark cloudy night
Chaseth away Phœbus bright,
Taking his course towards the West,
God send my Sparrow's soul good rest!
Requiem eternam dona eis, Domine!

This dirge on Philip Sparrow may read as doggerel, yet Skelton, when he chose, could write fine poetry, and in this there is no question that his music helped him. There is the lilt of dance music in his lyric to Mrs. Margaret Hussey:

> *Merry Margaret*
> *As midsummer flower,*
> *Gentle as falcon*
> *Or hawk of the bower;*
> With solace and gladness,
> Much mirth and no madness,
> All good and no badness;
> So joyously
> So maidenly,
> So womanly
> Her demeaning
> In everything
> Far, far passing
> That I can indite
> Or suffice to write
> *Of Merry Margaret*
> *As midsummer flower,*
> *Gentle as falcon*
> *Or hawk of the bower;*
>
> As patient and as still,
> And as full of good will,
> As fair Isiphil,
> Coliander,
> Sweet Pomander,
> Good Cassander,
> Steadfast of thought,
> Well made, well wrought,
> Far may be sought
> Ere you can find
> So courteous, so kind,

As Merry Margaret,
This midsummer flower,
Gentle as falcon
Or hawk of the bower.

The rhymes and stanzas in this are cunningly balanced so that there is no reason why it should not have been set to a definite tune with its four-line refrain.

Henry VIII, himself a composer, encouraged song-writers, and on that account may be forgiven many of his sins. One song that he used to sing with Sir Peter Carew is delightful, both in words and music:

By a bank as I lay,
Myself alone did muse:
    Hey ho!
A bird's sweet voice
Did me rejoice,
She sang before the Day.
Methought full well I wot her lay;
She said the Winter's past,
    Hey ho!

Down derry down, down derry down derry
   down, derry down derry down, down.

Master of Spring's sweet music,
The lusty nightingale,
    Hey ho!
Full merrily and secretly
She singeth in the thyke;
Within her breast a thorn doth prick
To keep off her from sleep,
    Hey ho!

Waken, therefore, young men,
All ye that lovers be,
    Hey ho!
This month of May
So fresh, so gay,
So fair by field and fen,
Hath flowered o'er each leafy den;
Great joy it is to see,
    Hey ho!

Brit. Mus. Royal App. 58, fol. 10B. Quoted in *English Melodies* (J. M. Dent & Sons Ltd.).

This song also appears in the "bunch of ballets and songs all ancient," which Captain Cox, a mason of Coventry, had ready to entertain Queen Elizabeth while she was the guest of the Earl of Leicester at Kenilworth.

"In a letter from Sir John Harrington to the Lord Treasurer Burleigh," says Burney, "mention is made of certain old monkish rhymes called, 'The Black Sanctus, or Monkes Hymn to Sancte Satan.'" The father of Sir John Harrington who had married a natural daughter of Henry VIII, named Esther, and was very well skilled in music, "having learned it," as the letter says, "in the fellowship of good Master Tallis," set this hymn to music in a canon of three parts, and King Henry was used "in pleasant mood to sing it."

Another old favourite of Henry's was, "As I walked the woods so wild."

For the king himself, being much delighted to sing, and Sir Peter Carew having a pleasing voice, the king would often use him to sing with him certain songs, as namely "By the bank I lay," and "As I walked the woods so wild."—JOHN NOWELL.

This must have remained a popular song, for it was arranged for the virginals sixty years later by Orlando Gibbons.

Shall I go walk the woods so wild,
Wandering, wand'ring here and there,
As I was once full sore beguiled?
Alas! for love I die with woe.

From *Pammelia* (1609). Quoted in Chappell's *Popular Music of the Olden Time*.

On his accession to the throne, Henry restored to favour at court that admirable poet, musician, and occasional jailbird, William Cornysshe, who wrote, "Blow thy horn, Hunter":

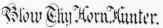

Blow thy horn, Hunter,
Come blow thy horn on high;
In yonder wood there lies a doe,
In faith she will not die,
Come blow thy horn, Hunter,
Come blow thy horn, jolly Hunter.

Fare thee well, Lady,
The day doth break on high;
And hounds and horn proclaim the morn
Is surely passing by;
So fare thee well, lady;
Now fare thee well, dearest lady.

Brit. Mus. MSS. Reg. App. 58. Quoted in Chappell's *Popular Music of the Olden Time*.

Cornysshe was in charge of the music at the Field of the Cloth of Gold, in which the choristers of the two Chapels Royal of France and England sang together a mass by Perino, accompanied by an organ with trombones and cornets. He set the music for at least one of Skelton's songs, and one suspects that they were birds of a feather. Another of Henry's protégés was one Gray, who wrote "certain merry ballads whereof one chiefly is, 'The Hunt is Up'":

The hunt is up, the hunt is up,
And it is wellnigh day:
And Harry, our King, is gone hunting
To bring his deer to bay.

The east is bright with morning light,
And darkness it is fled:
The merry horn wakes up the morn
To leave his idle bed.

Behold, the skies with golden dies
Are glowing all around:
The grass is green and so are the treen,
All laughing at the sound.

The horses snort to see the sport,
The dogs are running free,
The woods rejoice at the merry noise
Of "hey tantara tee ree."

The sun is glad to see us clad
All in our lusty green,
And smiles in the sky as he riseth high
To see and to be seen.

Awake, all men, I say again,
Be merry as you may;
For Harry, our King, is gone hunting
To drive his deer to bay.

From *Music's Delight on the Cittern* (1666), quoted in Chappell's *Popular Music of the Olden Time*. Cf. *English Melodies* (J. M. Dent & Sons Ltd.), where another tune is also given. Mentioned as a dance tune in *The Complaint of Scotland*, 1549.

From the same manuscript as contains "Blow thy horn, Hunter" are three lyrics set to music, perhaps of an earlier date, but pricked down, no doubt, for this tuneful monarch.

For the first of these the original manuscript has a delightful initial letter drawn by a musical scribe who seems to have been carried away by the spirit of the ballad. Those who cannot personally visit the British Museum to inspect this manuscript may find an accessible facsimile reproduction in the first volume of Chappell's *Popular Music of the Olden Times*.

Ah, the sighs that come fro' my heart,
They grieve me passing sore;
Sith I must fro' my love depart,
Farewell my joy for evermore.

Oft to me with her goodly face
She was wont to cast an eye;
And now absence to me in place—
Alas, for woe I die, I die!

I was wont her to behold
And take her in armes twain;
And now with sighes manifold
Farewell my joy and welcome pain!

Cornysshe, who is credited with the composition of this song, received on one occasion the sum of 13s. 4d. "for setting of a carol upon Christmas Day."

Brit. Mus. MSS. Reg. App. 58, attributed to W. Cornysshe. Facsimile in Chappell, *Popular Music of the Olden Time.*

The second of the lyrics has perhaps greater poetical merit:

Brit. Mus. MSS. Reg. App. 58. (Quoted in *The Minstrelsy of England*, Vol. II, appendix (Augener, Ltd.).

The little pretty nightingale
Among the leavës green,
I would I were with her all night;
But yet ye wot not whom I mean.

The nightingale sat on a briar
Among the thornës sharp and keen
And comfort me with merry cheer;
But yet ye wot not whom I mean.

She did appear of all her kind
A lady right well to be seen;
With words of love told me her mind;
But yet ye wot not whom I mean.

It did me good on her to look,
Her corse was clothed all in green;
Away from me her heart she took;
But yet ye wot not whom I mean.

Very plaintive is the melody of the third of these lyrics:

Western wind, when wilt thou blow?
The small rain down doth rain.
O gentle death, when wilt thou come?
For I of my life am weary.

Mart'mas wind, when wilt thou blow?
The small rain down can rain.
The green leaves fall from off the tree,
And I to my love do call in vain.

Western wind, when wilt thou blow?
The small rain down doth rain.
O if my love were in my arms,
Or I in my bed again.

Henry himself is credited with several songs of which one has survived on its merits, namely, "Pastime with good company." Whether the melody is due to Henry is doubtful, as one manuscript copy refers to it as "The Poor Man's Dump," suggesting an old dance tune. The music is here printed in such a way as to illustrate the dance form.

Pastime with good company
I love, and shall, until I die;
Grudge who will, but none deny,
So God be pleased, this life will I
For my pastance,
Hunt, sing and dance;
My heart is set,
All goodly sport,
To my comfort,
Who shall me let?

Youth will needs have dalliance,
Of good or ill some pastance;
Company me thinketh the best
All thoughts and fantasies to digest:
For idleness
Is chief mistress
Of vices all:
Then who can say
But pass the day
Is best of all?

Company with honesty
Is virtue sure and vice to flee:
Company is good or ill,
But every man has his free will.
The best I sue,
The worst eschew:
My mind shall be
Virtue to use,
Vice to refuse,
I shall use me.

D

Brit. Mus. MSS. Reg. App. 58. Quoted in *English Melodies* (J. M. Dent & Sons Ltd.).

Brit. Mus. Add MSS. 5665. Quoted in *English Melodies* (J. M. Dent & Sons Ltd.).

One of the charms that drew this monarch to Anne Boleyn was her skill in music. At the court of France she had learned "to dote on the compositions of Josquin de Pres," and she has been credited with the writing of a very beautiful song, "O Death, rock me on sleep," said to have been written in prison shortly before her execution. Others have attributed this to her brother, Viscount Rochford, with about as much authority as those who say that the Odyssey was written, not by Homer, but by another man of the same name.

O Death, rock me on sleep,
Bring me on quiet rest;
Let pass my very guiltless ghost
Out of my careful breast.
Toll on the passing bell,
Ring out the doleful knell;
Let the sound my death tell,
For I must die:
There is no remedy,
For now I die.

Alone in prison strong
I wail my destiny;
Woe worth this cruel hap that I
Should taste this misery.
Toll on, etc.

Farewell my pleasures past,
Welcome my present pain;
I feel my torments so increase
That life cannot remain.
Cease now the passing bell,
Rung is my doleful knell;
For the sound my death doth tell;
Death doth draw nigh;
Sound my end dolefully
For now I die.

Brit. Mus. Add. MSS. 15117. Cf. Chappell's *Popular Music of the Olden Time*; also Arnold Dolmetsch, *Select English Songs and Dialogues* (Boosey & Co. Ltd.), and *King's Music* (Augener Ltd.).

Music meant much to a Tudor, and it may have been partly her dislike of music that caused Henry to discard Anne of Cleves.

The poets of these days seem to have lived precarious lives. Both Wyatt and Surrey came to an untimely end, and both Wyatt and Surrey are poets who tuned their lyrics to the lute. Wyatt and Cornyshe are associated in a song which Shakespeare refers to in *Twelfth Night*:

Hey Robin, jolly Robin.

"Hey Robin,
Gentle Robin,
Tell me how thy lemman doth,
And thou shalt know of mine.

"My lady is unkind, I wis,
Alack, why is she so?
She loveth another better than me,
And yet she will say no."

Response:

"I cannot think such doubleness,
For I find women true;
In fact my lady loveth me well,
She will change for no new."

Le Plaintiff:

"Thou art happy while that doth last,
But I say as I find,
That woman's love is but a blast,
And turneth like the wind."

Response:

"Such folk shall take no harm by love
That can abide their turn;
But I alas! can no way prove
In love but lack and mourn."

Le Plaintiff:

"But if thou wilt avoid thy harm
Learn this lesson of me:
At other fires thyself to warm,
And let them warm with thee."

Brit. Mus. Add MS. 31922, fol. 54. Music by
W. Cornyshe. Quoted in *Shakespere Music,*
E. W. Naylor (J. Curwen & Sons Ltd.).

Of Sir Thomas Offley, who lived early in the sixteenth century, it is
written that in his youth, "because he had a sweet voice he was put to
learn pricksong among the choristers of St. Paul's, for that learned
Mr. (William) Lillie (the grammarian, high-master from 1509–22) knew
full well that knowledge in music was a help and a furtherance to
all arts."

Surrey was a typical courtier of his time, when "every person of good
education played on the lute. Surrey excelled on that instrument," and
according to an early biographer, "composed to it several elegant airs."

The gravedigger sings in *Hamlet* a broken-down form of a song attributed by some to Surrey, who, however, used a different tune from that traditionally used in the play.

I loathe that I did love,
In youth that I thought sweet;
As time requires for my behove,
Methinks they are not meet.

For age with stealing steps
Hath claw'd me in his crowch;
And lusty youth away he leaps,
As there had been none such.

A pikeaxe and a spade
And eke a shrowding sheet,
A home of clay for to be made
For such a guest most meet.

Tune said to have been that favoured by the Earl of Surrey. Cf. Chappell's *Popular Music of the Olden Time.*

For the original song "In youth when I did love" with another tune cf. *English Melodies* (J. M. Dent & Sons Ltd.).

This song has also been ascribed to Lord Vaux, another of the contributors to Tottel's *Miscellany.* A song to which Vaux's name has been attached with less dispute has been preserved with music that appears to be contemporary:

How can the tree but waste and wither away,
That hath not sometime comfort of the sun?
How can the flower but fade and soon decay,
That always is with dark clouds overrun?
    Is this a life?
    Nay, death I may it call,
That feels each pain, and knows no joy at all.

What foodless beast can live long in good
        plight?
Or what's the life where senses there be
        none?
Of what availeth eyes without their sight?
Or else a tongue to him that is alone?
    Is this a life? etc.

Whereto serve ears if that there be no sound
Or such a head where no device doth grow,
But of all plaints, since sorrow is the ground
Whereby the heart doth pine in deadly woe?
    Is this a life? etc.

Tune from W. Barley's *New Book of Tablature* (1596). Quoted in *English Melodies* (J. M. Dent & Sons Ltd.).

An interesting reference to these musical poets is made by Sir Walter Scott in *The Lay of the Last Minstrel*:

> As ended Albert's simple lay,
> Arose a bard of loftier port,
> For sonnet, rhyme and roundelay
> Renowned in haughty Henry's court,
> There rung thy harp, unrivall'd long,
> Fitztraver of the silver song.
> The gentle Surrey loved his lyre. . . .

From an anonymous song-sheet comes this charming lyric to a dainty tune:

My little pretty one,
My pretty honey one,
She is a jolly one
And gentle as can be.
With a beck she comes anon,
With a wink she will be gone;
No doubt she is alone
Of all that ever I see.

Brit. Mus. Add MS. 4900, fol. 59.   Quoted in
The Minstrelsy of England, Vol. I (Augener Ltd.).
Cf. also Arnold Dolmetsch, *Select English Songs
and Dialogues* (Boosey & Co. Ltd.).

CHAPTER IV

Edward VI—Translations of the Psalms by Clément Marot, and Sternhold and Hopkins—Sidney—Wedderburn—Martin Luther's hymns—Day's Psalter—Este's Psalter—William Byrd.

THE brief life of the precocious youth known as Edward VI, marked a prolific output of metrical versions of the scriptures for music intended to supplant the Romish plainsong. Edward himself played the lute, and had as musical preceptor Christopher Tye, who, among other activities, translated the Acts of the Apostles into ballad metre, and set these as four-part songs for the delectation of his royal pupil. In his preface, Tye wrote:

> Your Grace shall herein find
> By notes set forth to sing or play
> To recreate the mind.
>
> That such good things your Grace might move
> Your Lute when ye essay,
> Instead of songs of wanton love,
> These stories then to play.

Sternhold, a groom of the royal household, translated a number of the psalms into a similar "Chevy Chase" ballad metre, and was overheard by Edward singing these for his own solace at the organ. Sternhold may have desired to emulate the example of Clément Marot, who had made the singing of metrical psalms popular at the court of Francis I, by assigning specific psalms with tunes to the leaders of that court. Marot, however, was happier than the English psalmodists through his choice of melodies. By taking popular love and hunting songs as his models, he was able to introduce a variety of metres into his versions, which makes them of more literary interest than the jog-trot rhymes of the English. Queen Elizabeth in turn encouraged the fashion by herself attempting metrical translation, and psalm-singing became a social diversion in the households of her day. In her Forty-ninth Injunction of 1559 she announced:

For the comforting of such as delight in music, it may be permitted that in the beginning or end of Common Prayer, either at morning or evening, there may be sung an hymn or such-like song to the praise of Almighty God in the best melody and music that may be devised, having respect that the sentence of the hymn may be understood and perceived.

The list of metrical translators includes some notable names, such as Edmund Spenser, Sir Philip Sidney, John Donne, Michael Drayton, Phineas Fletcher, Lord Bacon, George Herbert, Richard Crashaw, and George Wither. Two of these poets made translations which were closely associated with music, namely Sir Philip Sidney and George Wither, as will be discussed in later chapters.

The version of the Hundredth Psalm, which has become an accepted classic, was made by a Scottish divine, William Kethe. But it is another Scot, John Wedderburn, who wrote the most notable of the religious lyrics in this time of Reformation. Some of the *Gude and Godlie Balates* are merely religious parodies, such as:

> With hunt is up,
> With hunt is up,
> It is now perfect day.
> Jesus, our King,
> Is gone hunting—
> Who likes to speed, they may.

In others, Wedderburn touches true poetry:

> Go, heart, unto thy lamp of light,
> Go, heart, do service and honour.
> Go, heart, and serve Him day and night,
> Go, heart, unto thy Saviour.
> Go, heart, unto thy only remede,
> Descending from thy heavenly tour,
> Thee to deliver from pain and dread,
> Go, heart, unto thy Saviour.

One of Luther's hymns—the carol written for his son, Hans—was rendered by Wedderburn in a translation written not to Luther's original tune, but to a Scots lullaby which he designates as "Baw Lulalaw." There is reason to believe this is the tune used in a later century for "Can ye sew cushions?" The old version of this tune is here printed with Wedderburn's translation—the first line of which contained an obvious misprint in the original edition:

I come from heaven high to tell
The best nowels that ever befel:
To you their tidings true I bring,
And I will of them say and sing.

This day to you is born ane child,
Of Mary meek and virgin mild:
That blessed bairn, benign and kind,
Sall you rejoice, baith heart and mind.

I Come From Heaven High

I come from hea-ven high to tell The best now-els that e-ver be-fel To

And were the warld ten times so wide,
Clad over with gold and stanes of pride,
Unworthy yet it were to Thee,
Under Thy feet ane stool to be.

The silk and sandal Thee to ease,
Are hay and simple swaddling claes,
Wherein thou glories, greatest King,
As Thou in heaven were in Thy ring.

O my dear heart, young Jesus sweet,
Prepare Thy cradle in my sprite,
And I shall rock Thee in my heart,
And never mair from Thee depart.

But I shall praise Thee evermore,
With sanges sweet until Thy gloire;
The knees of my heart sall I bow,
And sing that richt *Balulalow*.

Tune from Johnson's *Musical Museum*, "O can
ye sew cushions?"

Martin Luther, whom Hans Sachs called "the Wittenberg nightingale,"
had early in the century launched his evangel on a tide of music. With
the help of his "house choir," consisting of Johann Walther, Konrad
Rupff, and Philip Melanchthon, he adapted popular melodies and composed new tunes to translations from the Psalms of David, metrical
versions of texts such as the Lord's Prayer, and hymns of which "Ein
feste Burg ist unser Gott" is the supreme example. Himself a singer
and player on the flute, he called music "a beautiful and glorious gift of
God." Writing of the forms of the Catholic Church, he says:

> In the same way have they much noble music, especially in the abbeys and parish
> churches, used to adorn most vile idolatrous words. Therefore have we undressed
> these lifeless, idolatrous, crazy words, stripping off the noble music, and putting it
> upon the living and holy word of God, wherewith to sing, praise and honour the same;
> that so the beautiful ornament of music, brought back to its right use, may serve its
> blessed Maker and his Christian people.—Translation by E. DICKINSON, *Music in the
> Western Church*.

As a result, Luther's hymns were sung wherever German was spoken.
John Calvin at Geneva followed suit, and with the aid of Clément
Marot and Theodore Beza produced a metrical and musical psalter tuned
chiefly to old French melodies. The metrical version of the psalms,
commenced in England by Sternhold and Hopkins, and continued in
Geneva by Whittinghame, Kethe, and others, captured the English
Protestant fancy as soon as Elizabeth came to the throne, and though, as
Fuller says, the piety of the translators was better than their poetry, and
"they had drunk more of Jordan than of Helicon," the tunes were simple
and impressive, and the psalms were sung in streets and country places,
in church and at home, or by congregations of as many as six thousand

worshippers after the sermons at St. Paul's Cross.   Margaret, Lady Hoby, a Puritan lady of Elizabeth's day, refers frequently to the psalm-singing in her household.

In Shakespeare's *Merry Wives of Windsor* (Act II, scene i), Mrs. Ford says of Falstaff:

I would have sworn his disposition would have gone to the truth of his words; but they do no more adhere and keep pace than the Hundredth Psalm to the tune of "Green Sleeves."

In this reference to two old melodies, we find two currents of popular song, sacred and secular, which run through the Elizabethan age.   An edition of Sternhold and Hopkins's *Old Version* with music was printed by Day in 1583, two years before Shakespeare came to London.   *The Merry Wives of Windsor* has another reference to Day's Psalter in Psalm 137, when Sir Hugh Evans interjects a loosely-remembered line,

Whenas I sat in Pabylon,

into the second and third verses of Christopher Marlowe's song, quoted in *The Passionate Pilgrim*, "Come live with me and be my love."

DAY'S PSALTER:

When we did sit in Babylon
The rivers round about,
Then in remembrance of Sion
The tears of grief burst out.
We hang'd our hearts and instruments
The willow tree upon,
For in that place men for their use
Had planted many one.

MARLOWE'S SONG (*second and third verses*):

And we will sit upon the rocks,
And see the shepherds feed their flocks
By shallow rivers, to whose falls
Melodious birds sing madrigals.

And I will make thee beds of roses,
And a thousand fragrant posies;
A cap of flowers, and a kirtle
Embroider'd all with leaves of myrtle.

Tune from *Day's Psalter*.

The interest of musical as well as strictly religious circles in the Psalter is shown in the handsome edition, published by Thomas Este in 1592 and again in 1594, finely engraved with harmonies, "composed into four parts" by some of the leading musicians of the day, including Shakespeare's reputed friend, the lutenist, John Dowland, who gives a setting of the Old Hundredth which is still sung in some English cathedrals. In the introduction to this edition, Este says:

> Some have pleased themselves with pastorals, others with madrigals, but such as are endued with David's heart desire with David to sing unto God Psalms and Hymns and Spiritual Songs.

This same Thomas Este, or East, published for William Byrd, the greatest of English composers of that time, *Psalms, Sonets and Songs of Sadness and Pietie—for the recreation of all such as delight in Musicke* (1588), in which are "reasons briefly set down by the author to persuade every one to learn to sing:

> First, it is a knowledge easily taught and quickly learned, where there is a good master and an apt scholar.
> 2. The exercise of singing is delightful to nature, and good to preserve the health of man.
> 3. It doth strengthen all parts of the breast, and doth open the pipes.
> 4. It is a singular good remedy for a stutting and stammering in the speech.
> 5. It is the best means to procure a perfect pronunciation, and to make a good orator.
> 6. It is the only way to know where nature hath bestowed the benefit of a good voice: which gift is so rare as there is not one among a thousand, that hath it: and in many that excellent gift is lost because they want art to express nature.
> 7. There is not any music of instruments whatsoever comparable to that which is made of the voices of men, where the voices are good, and the same well sorted and ordered.
> 8. The better the voice is, the meeter it is to honour and serve God therewith: and the voice of man is chiefly to be employed to that end.

> > Since singing is so good a thing,
> > I wish all men would learn to sing."

This provides an interesting comparison with the earlier pronouncement of Miles Coverdale in his *Ghostly Psalms and Spiritual Songs* (1538), where he says:

> Would God that our minstrels had none other thing to play upon, neither our carters and plowman other thing to whistle upon save psalms, hymns and such like godly songs . . . and if women at the rocks (distaff) and spinning at the wheels had none other songs to pass their time withal than such as Moses' sister sung before them, they should be better occupied than with "Hey nonny nonny"—"Hey trolly trolly," and such like fantasies.

One of these "Hey trolly trolly" songs has been preserved for us in Ravenscroft's *Deuteromelia* (1609):

Willy, prithee go to bed,
For thou wilt have a drowsy head,
To-morrow we must a-hunting
And betimes be stirring
With a hey trolly lolly lolly lo
  lolly lo lolly lo lolly lo lolly lo,
Hey trolly lolly, hey trolly lolly lo.

It is like to be fair weather,
Couple all my hounds together,
We will go a-hunting
And betimes be stirring
With a hey trolly lolly lolly lo, etc.

Prick the path and down the lane,
She uses still her old strain,
She's gone to what-call wood
Where we are like to do no good,
With a hey trolly lolly lolly lo, etc.

Second and third verses from D'Urfey's *Wit and Mirth, or Pills to Purge Melancholy.*

Melody of "Trenchmore," a popular dance tune referred to in 1564, from *Deuteromelia*, which gives two versions. Cf. *English Melodies* (J. M. Dent & Sons Ltd.), also Chappell's *Popular Music of the Olden Time.*

Byrd clearly was not quite so Puritanic as Miles Coverdale, for he made an arrangement of the melody of "The Carman's Whistle" for the so-called *Queen Elizabeth's Virginal Book* (1550–1620), a manuscript now in the Fitzwilliam Museum, Cambridge.

CHAPTER V

Ballads and ballad tunes—Anthony Munday—Thomas Deloney—Ballad tunes arranged
for virginals by Byrd and Bull—"Fortune My Foe"—Robin Hood ballads.

IN the reign of Mary Tudor, herself a player on lute and virginals, and
during the early years of Queen Elizabeth, appear several tunes to which
a great many songs and ballads were written. Of these, one which has
lived to our own day is "The Leather Bottel," clearly an old tune with
much of the old verse remaining:

When I survey the world around,
The heav'ns, the earth and all therein,
The ships that on the sea do swim,
To guard from foes that none come in;
And let them all do what they can,
'Twas for one end, the good of man,
So I wish in heaven his soul may dwell
That first found out the leather bottel.

Now what do you say to these cans of wood?
O no, in faith, they cannot be good;
For if the bearer fall by the way,
Why, on the ground your liquor doth lay!
But had it been in a leather bottel,
Although he had fallen, all had been well;
So I wish, etc.

Then what do you say to these glasses fine?
O they shall have no praise of mine,
For if you chance to touch the brim,
Down falls the liquor and all therein;
But had it been in a leather bottel
And the stopple in, all had been well;
So I wish, etc.

Melody quoted in Chappell's *Popular Music
of the Olden Time*, and *English Melodies* (J. M.
Dent & Sons Ltd.).

To this tune seems to have been written an interesting ballad on Queen
Mary, of which the following is a verse:

To Mary our Queen, that flower so sweet,
This Marigold I do apply,
For that the name doth seem so meet
And properly in each party,

44

For her enduring patiently
The storms of such as list to scold
At her doings, without cause why,
Loth to see spring this Marigold.

It is advisable to make oneself familiar with these ballad tunes, as they account for some otherwise inexplicable metres. Take, for instance, the tune of "Row well, ye mariners," from which comes the curious rhythm at the close of each stanza of ballads which have been written to it. One of the earliest of the ballads to this tune is here printed:

The Doleful Lover

As one without refuge
For life doth plead with panting breath
And ruefully the Judge
Beholds (whose doom grants life or death),
So fare I now, my only Love,
Whom I do tend as turtle dove,
Whose tender looks (O jolly joy)
Shall win me sure your loving boy.
Fair looks, sweet Dame,
Or else (alas) I take my bane;
Nice talk, coying,
Will bring me sure to my ending.

. . . . .

As nature hath you deck'd
With worthy gifts above the rest,
So to your praise most great,
Let pity dwell within your breast,
That I may say with heart and will,
Lo, this is she that might me kill:
For why? in hand she held the knife,
And yet (forsooth) she saved my life.
Hey-ho, darling,
With lusty love now let us sing;
Play on, Minstrel,
My Lady is my only girl.

Words from *A Handful of Pleasant Delights*, 1584. Melody from Thos. Robinson's *School of Musick*, fol. 1603, quoted in Chappell's *Popular Music of the Olden Time*.

This rhythm of four beats to a short line is used by George Peele, in *The Love of David and Fair Bethsade*:

Hot sun, cool fire,
    tempered with sweet air,
Black shade, fair nurse,
    shadow my sweet hair.
Shine sun, burn fire,
    breathe air, and ease me;
Black shade, fair nurse,
    shroud me and please me.

The same rhythm is used by Michael Drayton in the seventh eclogue of his *Shepheard's Garland* (1593):

> Thought's grief, heart's woe,
> Hope's pain, body's languish,
> Envy's rage, sleep's foe,
> Fancy's fraud, soul's anguish.

As the tune of "The Doleful Lover" was a popular dance tune, the probability is that this was a dance rhythm.

"John Dory" is an old ballad tune to a variant of which is sung a famous song in *Gammer Gurton's Needle*, one of the earliest Elizabethan plays:

I cannot eat but little meat,
My stomach is not good;
But sure I think that I can drink
With him that wears a hood.

Though I go bare, take ye no care,
I nothing am a-cold;
I stuff my skin so full within
Of jolly good ale and old.

Back and side go bare, go bare,
Both foot and hand go cold;
But belly, God send thee good ale enough,
Whether it be new or old.

Tune from Stafford's *Musica Antiqua*. The type version of the "John Dory" tune is printed in chapter xii, p. 126.

I love no roast but a nut-brown toast,
And a crab laid in the fire;
A little bread shall do me stead,
Much bread I not desire:

No frost nor snow, no wind, I trow,
Can hurt me if I would,
I am so wrapt and throughly lapt
Of jolly good ale and old.

One ballad tune beloved of Shakespeare is "Heartsease," to which a song in the early play, *Misogonus* (1560) was sung. The first half of this tune seems to have been used in the street cry of the coopers, as it appears as such in Deering's *Cries of London*. (Cf. chapter xi, p. 100.)

Sing care away, with sport and play,
Pastime is all our pleasure,
If well we fare, for nought we care,
In mirth consists our treasure.

What doth avail, far hence to sail
And lead our life in toiling,
Or to what end shall we here spend
Our days in irksome moiling?

The merry man with cup and can
Lives longer than doth twenty:
The miser's wealth doth hurt his health,
Examples we have plenty.

With Bess and Nell we love to dwell
In kissing and in talking:
But whoopho, holly, with trolly lolly!
To them we'll now be walking.

The pilgrimages to Walsingham ceased when Henry appropriated the treasures of the shrine, but the tune of "Walsingham," attached to ballads associated with that pilgrimage, remained so popular that even in the seventeenth century it was taught to singing-birds.

Deloney's ballad to this tune, which finds an echo in a snatch of song sung by Ophelia in *Hamlet*, is quoted in Percy's *Reliques*:

Tune from Playford's *Dancing Master*. Quoted in Chappell's *Popular Music of the Olden Time*.

As ye came from the holy land
Of blessed Walsingham,
O met you not my true love
As by the way ye came?

"How should I know your true love,
That have met many a one,
As I came from the holy land,
That have both come and gone."

My love is neither white nor brown,
But as the heavens fair;
There is none hath her form divine,
Either in earth, or air.

Melody from setting by W. Byrd. Quoted in Chappell's *Popular Music of the Olden Time*.

"Such an one did I meet, good sir,
With an angelic face:
Who like a nymph, a queen appear'd
Both in her gait, her grace."

Yes, she hath clean forsaken me,
And left me all alone,
Who sometime loved me as her life,
And called me her own.

"What the cause she leaves thee thus,
And a new way doth take,

That sometime loved thee as her life,
And thee her joy did make?"

I that loved her all my youth,
Grow old now as you see;
Love liketh not the failing fruit
Nor yet the withered tree.

The ballad-mongers thrived on topical verse, and wrote what may be termed the journalese of their day. Two whose lyrics occasionally rise to a higher level are Anthony Munday and Thomas Deloney, the latter being also a prose-writer of considerable charm. To Deloney is now given the song once credited to Shakespeare:

> Crabbed Age and Youth
> Cannot live together;
> Youth is full of pleasure,
> Age is full of care.

One of the songs in Deloney's novel, *The Gentle Craft*, has a subtle charm that one misses in the more sophisticated Elizabethans:

Would God that it were holiday,
Hey derry down, down derry,
That with my love I might go play;
With woe my heart is weary.
My whole delight
Is in her sight;
Would God I had her company,
        Her company,
Hey derry down, down-a-down.

My love is fine, my love is fair,
Hey derry down, down derry,
No maid with her may well compare
In Kent or Canterbury.
From me my love
Shall never move;
Would God I had her company,
        Her company,
Hey derry down, down a-down.

Deloney's ballad of "The Spanish Lady" is associated with an enchanting melody.

Will you hear a Spanish lady,
How she woo'd an Englishman?
Garments gay and rich as may be
Deck'd with jewels she had on.
Of a comely countenance and grace was she,
And by birth and parentage of high degree.

As his prisoner there he kept her,
In his hands her life did lie;
Cupid's bands did tie them faster
By the liking of an eye.
In his courteous company was all her joy,
To favour him in anything she was not coy.

From PERCY'S *Reliques.*

The Spanish Lady

Will you hear a Spanish la-dy How she vow'd an Englishman? Garments gay and rich as may be Deck'd with jewels she had on of a comely countenance and grace was she And by birth and parentage of high de gree

Tune in Skene MS. *c.* 1615). Cf. *English Melodies* (J. M. Dent & Sons Ltd.).

These ballad tunes were not known merely to the ballad singers. They were adapted to the virginals by courtly musicians, who knew them and used them as dance tunes. "Walsingham," for instance, was so arranged by William Byrd and Dr. John Bull, while Byrd also made a setting of "Sellinger's Round," and did not disdain the simple melody of "Peascod Time."

A ballad, identified with the most famous of Elizabethan melodies, the "hanging tune" of "Fortune My Foe," was registered with the Stationers' Company in 1565–6. As Chappell says, the ballads written to this tune are "too many for enumeration." "Fortune My Foe" itself used to be sung by the crowds waiting for public executions, and owing to the frequency of such executions, was easy to keep in mind. Shakespeare mentions it in *The Merry Wives of Windsor* (Act III, scene iii):

Fortune my foe, why dost thou frown on me
And will thy favours never greater be?
Wilt thou, I say, for ever breed me pain,
And wilt thou ne'er restore my joys again?

Fortune hath wrought me grief and great annoy;
Fortune hath falsely stolen my love away;
My love and joy whose sight did make me glad:
Greater misfortune never young man had.

Melody from William Ballet's *Lute Book* (1594). Cf. Chappell's *Popular Music of the Olden Time*, and *English Melodies* (J. M. Dent & Sons Ltd.).

Whenever there is a good tune in this, or, indeed, any period of British balladry, the ingenious Dr. W. H. Gratton Flood comes along and claims it as Irish. "Fortune My Foe" naturally could not escape the net of this acquisitive Irishman, and with it have gone ten other ballad tunes referred to by Shakespeare, of which one, "Light o' Love," is said by tradition to have been the poet's favourite. He mentions it in *Two Gentlemen of Verona*, and *Much Ado About Nothing*. If it was Irish, the Irish must have danced to some six-eight measure at the time, for it is clearly a dance tune (see next chapter).

Another of these ballads for which more convincing evidence is given of its Irish origin is "Calen o Casture Me," registered with the Stationers' Company in 1581, and referred to in the anthology *A Handful of Pleasant Delights* of 1584. William de Bathe, an Irish student at Oxford University, who published an *Introduction to Art of Music* in 1584 while still a student, and who shortly afterwards became a favourite of the queen, is credited with making Irish airs popular at court in the later years of Elizabeth's reign.

E

Whenas I view your comely grace,
Your golden hairs, your angel face,
Your azured veins much like the skies
Your silver teeth, your crystal eyes,
Your coral lips, your crimson cheeks,
That Gods and men both love and leekes,

.   .   .   .   .

My soul with silence moving sense
Doth wish of God with reverence
Long life and virtue you possess,
To match these gifts of worthiness:
And love and pity may be spied
To be your chief and only guide.

Melody from W. Byrd's arrangement in Queen Elizabeth's *Virginal Book.* Cf. *Shakespeare Music,* edited by E. W. Naylor (J. Curwen & Sons Ltd.).

The "Robin Hood" ballads were never so popular as in the sixteenth century. The daybook of John Dorne, bookseller at Oxford, shows for the year 1520, "quantities of ballads, among which the celebrated 'Nut-Brown Maid,' 'Christmas Carols,' poems about Robin Hood and about Robert the Devil" (Jusserand). One of the "Robin Hood" ballads, which Sir Toby in *Twelfth Night* evidently knew, was "Arthur a Bland," or "Robin Hood and the Tanner."

This bustling ballad of thirty-seven stanzas as quoted by Child (his No. 126) is too long to be printed here, but half a dozen verses will give the swing of it:

In Nottingham there lives a jolly tanner,
With a hey down down a down down,
His name it is Arthur a Bland.
There is ne'er a squire in Nottinghamshire
Dare bid bold Arthur stand.

With a long pikestaff upon his shoulder
So well he can clear his way;
By two and three he makes them to flee,
For he hath no list to stay.

And as he went forth, in a summer's morning,
Into the forest of merry Sherwood,
To view the red deer, that range here and there,
There met he with bold Robin Hood.

.   .   .   .   .

(*They fight and are reconciled.*)

Tune, sometimes called "Hey down a down," has been traced back to 1640. Cf. *The Minstrelsy of England,* Vol. II, p. 64 (Augener Ltd.).

Then Robin Hood blew on the bugle horn,
He blew full loud and shrill,
But quickly anon appear'd Little John,
Came tripping down a green hill.

. . . . .

Then Robin Hood took them both by the hand
And danced round about the oak-tree;
"For three merry men, and three merry men,
And three merry men we be.

"And ever hereafter, as long as I live,
We three will be all one;
The wood shall ring, and the old wife sing
Of Robin Hood, Arthur and John."

"All in a garden green" seems to have been the opening line of several ballads of this period, for those indicated as being sung to a tune of this name do not all have the same metre. One tune in William Ballet's *Lute Book* (1594), to which words have been found, is still a favourite with country dancers, who know it under the name of "Gathering Peascods."

All in a garden green
Two lovers sat at ease,
As they could scarce be seen among,
Among the leafy trees.
They long had lov'd y-fere
And no longer than truly,
In that time of the year
Cometh 'twixt May and July.

. . . . .

She listed to his song,
And heard it with a smile,
And innocent as young
She dreamed not of guile.
No guile he meant, I ween.
For he was true as steel,
As was thereafter seen
When she made him her weal.

Cf. Chappell's *Popular Music of the Olden Time*.

CHAPTER VI

Ballads sung to dance tunes ("Sellinger's Round" and "Green Sleeves")—Dances mentioned in Shakespeare—Words of lyrics fitted to dance rhythms—Popularity of dancing in Tudor times—Dance songs in masques—A Saraband rhythm— Dance tunes—"Robin lend to me thy bow."

SOME of these ballad tunes at first were probably dance tunes such as "Sellinger's Round." One of the earliest poems associated with "Sellinger's Round" is "Farewell, adieu, that courtly life":

Farewell, adieu, that courtly life,
To war we tend to go;
It is good sport to see the strife
Of soldiers in a row.
    How merrily they forward march
    These enemies to slay:
    With hey trim and trixie too,
    Their banners to display.

Now shall we have the golden cheats
When others want the same;
And soldiers have full many feats
Their enemies to tame:
    With cocking here and booming there
    They break their foes array:
    And lusty lads among the fields
    Their ensigns do display.

The drum and flute play lustily,
The trumpet blows amain,
And venturous knights courageously
Do march before their train:
    With spears in rest so lively drest
    In armour bright and gay;
    With hey trim and trixie too,
    Their banners they display.

From John Pickering's *A New Interlude of Vice*, containing the "History of Horestes," 1567.

Melody from *Queen Elizabeth's Virginal Book*. Quoted in *English Melodies* (J. M. Dent & Sons Ltd.), with words of a later ballad.

"Green Sleeves," another dance tune, still a favourite with Morris dancers, is twice mentioned in *The Merry Wives of Windsor*, and was already old in Shakespeare's day. Chappell, indeed, traces it back to the time of Henry VIII. The ballad with which it was registered as a tune in 1580, is printed in *A Handful of Pleasant Delights* (1584 edition).

Alas, my love, ye do me wrong,
To cast me off discourteously,
And I have lovèd you so long,
Delighting in your company.

    Green Sleeves was all my joy,
    Green Sleeves was my delight:
    Green Sleeves was my heart of gold
    And who but Lady Green Sleeves?

I have been ready at your hand
To grant whatever you did crave.
I have both wagéd life and land
Your love and good will for to have.

    Green Sleeves was all my joy, etc.

I bought thee kerchers to thy head,
That were wrought fine and gallantly
I kept thee both at board and bed,
Which cost my purse well favouredly.

    Green Sleeves was all my joy, etc.

My men were clothed all in green,
And they did ever wait on thee;
All this was gallant to be seen;
And yet thou wouldst not love me.

    Green Sleeves was all my joy, etc.

Thou couldst desire no earthly thing,
But still thou hadst it readily:
Thy music still to play and sing:
And yet thou wouldst not love me.

    Green Sleeves was all my joy, etc.

Melody from William Ballet's *Lute Book* (1594). Quoted in Chappell's *Popular Music of the Old Time.*

Well I will pray to God on High,
    That thou my constancy mayst see;
And that yet once before I die,
    Thou wilt vouchsafe to love me.

    Green Sleeves was all my joy, etc.

A ballad with a gay dance tune, the words of which link up with the French pastourelles of the fifteenth century is to be found in Ravenscroft's *Deuteromelia,* incorporating "King Henry's Mirth, or Freeman's Songs," published in 1609, but containing many numbers that are clearly of older date.

The theme of the country girl importuned by an amorous knight for whom she is more than a match in wit takes us back to the earliest known comic opera, *Le Jeu de Robin et Marion,* of the trouvère Adam de la Halle, and survives in English folk-song of our own day, witness "Blow away the morning dew," with its climax:

> But when they came to the garden gate
> So nimble she popped in
> And said "There is a fool without
> And here's a maid within."

Compare this with the ballad in question: "The Baffled Knight."

Yonder comes a courteous knight,
Lustily raking over the lee;
He was well ware of a bonny lass,
As she came wandering over the way.
Then she sang downadown, hey down
  derry (*bis*).

"Jove you speed, fair lady," he said
Among the leaves that be so green;
"If I were a king and wore a crown,
Full soon, fair lady, shouldst thou be a
  queen."

"If you will carry me, gentle sir,
A maid unto my father's hall,
Then you shall have your will of me,
Under purple and under pall."

. . . . . .

When she came to her father's hall
It was well walléd round about;
She rode in at the wicket gate,
And shut the four-ear'd fool without.

Ravenscroft's *Deuteromelia* (1609). Quoted in Chappell's *Popular Music of the Olden Time*.

The relation between the tune and the ballad is worth analysis. "Light o' Love" is stated in *Much Ado About Nothing* to have been a dance song: Margaret will dance, if Beatrice will sing it (Act III, scene iv).

By force I am fixéd my fancy to write,
Ingratitude willeth me not to refrain;
Then blame me not, ladies, although I indite
What lighty love now amongst you doth
  reign.
Your traces in places to outward allure-
  ments
Do move my endeavour to be the more
  plain.
Your nicings and 'ticings with sundry
  procurements
To publish your lightie love do me constrain.

Words by Leonard Gybson,
LILLY'S *Ballads*.

Melody in William Ballet's *Lute Book* (1594). Quoted in Chappell's *Popular Music of the Olden Time*.

Shakespeare's many references to dancing indicate his interest. Of Morris dances he mentions by name one, "Trip and Go" (*Love's Labour's*

Lost) which is introduced as a dance song by Thomas Nashe in his *Summer's Last Will and Testament* (c. 1592), where it is sung and danced to by three clowns and three maids.

Trip and go, heave and ho,
Up and down, to and fro,
From the town to the grove
Two and two let us rove
A-maying, a-playing,
Love hath no gainsaying,
So trip and go, trip and go,
Merrily trip and go.

Melody from *Musick's Delight on the Cithern* (1666). Quoted in Chappell's *Popular Music of the Olden Time*.

Other dances named by Shakespeare are the galliard, cinq-pas, dump, coranto, passy-measure, pavane, jig, brawl, canary, hornpipe, hay, and bergomask.

Dance music may give us a possible clue to the tune Shakespeare may have had in mind when he wrote his lyric, "Under the greenwood tree" for *As You Like It*. In this, the words "Come hither, come hither, come hither" at once suggest a dance measure, and it is significant that the earliest tune associated with the words is a dance tune, although the words have not hitherto been printed to exactly fit this. Chappell, whose knowledge of old tunes has never been equalled, suggests that this tune may date back to Elizabeth's day. Indeed his reasoning might be carried further so as to identify it with the ballad of "Robin Hood and the Monk" (see p. 22) which takes us back to the year 1450, as this has an "Under the greenwood tree" end-line and can readily be sung to this melody. Some lutenist may have written another tune for the actual production of *As You Like It*, but Shakespeare may very well have had the old tune in his head when he wrote the words of the song we know. His words exactly fit this traditional tune if the line

Come hither, come hither, come hither,

is repeated, as lines and phrases are so often repeated when sung. The song is here printed with notation arranged in such a way as to show the dancing rhythm of words corresponding to the music:

Under the greenwood tree
Who loves to lie with me,
And turn his merry note
Unto the sweet bird's throat,
Come hither, come hither, come hither:
Here shall we see   (*bis*)
No enemy
But winter and rough weather.

Who doth ambition shun,
And loves to live i' the sun,
Seeking the food he eats,
And pleased with what he gets,
Come hither, come hither, come hither:
Here shall he see   (*bis*)
No enemy
But winter and rough weather.

If it do come to pass
That any man turn ass,
Leaving his wealth and ease
A stubborn will to please,
Ducdame, ducdame, ducdame: (*bis*)
Here shall he see
Gross fools as he,
And if he will come to me.

Tune from Playford's *Dancing Master*.

In Clement Robinson's *A Handful of Pleasant Delights* there are a number of dance tunes cited for the ballads printed, such as "Quarter Braules," "Cecilia Pavan," "Black Almaine," "Kypascie" ("Qui passe"), and the "New Almaine." One of the most delightful songs of the period is said to be written to a dance tune, "Brangill of Poictu":

We be three poor mariners
Newly come from the seas;
We spend our lives in jeopardy
While others live at ease.
Shall we go dance the round, the round,
    the round?
Shall we go dance the round, the round,
    the round?
And he that is a bully boy
Come pledge me on the ground, the ground,
    the ground.

From *Deuteromelia* (1609). Cf. *English Melodies* (J. M. Dent & Sons Ltd.).

We care not for these martial men
That do our states disdain;
But we care for these merchantmen
Who do our states maintain.
To them we dance this round, around, around;
To them we dance this round, around, around;
And he that is a bully boy
Come pledge me on the ground, aground, aground.

Anthony Munday, who is the Antonio Balladino of Ben Jonson's play *The Case is Altered* (1599), published in 1588 *A Banquet of Dainty Conceits*—"furnished with very delicate and choice inventions to delight their minds who take Pleasure in Musique, and therewithal to sing sweet Ditties, either to the Lute, Bandora, Virginals or any other Instrument." The twenty-two tunes to which his moralizing ballads in this quaint production are written are, with one possible exception, all dance tunes, such as "Allemaines," "Galliardes," and "Pavanes."

In a modest preface addressed "to the gentle and friendly reader," the balladist remarks: "If any ditty shall chance to limp a little in the note—yet I pray thee condemn me not, in that I have no jot of knowledge of music, but what I have done and do is only by the ear; for had I skill in musique, they should have been far better than they be."

If Munday is the author of that truly charming lyric "Beauty sat bathing by a spring" he had certainly cause to apologize for some of these *Dainty Conceits*, although some are fair enough.

Beauty sat bathing by a spring
Where fairest shades did hide her;
The winds blew calm, the birds did sing,
The cool streams ran beside her.
My wanton thoughts enticed mine eye,
To see what was forbidden:
But better memory said Fie!
So vain desire was chidden—
Hey nonny nonny O, hey nonny nonny!

Into a slumber then I fell,
When fond imagination
Seemed to see, but could not tell
Her feature or her fashion;
But even as babes in dreams do smile
And sometimes fall a-weeping,
So I awaked, as wise that while
As when I fell a-sleeping.

Music by R. Jones, *Ultimum Vale*. Reproduced with original harmonies in *Eight Ayres*, edited by Peter Warlock and Philip Wilson. Transcribed by permission of the Publishers, Enoch & Sons (1927) Ltd., Boosey & Co. Inc., U.S.A. and Canada, Oxford University Press (for all other countries).

Typical of Munday's ballads to dance tunes is that written to a Spanish Pavan which served for a number of other ballads of the period:

Two friends that had a shock of corn
One day did part it equally,
But left it in the garner still
For want of other remedy.
One of these thought his friend had most,
Which caused him, discourteously,
To seek it to steal thence,
Not minding friendly amity.

His friend that not mistrusted him
Did walk about his business—
The other to the garner comes
To make assured his craftiness;
And on his friend's heap cast his cloak
Lest he should miss of his device;
For he that steals in the dark
May be deceived twice.

He being gone, within a while
The other partner thither came,
Who, seeing his friend's cloak on the heap,
Did very kindly take the same,
Thinking his friend had left the cloak.

To save his portion from the dust,
Therefore he thought again
To show his friendship just.

.   .   .   .   .

His partner carried thence his corn,
And he went home full heavily,
Not daring to reveal his harm
Lest all should know his treachery.
See how Deceit deceived himself,
Mark well the practice and the end;
I would the like might hap
To every faithless friend.

Tune of the Spanish Pavan.

When Samson was a tall young man

His pow'r and strength in creased then

And in the host and tribe of Dan

The Lord did bless him al·· way·

It chanced so up on a day

As he was walking on his way

He saw a maiden fresh and gay

In Timnath, in Timnath.

Tune from Chappell's *Popular Music of the Olden Time* in which another ballad is cited:

"When Samson was a tall young man
His pow'r and strength increased then
And in the host and tribe of Dan
The Lord did bless him alway.
It chanced so upon a day
As he was walking on his way
He saw a maiden fresh and gay
In Timnath, in Timnath."

This dance (the Spanish Pavan) came to England perhaps with Katharine of Aragon, and was highly popular at the court of Elizabeth and James II. The other ballads to this tune have no particular lyrical merit, but the one commencing "When Samson was a tall young man" introduces a rhyme succession in the second half of the verse which Dryden follows in a song for *The Spanish Friar*, to be used again with great lyrical charm by Swinburne in his "Garden of Proserpine."

Dryden:	Swinburne:
Farewell, ungrateful traitor,	Here, where the world is quiet;
Farewell, my perjured swain,	Here, where all trouble seems
Let never injured creature	Dead winds' and spent waves' riot
Believe a man again.	In doubtful dreams of dreams;
The pleasure of possessing	I watch the green field growing
Surpasses all expressing,	For reaping folk and sowing,
But 'tis too short a blessing,	For harvest-time and mowing,
And love too long a pain.	A sleepy world of streams.

W. P. Ker, in his London lectures on *Form and Style*, points out the recurrence of this stanza form in the ballad poetry of Catalonia, and refers to it as a sort of abstract form coming into the minds of men and being associated with words. The recurrence of this form in ballad poetry may, however, be more definitely traced to the original meaning of ballad, which is "dance-song." The rhythms of this ballad metre go back to original dance-song measures.

Webbe in his *Discourse of English Poetry* (1580) wrote:

Neither is there any tune or stroke which may be sung or played on instruments which hath not some poetical ditties framed according to the numbers thereof: some to Rogero, some to Trenchmore, to Downright Squire, to Gaillardes, to Pavanes, to Jigs, to Brawles, to all manner of tunes which every fiddler knows better than myself.

The usual explanation of these dance tunes is that they were adapted to dances from ballads, but this does not account for the large number of dance tunes for which no words are known.

When one remembers how popular dancing was in Tudor days in every class of life, one readily understands the influence that dance tunes may have had on poets accustomed to writing lyrics to music. After a certain diplomatic banquet in 1517, Henry VIII and his guests "betook themselves into another hall where the damsels of the most serene queen were, and dancing went on there for two hours."

Anne Boleyn, according to Chateaubriand, "danced the English dances, leaping and dancing with infinite grace and agility." A picture at Penshurst shows Queen Elizabeth engaged in an ague lavolta with the Earl of Leicester. Here was a court where dancing was a courtier's best equipment. "The Queen," wrote Sir John Stanhope in 1589, "is well, I assure you. Six or seven galliards in a morning, beside music and singing, is her usual exercise."

One of Dowland's most celebrated songs is frequently referred to as the "Frog Galliard." The tune was afterwards used by a number of ballad writers, and Chappell conjectures that Dowland wrote the music originally as a dance tune, adding the words later:

Now, O now, I needs must part,
Parting though I absent mourn.
Absence can no joy impart,
Joy once fled cannot return.
While I live I needs must love;
Love dies not when Hope is gone.
Now at last Despair doth prove
Love divided loveth none.

    Sad despair doth drive me hence;
    This despair unkindness sends.
    If that parting be offence
    It is she that then offends.

Dear, when I am from thee gone,
Gone are all my joys at once.
I loved thee and thee alone
In whose love I joyéd once.
And although your sight I leave,
Sight wherein my joys do lie,
Till that death do sense bereave,
Never shall affection die.

    Sad despair, etc.

The lavolta was a French dance
which gave English poetry at least
one interesting dactylic measure:

Henry our royal king
Would ride a-hunting
To the green forest so pleasant and fair,
To see the harts skipping
And dainty does tripping
Unto merry Sherwood his nobles repair.
Hawk and hound were unbound,
All things prepared
For the game in the same
With good regard.

All a long summer's day
Rode the king pleasantly
With all his princes and nobles each one;
Chasing the hart and hind
And the bucks gallantly
Till the dark evening forc'd all to turn home.
Then at last riding fast
He had lost quite
All his lords in the wood
Late in the night.

Dowland's *First Book of Songs* (1597). Cf.
Chappell's *Popular Music of the Olden Time*
and *English Melodies* (J. M. Dent & Sons Ltd.).

Tune found by Rimbault. Cf. Chappell's *Popular Music of the Olden Time*.

In the masque which Campian wrote for the festivities at the marriage of Lord Hayes, performed at Whitehall on Twelfth Night before King James, there is a dance song in which the words are knit admirably to the rhythm and melody of the music. The description is taken from the original:

This spoken, the four Silvans played on their instruments the first strain of this song following: and at the repetition thereof the voice fell in with the instruments which were thus divided: a treble and a base were placed near His Majesty and another treble and base near the grove, that the words of the song might be heard of all, because the trees of gold instantly at the first sound of their voices began to move and dance according to the measure of the time which the musicians kept in singing, and the nature of the words which they delivered.

Move now with measured sound,
You charmed grove of gold;
Trace forth the sacred ground
That shall your forms unfold.
Diana and the starry night,
For your Apollo's sake,
Endue your sylvan shapes with power
This strange delight to make.
Much joy must needs the place betide
Where trees for gladness move;
A fairer sight was ne'er beheld,
Nor more expressing love.

The full song may be found in *The Minstrelsy of England*, Vol. II, edited by Edmondstoune Duncan (Augener Ltd.), or in *Masque in Honour of the Marriage of Lord Hayes* (Joseph Williams).

The first half of this tune appears, strangely enough, as the opening half of the Swedish Ox-dance tune used for a burlesque dance by students of the University of Upsala during the reign of Gustavus Adolphus. Whether the Swedes took the tune from Thomas Campian, or Campian adopted a Swedish dance tune, remains for some musicologist to discover.

Melody obtained from a Swedish folk-dancer in Winnipeg.

In this masque, Thomas Giles, the director of the dancing, composed a dance tune for which Campian wrote the words, "Triumph now with joy and mirth":

Triumph now with joy and mirth,
The God of peace hath blest our land.
We enjoy the fruits of earth
Through favour of his bounteous hand.
We through his most loving grace
A King and kingly seed behold,
Like a sun with lesser stars
Or careful shepherd to his fold:
Triumph then and yield him praise
That gives us blest and joyful days.

In the masque written by Thomas Campian for the entertainment given by Lord Knowles to Queen Anne at Cawsome House, near Reading, in 1613, there is another dance song with metre evidently suited to the music, followed by some doggerel verses swinging to the music of a coranto.

Dance tune by Thomas Giles. The full song may be found in *The Minstrelsy of England*, Vol. II, edited by Edmondstoune Duncan (Augener Ltd.), or in *Masque in Honour of the Marriage of Lord Hayes* (Joseph Williams).

The ballets or dance-songs introduced into England under the influence of Italian music provide some lively metres. Of these English ballets, perhaps the best known is Thomas Morley's "Now is the month of maying":

Now is the month of Maying
When merry lads are playing,
Each with his bonny lass
Upon the greeny grass.

The Spring clad all in gladness
Doth laugh at Winter's sadness,
And to the bagpipe's sound
The nymphs tread out their ground.

Fie then! Why sit we musing,
Youth's sweet delight refusing?
Say, dainty nymphs and speak,
Shall we play barley-break?

Melody from Morley's *Ballets for Five Voices* (1595), to be found in *The Minstrelsy of England*, Vol. I (Augener Ltd.). An original copy of the songbook is in the Congressional Library, Washington, D.C.

Ben Jonson in *The Staple of News* makes good-natured comedy out of the poet who writes his verses to dance tunes:

MADRIGAL.	It is a madrigal; I affect that kind of poem much.
PENNYBOY JR.	And thence you have the name.
FITBON.	It is his rose, he can make nothing else.
MAD.	I made it to the tune the fiddlers played, That we all liked so well.
P. JR.	Good! Read it.
MAD.	The sun is father of all metals, you know, *Silver and Gold.*
P. JR.	Ay, leave your prologues, say.
MAD.	*As bright as is the sun her sire,* *Or earth, her mother, in her best attire,* *Or Mint, the midwife, with her fire,* *Comes forth her grace!*
P. JR.	That Mint, the midwife, does well.
MAD.	*The splendour of the wealthiest mines,* *The stamp and strength of all imperial lines,* *Both majesty and beauty shines,* *In her sweet face.*
FIT.	That 's fairly said of money.
MAD.	*Look how a torch of taper light,* *Or of that torch's flame a beacon bright.*
P. JR.	Good!
MAD.	Now there! I want a line to finish, sir.
P. Jr.	*Or of that beacon's fire, moonlight.*
MAD.	*So takes she place!*
FIT.	'Tis good.
MAD.	And then I have a saraband—— *She makes good cheer, she keeps full boards,* *She holds a fair of knights and lords,* *A market of all offices,* *And shops of honours more or less,* *According to Pecunia's grace,* *The bride hath beauty, blood, and place;* *The bridegroom, virtue, valour, wit,* *And wisdom as he stands for it.*
P. JR.	Call in the fiddlers!

Now here we have the character of a poet, evidently studied from the life, who writes his verse to dance tunes. If one were not told that the second half of his poem were written in saraband rhythm, one might not have suspected it, as the eye reads it as purely octosyllabic verse.

In order to show how Madrigal pronounced and probably sang this verse, I have taken a typical saraband tune from Playford's *Dancing Master*, and arranged the words to fit the musical accent. After hearing a verse of this, no wonder that Pennyboy Junior interrupted with "Call in the fiddlers."

Edmund Waller (1606–87) has a poem "Made to a Saraband" which has a rhythm governed in the same way by this type of dance tune:

Hylas O Hylas, why sit we mute,
Now that each bird saluteth the spring?
Wind up the slacken'd spring of thy lute,
Never canst thou want matter to sing.
For love thy breast does fill with such a fire
That whatsoe'er is fair moves thy desire.

It is only natural that dance rhythms should be reproduced in the metres of the lyrics which were written to their tunes. The rhythms of country dance tunes account for broken line metres, such as, for instance, Herrick affects—lines which correspond with the "set and turn single" of country dance steps. One of Herrick's lyrics in such measure is headed with the title of a country dance, "Up Tails All," while another dance tune reflected in his metres is, "Pepper is Black."

Melody from Playford's *Dancing Master*, 1665.

Tune mentioned by Nashe, from Playford's *Dancing Master*, cf. p. 175.

PREPARE YE TO THE PLOUGH

Look up my lords
And mark my words
And hear what I shall sing ye;
And subjects all
Both great and small,
Now mark what I shall bring ye.

Ballad by W. Elderton, to the tune of "Pepper is Black."

AN HYMN TO LOVE

I will confess
With cheerfulness
Love is a thing so likes me,
That let her lay
On me all day,
I'll kiss the hand that strikes me.

R. Herrick, in the same metre which he used for three other poems.

In Ben Jonson's *Masque of Christmas,* Christmas and the Company enter singing a ballad to the dance rhythm of "Up Tails All."

Now God preserve,
As you well deserve,
Your Majesties all two there;
Your Highness small,
With my good lords all,
And ladies, how do you do there?

Give me leave to ask,
For I bring you a masque
From little, little, little London;
Which say the king likes,
I have passed the pikes,
If not, old Christmas is undone.

It is not without significance that this should be the rhythm which Herrick used for his lyric on "Ceremonies for Christmas."

Ben Jonson uses the same rhythm in the dance song he introduces into the *Masque of Augurs* (1622), where "Enter John Urson with his bears," who dance while he sings the following;

Though it may seem rude
For me to intrude
With these my bears by chance-a,
'Twere sport for a king
If they could sing
As well as they can dance-a.

But such dance rhythms in the English lyric date back much earlier than Herrick and Ben Jonson—one finds them, for instance, in Henry VIII's "Pastime with good company," written apparently to a dance tune, entitled "The Poor Man's Dump" (see Chapter III).

Two dance tunes which served to carry many a ballad are "Lusty Gallant," and "Turkeyloney." One of the earliest and best of the ballads associated with "Lusty Gallant" is

Fain would I have a pretty thing
To give unto my lady.
I name no thing and mean no thing,
But as pretty a thing as may be.

Twenty journeys would I make
And twenty ways would hie me
To make adventure for her sake,
To set some matter by me.

Some do long for pretty knacks
And some for strange devices;
God send me that my lady lacks,
I care not what the price is.

I walk the town and tread the street
In every corner seeking:
The pretty thing I cannot meet
That 's for my lady's liking.

Tune from William Ballet's *Lute Book* (1594). Quoted in Chappell's *Popular Music of the Olden Time.*

F

The mercers pull me going by,
The silk wives say, "What lack ye?"
The thing you have not, then say I,
Ye foolish fools, go pack ye.

It is not all the silk in Cheape,
Nor all the golden treasure:
Nor twenty bushels in a heap
Can do my lady pleasure.

The gravers of the golden shows,
With jewels do beset me.
The seemsters in the shops that sowes
May do nothing but let me.

But were it in the wit of man
By any means to make it,
I could for coney buy it then,
And say, "Fair lady, take it."

O Lady, what a luck is this,
That my good willing misseth:
To find what pretty thing it is
That my good lady wisheth.

Thus fain would I have had this pretty
   thing
To give unto my lady.
I said no harm, nor I meant no harm,
But as pretty a thing as may be.

This can be traced as far back as 1565, and equally old is "Turkey-loney," with words which were entered at Stationers' Hall in 1557:

IF EVER I MARRY I'LL MARRY A MAID

If ever I marry, I'll marry a maid:
To marry a widow I'm sore afraid;
For maids they are simple and never will
   grouch,
But widows full oft, as they say, know too
   much.

A maid is so sweet and so gentle of kind
That a maid is the wife I will choose to
   my mind;
A widow is froward and never will yield,
Or if such there be you will meet them but
   seeld.

.   .   .   .   .

Then if ever I marry, give me a fresh maid,
If to marry with any I be not afraid;
But to marry with any, it asketh much care,
And some bachelors hold they are best as
   they are.

Tune in William Ballet's *Lute Book* (1594).
Quoted in Chappell's *Popular Music of the
Olden Time*.

A delightful song of this period, mentioned in a play which was registered in 1568–9, has all the earmarks of being a singing game.

The play was "A very merry and pithy comedy, called *The longer thou livest, the more fool thou art*" and the song in question was introduced by "Moros, counterfeiting a vain gesture and a foolish countenance, singing the foot of many songs, as fools were wont."

Now Robin, lend to me thy bow,
Sweet Robin, lend to me thy bow,
For I must now a-hunting with my lady go,
With my sweet lady.

And whither will thy lady go?
Sweet Wilkin, tell it unto me;
And thou shalt have my hawk, my hound
    and eke my bow
To wait on thy lady.

My lady will to Uppingham,
To Uppingham forsooth will she;
And I myself appointed for to be the man
To wait on my lady.

Adieu, good Wilkin, all beshrewd,
Thy hunting nothing pleaseth me;
But yet beware thy babbling hounds stray
    not abroad
For ang'ring of thy lady.

From *Pammelia* (1609), a collection of "Pleasant Roundelais and delightful Catches," edited by Thomas Ravenscroft.

My hounds shall be led in the line,
So well I can assure it thee;
Unless by strain of view some pursue
    I may find
To please my sweet lady.

With that the lady she came in,
And will'd them all for to agree;
For honest hunting never was accounted
    sin,
Nor never shall for me.

CHAPTER VII

Queen Elizabeth and music—Sir Philip Sidney—Sidney and the Huguenot Psalter
compared—William Byrd

QUEEN ELIZABETH played the lute and viol before she was ten years old.
Roger Ascham, her tutor, said of his royal pupil when she was sixteen,
"In music she is very skilful, but does not greatly delight." Seven years
later at Hatfield she is described as playing on the virginals accompanying
one of the children choristers of St. Paul's, while William Camden, the
antiquarian friend of Ben Jonson, speaks of her as "being able to sing
and play on the lute prettily and sweetly." William Byrd, one of the
greatest of English musicians, was her music teacher. During her
progresses through the country, Elizabeth, not content with the music
that might be offered by her hosts, took in her retinue a choir from the
Chapel Royal, comprising six gentlemen and six children. The duties
of a maid of honour included those of playing and singing to the queen.
On 24 February, 1601, the morning of the execution of her late favourite,
the Earl of Essex, Elizabeth distracted her thoughts by playing on the
virginals.

The Courtier of Castiglione, translated in 1561 by Sir Thomas Hoby,
governed the conduct of those Englishmen who pretended to good
breeding. The chief conditions and qualities of a courtier as laid down
in this book include:

> To sing well upon the book,
> To play upon the lute and sing to it with the ditty,
> To play upon the viol and all other instruments with frets.

The pattern courtier of his age was Sir Philip Sidney, of whose poems
eight are definitely stated to have been written to a specified tune. As
he lay dying, he composed a poem, "La Caisse Rompue," which he caused
to be set to music, and sung at his bedside. "The poet," he wrote in his
Apologie for Poetrie, "cometh to you with words set in delightful proportion, either accompanied with or prepared for the well-enchanting
skill of music." Sidney was greatly influenced by the contemporary
poetry of France which, under the leadership of Ronsard, was closely
associated with music. Clément Marot had set his own translations
of the psalms to popular tunes, and Ronsard maintained that "music is
the elder sister of poetry—without music, poetry is without grace, just
as music without the melody of verse is inanimate and without life."

While Sidney claimed in a famous sonnet:

> My Muse, to some ears not unsweet
> Tempers her words to trampling horses' feet
> More oft than to a chamber melody,

he was not indifferent to the charm of that music. Writing in 1574 from Venice to his friend, Hubert Languet, Sidney says he is "getting a knowledge of music," and again, six years later, to his brother Robert, "Now, sweet brother, take a delight to keep and increase your music; you will not believe what a want I feel of it in my melancholy times." Sir Robert Sidney seems to have followed this injunction, for the lutenist, Robert Jones, dedicated to him in 1600 his first book of songs, "the unworthy labours of my musical travels." In Philip Sidney's *Arcadia* one finds "here a shepherd's boy piping, as though he should never be old; there a young shepherdess knitting and withal singing; and it seemed that her voice comforted her hands to work, and her hands kept time to her voice and music." *Arcadia* is littered with the names of musical instruments to accompany the songs there cited to be sung. Two of these are sung to the harp, one to a gitterne, one to a consort of five viols with as many voices taking parts. One is sung with a base lyra, another to a cittern, and yet another to a lute. "Green Sleeves" is a tune that must have caught his fancy, for in *The Fairy Pastorall or Forest of Elves*, by William Percy, a poem to this tune is credited to "Philip Sydneye Knight":

> The time hath been that a tawdry lace,
> Or a bonnet for my Lady's grace,
> A ring of a rich or a needle's case
> Would make my lady to love me.
> But now the world is grown so rich
> They will leave it be in ne'er so mich;
> Yet by your leave they will keep no tich,
> For which doth not a little move me.
> Fie upon honesty, fie,
> Your head is full of jealousy.
> There is no fault in my Lady
> For to suspect the contrary.

In *The Life of the Renowned Sir Philip Sidney*, by Sir Fulke Greville, there is a reference to the mutual admiration entertained by the courtly English poet and the Dutch Prince William of Nassau, whose simple dress, unbuttoned doublet, and woollen waistcoat seem to have greatly impressed the worthy biographer. William of Nassau was also the hero of a song, the tune of which was taken from the French to serve as the Dutch national anthem, and this tune appealed so much to Sidney that he wrote a lyric adapted to its measures. There are two rhythms in this melody, and Sidney must have had a good ear, otherwise he could not have fitted the words so closely to the music.

Sidney must have heard this tune many a time, as he paid several visits to the Netherlands during Prince William's life, and was himself appointed Governor of Flushing and Rammekins in 1585. It was at Zutphen in

the Netherlands that he received his fatal wound.   The lyric written to
the tune "Wilhelmus van Nassauen" here follows:

Who hath his fancy pleasèd,
With fruits of happy sight,
Let here his eyes be raisèd
On Nature's sweetest light.
A light which doth dissever
And yet unite the eyes;
A light which, dying never,
Is cause the looker dies.

She never dies, but lasteth
In life of lover's heart;
He ever dies that wasteth
In love his chiefest part.
Thus is her life still guarded
In never dying faith,
Thus is his death rewarded,
Since she lives in his death.

Look then and die.   The pleasure
Doth answer well the pain.
Small loss of mortal treasure,
Who may immortal gain.
Immortal be her graces,
Immortal is her mind:
They, fit for heavenly places,
This heaven in it doth bind.

Dutch national air, "Wilhelmus van Nassauen," a sixteenth-century French melody
used for a satirical ballad on the Huguenots
adopted by the followers of William of Nassau
for a song, published in 1581, which became a
national hymn.

Although the old song of "Wilhelmus van Nassauen" has remained the
national anthem of the Dutch to this day, it is a curious comment on the
alertness of the scholars who have edited Sidney's works that they say
nothing about it.

Of the other tunes actually named in the early printed editions of
Sidney's poems, four are Italian and one Spanish.   The Italian tunes
Sidney probably picked up during a visit he paid to Italy in 1574.
Spanish tunes were frequently to be heard at the court of Elizabeth.

Another connection with music overlooked by the scholars is to be
found in the metres used by Sidney for his translations of the psalms.
Unlike the metrical versions of Sternhold and his host of followers, these
do not as a rule conform to the "Chevy Chase" form, but tread an infinite
variety of measures.   In Julian's *Dictionary of Hymnology* these are
described as "the fantastic and capricious measures of the lighter Elizabethan style."   The truth is, however, that the source of this variety

is to be found in the Huguenot Psalter, which Sidney learned to know through his friendship for Languet.

> The song I sang old Languet had me taught,
> Languet, the shepherd best swift Ister knew,
> For clerkly rede, and hating what is naught,
> For faithful heart, clean hands, and mouth as true:
> With his sweet skill my skilless youth he drew,
> To have a feeling taste of Him that sits
> Beyond the heaven, far more beyond our wits.
>
> He said the music best thilk power pleased
> Was jump concord between our wit and will;
> Where highest notes to godliness are raised,
> And lowest sink not down to jot of ill:
> With old true tales he wont mine ears to fill,
> How shepherds did of yore, how now they thrive,
> Spoiling their flock, or while 'twixt them they strive.
>
> He likèd me, but pitied lustful youth;
> His good strong staff my slipp'ry years upbore;
> He still hop'd well, because I lovèd truth:
> Till forc'd to part with heart and eyes e'en sore
> To worthy Corydon he gave me o'er.
> But this in oaks' true shade recounted be,
> Which now in night's deep shade sheep heard of me.

The Huguenot Psalter incorporates tunes of popular airs selected by Clément Marot as *timbres* for his psalm translations, and it was with these in his head that Sidney translated.

In Psalm 3 we have a stanza of six short lines, the origin of which is clearly shown by the music:

Psalm 3

SIDNEY:

Lord, how do they increase
That hateful never cease
To breed my grievous trouble;
How many ones there be
That all against poor me
Their numbers' strength redouble.

HUGUENOT PSALTER:

O Seigneur, que de gens
A nuire diligens
Qui me troublent et grevent;
Mon Dieu, que d'ennemis
Qui aux champs se sont mis
Et contre moy s'eslèvent.

Psalm 40 has a peculiar metre which one might have thought would have stirred the curiosity of scholars. The model is once more found in the Huguenot Psalter where the translation is ascribed to Theodore Beza:

SIDNEY:

While long I did, with patient constancy,
The pleasure of my God attend,
He did himself to me-ward bend
And hearkened how and why that I did cry.
And me from pit bemired
From dungeon He retired
Where I in horrors lay;
Setting my feet upon
A steadfast rocky stone,
And my weak step did stay.

HUGUENOT PSALTER:

Aprés avoir constamment attendu
De l'Eternel la volonté,
Il s'est tourné de mon costé
Et à mon cri au besoin entendu;
Hors de fange et d'ordure
Et profondeur obscure
D'un gouffre m'a tiré
A mes piés affermis
Et au chemin remis
Sur un roc asseuré.

If there was one tune in this psalter that Sidney must have known it was the melody of the great battle hymn of the Huguenots. This tune was originally used by Marot for his translation of Psalm 36, but it was in connection with Beza's stirring version of Psalm 68 that it came to play its part in history. Sidney used it to form his metre for the translation of Psalm 32. His translations were widely circulated in manuscript, and in this form Ben Jonson may have noticed the metre. In his conversations with Drummond of Hawthornden Jonson remarks that "Sir P. Sidney had translated some of the Psalms which went abroad under the name of the Countess of Pembroke." Through his friendship with Elizabeth, Countess of Rutland, whom he calls "godlike Sidney's daughter," Jonson may very well have obtained special knowledge of the manner in which these translations were made, and of the tunes for which they were written. His own "Christmas Carol" so closely fits this Huguenot melody that one cannot help feeling it was in his mind.

This melody is supposed to have been taken from an old German chorale, and found its way in a modified form into the early Scottish and English psalters with a translation by William Kethe of the 113th Psalm:

> Ye children which do serve the Lord,
> Praise ye his name with one accord.

In this, however, the metre is changed in the third and sixth lines to allow for additional syllables, so that it cannot have formed the model for Sidney's translation or Ben Jonson's carol.

Of the Countess of Rutland, Jonson wrote:

> For what a sin 'gainst your great father's spirit
> Were it to think that you should not inherit
> His love unto the Muses, when his skill
> Almost you have, or may have when you will.

He had been a favoured guest at Penshurst, the seat of the Sidneys,

> whose liberal board doth flow
> With all that hospitality doth know.

For purpose of comparison, the music of this Huguenot tune is shown with (a) the original French of Beza's Psalm 68; (b) Sidney's translation of Psalm 32; (c) Ben Jonson's "Christmas Carol."

Que Dieu se monstre seulement,
Et on verra soudainement
Abandonner la place,
Le camp des ennemis espars
Et ses haineux de toutes pars
Fuir devant sa face.

Dieu les fera tous s'enfuir
Ainsi qu'on voit s'esvanouir
Un amas de fumée,
Comme la cire auprés du feu,
Ainsi des meschans devant Dieu
La force est consumée.

THEODORE BEZA.

Blessed is he whose filthy stain
The Lord with pardon does make clean,
Whose fault well hidden lyeth.
Blessed indeed to whom the Lord
Imputes not sins to be abhorred,
Whose spirit falsehood flyeth.

Thus I pressed down with weight of pain
Whether I silent did remain
Or roar'd, my bones still wasted;
For so both night and day did stand
On wretched me Thy heavy hand,
My life hot torments tasted.

Psalm 32, Sidney's translation.

I sing the birth was born to-night,
The Author both of life and light;
The angels so did sound it,
And like the ravish'd shepherds said,
Who saw the light and were afraid,
Yet searched, and true they found it.

The Son of God, th' eternal King,
That did us all salvation bring
And freed the world from danger;
He whom the whole world could not take,
The Lord which heav'n and earth did make,
Was now laid in a manger.

BEN JONSON.

William Byrd was a friend of the Sidneys, and it is more than likely that the poet and the composer should have discussed the relationship between poetry and music. As a madrigal writer, Byrd looked at poetry from a different point of view—his mission was to interpret an existing poem by means of music. In a Latin address prefacing his *Gradualia* in which he expounds his method of composition, Byrd says:

There is a certain hidden power, as I learnt by experience, in the thoughts underlying the words themselves: so that as one meditates upon the sacred words and constantly and seriously considers them, the right notes, in some inexplicable manner, suggest themselves quite spontaneously.—Translation by E. H. FELLOWES.

CHAPTER VIII

Musical education under Elizabeth at school and college—The Children of Paul's
—Lyrics—Lyly—Peele—Greene.

WHILE most of the Elizabethan youths of good family were educated by
private tutors, those who attended schools such as Westminster, St.
Paul's, and Merchant Taylors', went through classes in music. Win-
chester had its singing master, and boys sent to Eton would be put under
"a sufficient person to teach them to play on the viol and to sing."

Sir James Whitlocke, a fellow student at Oxford of John Donne, has
recorded:

I was brought up at school under Mr. Mulcaster, in the famous school of the
Marchantaylors in London, where I continued till I was well instructed in the Hebrew,
Greek, and Latin tongues. His care was also to increase my skill in musique, in which
I was brought up by daily exercise in it, as in singing and playing upon instruments,
and yearly he presented some plays to the court, in which his scholars were the only
actors, and I one among them, and by that means taught them good behaviour and
audacitye.

His widowed mother had set her heart on bringing her four sons up
"in as good a sort as any gentleman in England would do, as singing,
dancing, playing on the lute and other instruments."

At Westminster School the boys were under the choirmaster two
hours a week. This musical instruction may very well have had its
influence on the poet fledglings of that nest of the Muses. Any school
attached to an English cathedral was bound to have a musical atmosphere,
for the cathedrals upheld the tradition of two musical services a day, and
the voices of their boys were as the larks in the fields.

The Court at Whitehall and the Chapel Royal were outside the London
of that date, but in London was St. Paul's Cathedral with its choristers
and singing school. The Children of Paul's were favourites of the queen
and were summoned frequently to Court, particularly at Christmas, New
Year, and Twelfth Night. The plays interspersed with music which
John Lyly wrote and taught to them for the pleasure of the Court were
also played to the public, or at least to those of the public willing to pay
higher prices than were charged at the popular theatres. Evensong at
St. Paul's was much frequented by music-lovers of Elizabeth's day.
The City of London, too, encouraged music. Thomas Morley refers to
the excellent and expert musicians, "who adorned the Lord Mayor's

75

feasts and solemn meetings." The City Waits played outside the Royal Exchange on Sundays. The first Gresham lecture on music was delivered in 1597 by Dr. John Bull before the Aldermen and Commoners of the City of London, "with a great multitude of other people." Writing of the London of that time, Sir George Buck, Master of the Revels, said, "Here be also the best musicians of this kingdom, and equal to any in Europe for their skill either in composing and setting, or for playing upon any kind of instrument."

Oxford was another musical centre. The carriers between London and Oxford did an active business in the transport of lutes and virginals. No sooner did the young scholar take up residence than

> The Music School did teach him her sweet art.

The Earl of Leicester in his revision of the University Statutes had retained the medieval subject of "Music" as necessary to the degree of B.A.—two terms being allotted to it. The public lecturers in music, however, had sometimes indifferent attendance, perhaps because of the competition of the college teachers, or because they had to expound the dry and out-of-date method of Boethius.

In a community with such good choirs as those of Christ Church and Magdalen, there was music in plenty. John Milton's father, a notable composer in after days, was trained in the Christ Church choir. The music master is a recognized character in the Elizabethan novels touching on university life, and when the queen made her second visit to Oxford in September 1592, the third day's entertainment included "A lecture on music with the practice thereof by instrument in the Common Schools."

At certain colleges there were days of special musical debauch. At New College, for instance, according to Anthony à Wood:

> There was an ancient custom, viz., on Holy Thursday every year some of the Fellows of New College (with some of their acquaintance with them) did go to St. Bartholomew's Hospital, and there in the Chapel sing an anthem of two or five parts —then going up to a well or spring in the grove, which strewed with flowers round about for them, they sang a song of five parts, lately one of Mr. Wilbye's *principium*, "Hard by a crystal fountain," and after that they came home by Cheyney Lane and Heddington Hill, singing catches.

Two such musical celebrations at Oxford still survive, that at Magdalen, where

> the choral ministers of this house do, according to an ancient custom, salute Flora every year on the First of May, at four in the morning, with vocal music of several parts,

and that at Queen's, where on Christmas Day the boar's head is brought in with ceremonial music. Traditions of wine and song permeated this still medieval university, and account for the lyrical exuberance of John

Lyly, whose prose in *Euphues* has now only an antiquarian interest, but whose songs written for plays produced and sung by the Children of Paul's have still an abiding charm. Gabriel Harvey characterized Lyly under the guise of "Pappe" as "a mad lad as ever twanged," and, "sometime the fiddlestick of Oxford and the very babble of London." As vice-master of the choristers at St. Paul's, his duties seem to have included the preparation and presentation of plays for the Children of Paul's at Court. These were interspersed with music, mostly part-songs for boys' voices of which only the words survive, and these not in every case. Lyly himself has been credited with the music, and certainly the words of the lyrics were written by one who could sing, but it is not unlikely that Sebastian Westcott and Thomas Gyles, his successor as master of the choristers, may at least have helped in the settings. The plays were evidently made for a musical company, for in *Alexander and Campaspe* eight of the actors sing; in *Endymion* there are ten singing voices; *Midas* is built round a musical competition between Apollo and Pan, and is memorable for two lyrics alive with music.

1. Apollo's "Song of Daphne," sung to the lute:

> My Daphne's hair is twisted gold,
> Bright stars a-piece her eyes do hold,
> My Daphne's brow enthrones the Graces,
> My Daphne's beauty stains all faces;
> On Daphne's cheek grow rose and cherry,
> On Daphne's lip a sweeter berry;
> Daphne's snowy hand but touched does melt,
> And then no heavenlier warmth is felt;
> My Daphne's voice tunes all the spheres,
> My Daphne's music charms all ears.
> Fond am I thus to sing her praise;
> These glories now are turned to bays.

2. Pan's "Song of Syrinx," sung unaccompanied after piping the tune:

> Pan's Syrinx was a girl indeed,
> Though now she 's turned into a reed;
> From that dear reed Pan's pipe does come,
> A pipe that strikes Apollo dumb;
> Nor flute, nor lute, nor gittern can
> So chant it as the pipe of Pan:
> Cross-gartered swains and dairy girls
> With faces smug and round as pearls,
> When Pan's shrill pipe begins to play,
> With dancing wear out night and day;
> The bagpipe's drone his hum lays by,
> When Pan sounds up his minstrelsy.
> His minstrelsy! O base! this quill
> Which at my mouth with wind I fill,
> Puts me in mind, though her I miss,
> That still my Syrinx' lips I kiss.

In *Sappho and Phao*, Lyly makes his poetess both sing and play the lute. Of all the lyrics in Lyly's plays perhaps the happiest and most melodious is the trio in *Alexander and Campaspe*:

GRANICHUS. O for a bowl of fat canary!
      Rich Palermo! Sparkling sherry!
      Some nectar also from Juno's dairy,
      O, these draughts would make us merry!

PSYLLUS. O for a wench, (I deal in faces,
      And in other daintier things)
      Tickled am I with her embraces—
      Fine dancing in such fairy rings!

MANES.   O for a plump fat leg of mutton!
      Veal, lamb, capon, pig and coney!
      None is happy but a glutton,
      None an ass but who wants money.

Chorus.   Wines, indeed, and girls are good,
      But brave victuals feast the blood.
      For wenches, wine and lusty cheer,
      Jove would leap down to surfeit here!

Two other lyrics in the same play were evidently also made for music:

SONG BY APELLES

Cupid and my Campaspe played
At cards for kisses. Cupid paid.
He stakes his quiver, bows and arrows,
His mother's doves and team of sparrows;
Loses them too. Then, down he throws
The coral of his lips, the rose
Growing on 's cheek (but none knows how);
With these, the crystal of his brow;
And then, the dimple of his chin.
All these did my Campaspe win!
At last he set her both his eyes;
She won, and Cupid blind did rise.
  O Love, has she done this to thee?
  What shall, alas! become of me?

The song by Trico is equally delicious:

What bird so sings, yet so does wail?
O, 'tis the ravished nightingale!
"Jug, jug, jug, jug, tereu!" she cries;
And still her woes at midnight rise.
Brave prick-song! Who is 't now we hear?
None but the lark so shrill and clear.
Now at heaven's gates she clasps her wings,
The morn not waking till she sings!
Hark, hark, with what a pretty throat
Poor Robin red-breast tunes his note!

Hark how the jolly cuckoos sing!
"Cuckoo" to welcome in the spring,
"Cuckoo" to welcome in the spring.

In Ravenscroft's *Melismata* (Musical Fancies Fitting the Court, City and Country Humours), 1611, there is a song so similar to the third song sung by the fairies in Lyly's *Endymion* that it helps us to imagine the kind of melody to which this song was sung:

SONG from *Melismata*

Dare you haunt our hallowed green?
None but fairies here are seen.
Down and sleep,
Wake and weep,
Pinch him black and pinch him blue
That seeks to steal a lover true.
When you come to hear us sing
Or to tread our fairies' ring,
Pinch him black and pinch him blue,
O thus our nails shall handle you.

FAIRIES' SONG from Lyly's *Endymion*

OMNES. Pinch him, pinch him black and
blue,
Saucy mortals must not view
What the Queen of Stars is doing
Nor pry into our fairy wooing.

1ST FAIRY. Pinch him blue

2ND FAIRY.   and pinch him black.

3RD FAIRY. Let him not lack
Sharp nails to pinch him blue and red
Till sleep has rocked his addlehead.

4TH FAIRY. For the trespass he hath done
Spots o'er all his flesh shall run,
Kiss Endymion, kiss his eyes,
Then to our midnight heidegyes.

From Ravenscroft's *Melismata* (1611).

Only a poet steeped in folklore and balladry could have written the enchanting fantasy, *The Old Wives' Tale* of George Peele. Frolic would sing out his ill fortune to the tune of "O man in desperation," but Antic suggests instead:

Three merry men, and three merry men
And three merry men be we,
I in the wood, and thou on the ground
And Jack sleeps in the tree.

Cf. Chappell's *Popular Music of the Olden Time*.

In Peele's *Arraignment of Paris*, Venus singeth an old song called "The Wooing of Colman." There were numerous old ballads making fun of a countryman's style of wooing, one of which dates back to the time of Henry VIII and may as likely as not have been the song in question:

Quoth John to Joan, "Wilt thou have me?
I prithee now wilt? And I'se marry with
      thee,
My cow, my calf, my house, my rents
And all my lands and tenements;
O say, my Joan, say, my Joan, will not
      that do?
I cannot come ev'ry day to woo.

"I've corn and hay in the barn hard by,
And three fat hogs pent up in the sty;
I have a mare and she is coal-black,
I ride on her tail to save her back.

"I have a cheese upon the shelf,
And I cannot eat it all myself;
I've three good marks that lie in a rag,
In the nook of the chimney instead of a bag.

"To marry I would have thy consent,
But faith, I never could compliment;
I can say nought but 'hoy, gee ho!'
Words that belong to the cart and the
      plough."

Tune in William Ballet's *Lute Book*. Quoted in Chappell's *Popular Music of the Olden Time*.

A ballad tune mentioned by Peele in his *Edward I*, is "Who list to lead a soldier's life," which we find also identified with Ophelia's song in *Hamlet*. "Good morrow! 'tis Saint Valentine's day." Attributed to Peele is the lilting ballad "It was a maid of my country," written and sung to the dance tune of "Donkin Dargason":

It was a maid of my country,
As she came by a hawthorn tree
As full of flow'rs as might be seen,
She marvell'd to see the tree so green.
At last she asked of this tree,
"How came this freshness unto thee,
And ev'ry branch so fair and clean?
I marvel that you grow so green."

The tree made answer by and by,
"I have come to grow triumphantly,
The sweetest dew that ever be seen
Doth fall on me to keep me green."

"Yes," quoth the maid, "but where you grow
You stand at hand for every blow,
Of every man for to be seen,
I marvel that you grow so green."

"Though many one take flowers from me,
And many a branch out of my tree,
I have such store they will not be seen,
For more and more my twigs grow green.
But you, fair maid, can not do so,
For when your beauty once does go,
Then will it never more be seen,
As I with my branches can grow green."

Tune, "Donkin Dargason" from Playford's *Dancing Master.* Quoted in Chappell's *Popular Music of the Olden Time.*

On three occasions Peele pays tribute to John Dowland, the most famous lutenist of his day, who had set the music for a song written by Peele in honour of Sir Henry Lee, Queen Elizabeth's personal champion. In *The Honours of the Garter* (1593), he refers to Dowland's skill as a poet,

that clothes conceit with well-made words.

Then he has a Latin epigram (1595) and a prefatory poem for Dowland's *First Book of Ayres*, published in 1597, in which the music of his song to Sir Henry Lee is printed. This song was sung at Westminster on 17 November, 1590, by Mr. Hales, Her Majesty's servant, "a gentleman in that art excellent, and for his voice commendable and admirable":

His golden locks time hath to silver turned,
O time too swift, O swiftness never ceasing!
His youth 'gainst time and age hath ever
      spurned,
But spurned in vain; youth waneth by
      increasing.
Beauty, strength, youth are flowers but
      fading seen;
Duty, faith, love are roots and ever green.

His helmet now shall make a hive for bees,
And lovers' sonnets turned to holy psalms.
A man-at-arms must now serve on his knees
And feed on prayers, which are age his alms.
But though from court to cottage he depart,
His saint is sure of his unspotted heart.

And when he saddest sits in homely cell, .
He'll teach his swains this carol for a song—

From Dowland's *First Book of Ayres*, reprinted and edited by E. H. Fellowes (Stainer & Bell). An original copy of the songbook is in the Henry E. Huntington Library, San Marino, California.

G

> "Blest be the hearts that wish my sovereign well,
> Curst be the souls that think her any wrong.
> Goddess, allow this aged man his right
> To be your beadsman now that was your knight."

George Peele was at Oxford at the same time as Lyly, and though he attended a different college (first Broadgates Hall, now Pembroke, then Christ Church), there were too many opportunities for kindred souls to meet at Oxford taverns to make it unlikely that these two university wits should not have met till they returned to London. Peele had been schooled at Christ's Hospital, where his father was a clerk. Here music was taught to the boys so that they might the more readily qualify as apprentices. Peele wrote his *Arraignment of Paris*, 1583, for the children of the Chapel Royal. There must have been a wealth of music with this play, for there were three choirs, and solos were sung by Pan, Œnone, Paris (who also pipes), Helen of Greece (who must have been bi-lingual, for her song was in Italian), Colin and Thestylis. Add to these a round in three voices by Nymph, Bacchus, and Mercury, and a trio in Latin by the three Fates, Clotho, Lachesis, and Atropos. Possibly more attention was paid to the music than the words, for the only lyric that stands out is the rather dainty duet:

> Fair and fair, and twice so fair,
> As fair as any may be;
> The fairest shepherd on our green,
> A love for any lady.

The Old Wives' Tale includes some captivating rhythms evidently linked with folk-melody, as in the Harvesters' Songs:

> All ye that lovely lovers be,
> Pray you for me,
> Lo, here we come a-sowing, a-sowing,
> And sow sweet fruits of love,
> In your sweet hearts well may it prove.
>
> Lo, here we come a-reaping, a-reaping,
> To reap our harvest fruit,
> And thus we pass the year so long
> And never be we mute.

Another lyric in the same play with dancing rhythm runs:

> Whenas the rye reach to the chin,
> And chopcherry, chopcherry ripe within,
> Strawberries swimming in the cream,
> And schoolboys playing in the stream;
> Then oh! then oh! then oh! my true love said,
> Till that time come again
> She could not live a maid.

In *David and Bathsabe*, Peele may have meant political satire under the guise of Biblical drama, but he was interested in David as a musician:

> Of Israel's sweetest singer now I sing . . .

> Upon the bosom of his ivory lute,
> The cherubims and angels laid their breasts,
> And when his consecrated fingers struck
> The golden wires of his ravishing harp,
> He gave alarum to the hosts of heaven.

> .   .   .   .   .

> Of this sweet poet, Jove's musician
> . . . I press to sing.

David was charmed by Bathsheba's singing. The play is enhanced by the music of shalmes, cymbals, and pipes on the death of Bathsheba's first babe, and there is the dancing and singing of shepherds.

In a sixteenth-century black-letter chronicle, *The Famous History of Friar Bacon*, which Robert Greene dramatized as *The Honourable History of Friar Bacon and Friar Bungay*, there is a song sung to a tune which is still popular in country dances under the name of "Newcastle." While the refrain is not given in that chronicle, it can be partly at least reconstructed from a fragment cited by Chappell in his *Popular Music of the Olden Time*:

To couple is a custom,
All things thereto agree;
Why should not I then love,
Since love to all is free?

But I'll have one that's pretty,
Her cheeks of scarlet dye,
For to breed my delight,
When that I ligge her by.

Though virtue be a dowry,
Yet I'll choose money store;
If my love prove untrue,
With that I can get more.

The fair is oft unconstant,
The black is often proud;
I'll choose a lovely brown—
Come, fiddler, scrape thy crowd.

Come, fiddler, scrape thy crowd,
For Peggie the brown is she
Must be my bride; God guide
That Peggie and I agree.

Tune "Newcastle" from Playford's *Dancing Master* (1650).

Greene's own lyrics have a more literary than singable quality. The succession of sibilants in lines such as

> Sweet are the thoughts that savour of content

and his conglomerations of consonants indicate that he had not the natural instincts of a singer.

CHAPTER IX

Italian influence on Elizabethan literature and music—The madrigal and canzonet—
Nicholas Yonge — Thomas Watson — Yonge's *Musica Trans-Alpina* — Thomas
Lodge—Importance of madrigal music in relation to poetry—Madrigal texts by
Sidney, Spenser, Raleigh—Lute songs.

"Ha! *Roma la Santa!* Italy for my money," cries Mirabel in *The Wild Goose
Chase* of John Fletcher.

ELIZABETHAN literature and music were strongly influenced by Italy.
Wyatt and Surrey, who introduced the sonnet from Italy to England
earlier in the century, were followed by Edmund Spenser, Sir Philip
Sidney, Samuel Daniel, Thomas Lodge, and Thomas Watson in translating the sonnets of Petrarch and Tasso. Queen Elizabeth herself studied
Italian, taking as her textbook Castiglione's *Il Cortegiano*, which, in Sir
Thomas Hoby's translation *The Courtier*, governed English etiquette for
sixty years. Robert Greene wrote love stories in the Italian manner,
frequently using Italian sources such as Boccaccio. His *Pandosto* served
as inspiration for Shakespeare's *Winter's Tale*. English translations were
published of Boccaccio's *Amorous Fiametta* (1587), Guazzo's *Civil Conversation* (1586); Tasso's *Amynta* (1587); Ariosto's *Orlando Furioso*, by
Sir John Harrington at the command of the Queen (1591); Tasso's
Jerusalem, by Richard Carew and Edward Fairfax (1600). As early as
1570 Roger Ascham in *The Schoolmaster* had denounced Italy as a Circe
whose enchantments mar men's manners in England—"by precepts of
fond books of late translated out of Italian into English, sold in every shop
in London, commended by honest titles the sooner to corrupt honest
manners." What did not come direct from the Italian, came by way of
French versions re-translated into English. Shakespeare in this way
found his sources for *Romeo and Juliet* (Bandello); *All's Well That Ends
Well* (Boccaccio); *The Taming of the Shrew* (Ariosto), and *Much Ado
About Nothing* (Bandello). Michael Angelo Florio, a Protestant preacher,
taught Italian in London, and John Florio, his son, who had been tutor
in several great English families before he was appointed to teach Italian
at Oxford, compiled an Italian-English dictionary of which Shakespeare
possessed a copy. Although the evidence is against the contention that
Shakespeare ever personally visited Italy, there was so much Italian
atmosphere and material in London that plays with Italian names and
places were quite acceptable to Elizabethan audiences. London had its
Italian colony where lived musicians such as Alphonso Ferrabosco, father

and son, Thomas Lupo the elder and the younger. English musicians such as John Dowland studied in Italy, and John Cooper, the lutenist, assumed for a time the name of Coperario. Five of the nine tunes named by Sir Philip Sidney as those to which he wrote his songs are specified as Italian. This Italian vogue was only natural when one remembers that Florence, Venice, Rome, and Milan had produced more great art in a century than the world had known for fifteen hundred years before. Although England was now officially Protestant, the chief composers, who were church musicians, were secretly, if not openly, in sympathy with Rome, always generous in its support of music. In secular music Italy had developed the madrigal or unaccompanied polyphonic part-song to a high degree of perfection when Nicholas Yonge published in 1588, his *Musica Trans-Alpina*, a collection of madrigals, mostly Italian.

Nicholas Yonge was a lay clerk at St. Paul's Cathedral, who attracted to his house in Cornhill "a great number of gentlemen and merchants of good account (as well of this realm as of foreign nations) for the exercise of music daily," importing music books from Italy for their use.

Following on this, Thomas Watson gave in his *Italian Madrigals Englished* (1590), renderings of sonnets by Petrarch and others which Luca Marenzio of Venice and other Italian composers had set as madrigals.

A vivid picture of the musical background to the life of the average Londoner is given in the manual of French conversation, entitled *The French Schoolmaster*, written by one Hollyband about the year 1572.

GOSSIP. What, have you not heard the minstrels and players of instruments, which did play so sweetly before the City's store-house, from midnight even unto the breaking of the day?

FATHER. Which were those singers and players of instruments?

GOSSIP. Perchance they were the minstrels of the town, with those of the Queen's, mingled with voices of Italians and Englishmen, which did sing very harmoniously.

FATHER. Would God I had heard them, and it had cost me a quart of wine.

GOSSIP. I would you had for your sake: for it would seem unto you to be ravished in an earthly paradise: you had heard first and foremost the Viols, Cornets, Harps, Hobois, Trumpets with four Flutes, the which did triumph.

FATHER. Is it true? In whose name did they play? Who had hired them?

GOSSIP. The best of the City! To plant the maypole in the market-place—Let us go and see it if you will. [*They set out in company.*

GOSSIP. What music do I hear there at the lane's end? Is it not some wedding?

FATHER. It is the bride of whom I told you. Let us go see that marriage.

At the Church of Saint Paul.

GOSSIP. Behold the church is all full of folks: how shall we enter in?

FATHER. Enter you first, and I will follow you: thrust hard, and cause the way to be made.

GOSSIP. Harken, I do hear sweet music: I never heard the like.

FATHER. See whether we may get to the choir, and we shall hear the fairest voices of all the Cathedral Churches in England.

GOSSIP. I believe you: who should have them, if the Londoners had them not?

FATHER. I think that the Queen's singing men are there, for I do hear her base.

GOSSIP. That may be; for to tell the truth, I never heard better singing.

FATHER. Harken, there is a good versicle.

GOSSIP. I promise you that I would hear them more willingly sing than eat or drink.

After dinner

FATHER. Roland, shall we have a song?

ROLAND. Yes, Sir: where be your books of musick? For they be the best corrected.

FATHER. They be in my chest: Katherine, take the key of my closet, you shall find them in a little till at the left hand: [KATHERINE *fetches the songs.*] Behold, there be fair songs at four parts.

ROLAND. Who shall sing with me?

FATHER. You shall have company enough: David shall make the base: John the tenor: and James the treble. Begin: James, take your tune: go to—Roland, drink before you begin, you will sing with a better courage.

ROLAND. It is well said—I should not be a singing man except I could drink well.

ANOTHER GUEST. There is a good song. I do marvel who hath made it.

FATHER. It is the Master of the Children of the Queen's Chapel.

GUEST. .What is his name?

FATHER. Master Edwards.

GUEST. Is he alive?

FATHER. I heard say that he was dead.

ANOTHER GUEST. It is already a good while ago: there are at the least five years and a half.

FATHER. Truly, it is a pity: he was a man of a good wit, and a good poet.

GUEST. It is time to depart, for they have rung twice to evening prayers.

The madrigal is described by Thomas Morley, a musical friend of Shakespeare, as "a kind of music made upon songs and sonnets such as Petrarcha and many poets of our time have excelled in." Canzonets were a lighter form of madrigal popularized at this time in England, and so, too, were "Neapolitans," which Thomas Morley described as "differing from canzonets in nothing save in name."

Seven of Morley's canzonets are translated from similar songs by the Italian Felice Amerio. The words often of his ballads are adaptations (made, according to some, by Michel Drayton) from Italian songs by Gastoldi, for instance the dainty "Sing we and chant it," of which a snatch is sung by Merrythought in Beaumont and Fletcher's *The Knight of the Burning Pestle*:

Sing we and chant it
While love doth grant it
Fa la la la la la la la
Not long youth lasteth
And old age hasteth.
Now is best leisure
To take our pleasure
Fa la la la la la la
Fa la la la la

All things invite us
Now to delight us.
Hence care, be packing!
No mirth be lacking!
Let spare no treasure
To live in pleasure.

Melody from Thomas Morley's *Ballets for Five Voices* (1595), reprinted and edited by E. H. Fellowes (Stainer & Bell). An original copy of the songbook is in the Congressional Library, Washington, D.C.

While William Byrd, who contributed to Yonge's *Musica Trans-Alpina*, had written madrigals before its publication, this collection established a fashion which for thirty years flourished among English composers. The fashion was of deep import to the English lyric, not only because of the great number of poems linked with madrigal music (E. H. Fellowes cites 850 individual English lyrics found in madrigal collections) but more especially through the intimate study of verse involved in close sympathy and intercourse between poets and musicians. For the essential excellence of a madrigal lay in interpreting by means of music the exact intention of the poet. Accurate time was the essential of good madrigal singing, as Shakespeare evidently knew:

> Music do I hear?
> Ha, ha! keep time—how sour sweet music is,
> When time is broken and no proportion kept!
> So is it in the music of men's lives.
> *Richard II*, Act V, sc. v.

Tybalt, the perfect swordsman in *Romeo and Juliet*, "fights as you sing prick-song, keeps time, distance and proportion; rests me his minim rest, one, two, and the third in your bosom."

There is a punning reference to part-song, in *Two Gentlemen of Verona*, a play usually ascribed to Shakespeare, of the date 1590–2.

> JULIA. Let's see your song. How now, minion!
> LUCETTA. Keep tune there still, so you will sing it out.
>   And yet methinks I do not like this tune.
> JULIA. You do not?
> LUCETTA.   No, madam, it is too sharp.
> JULIA. You, minion, are too saucy.
> LUCETTA. Nay, now you are too flat,
>   And mar the concord with too harsh a descant.
>   There wanteth but a mean to all your song.
> JULIA. The mean is drowned with your unruly bass.
> Act I, sc. ii.

Another possible reflection of the vogue for madrigals may be found in a stanza of Edmund Spenser's *Faerie Queene*. Richard Carlton, who wrote four madrigals from stanzas in the *Faerie Queene,* was a contemporary of Spenser at Cambridge. The second canto, which was not published till 1591, contains a stanza which takes the sounds of the elements as blending in harmony with the song of the mermaids:

> With that the rolling sea, resounding soft
> In his big base them fitly answerèd;
> And on the rock the waves, breaking aloft,
> A solemn mean unto them measurèd;
> The while sweet zephyrès loud whistelèd
> His treble—a strange kind of harmony,
> Which Guyon's senses softly tickelèd,
> That he the boatman bade row easily
> And let them hear some part of their rare melody.

Edmund Spenser was schooled at Merchant Taylors' where music was held to be a necessary study. Thomas Lodge was another Merchant Taylors' boy whose lyrics are identified with madrigal music. In *Rosalynd* (1590), the pastoral which gave Shakespeare the plot for *As You Like It,* Lodge gives the title of "Rosalynd's Madrigal" to one of the lyrics which is printed as to be sung:

ROSALYND'S MADRIGAL

> Love in my bosom like a bee
> Doth suck his sweet;
> Now with his wings he plays with me,
> Now with his feet.
> Within mine eyes he makes his nest,
> His bed amidst my tender breast;
> His kisses are his daily feast,
> And yet he robs me of my rest;
> Ah, wanton, will ye?

Lodge evidently knew something of Italian madrigals, for his lyric "When I admire the rose" in *William Longbeard* (1593), is a paraphrase of a madrigal by Bianciardi. A delightful contemporary setting of another of the songs in *Rosalynd* has been preserved. This is Francis Pilkington's ayre of four parts with tablature for the lute or orpherian with the viol de gamba; published 1605, but quite possibly the original melody, as Pilkington, who sang himself as well as composed for the lute, was born not later than 1565, and when he took his degree of Mus. Bac. at Oxford in 1595 had already been studying music for sixteen years.

The Phyllis of this ayre is a lady imported from the French of Ronsard and Desportes, whose songs and sonnets Lodge was assiduous in translating.

Down a down: thus Phyllis sung,
By fancy once oppressèd;
Who so by foolish love are stung,
Are worthily distressèd.
And so sing I with a down a down down.
When Love was first begot,
And by his mother's will
Did fall to human lot
His solace to fulfil,
Devoid of all deceit,
A chaste and holy fire
Did quicken man's conceit
And woman's breast inspire.
The gods that saw the good
That mortals did approve
With kind and holy mood
Began to talk of love.

But during this accord
A wonder strange to hear;
Whilst love in deed and word
Most faithful did appear,
False Semblance came in place
By Jealousy attended,
And with a double face
Both Love and Fancy blended;
Which made the gods forsake,
And men from Fancy fly,
And maidens scorn a mate.
Forsooth, and so will I.

Lyric by Thomas Lodge, quoted in
England's Helicon.

The madrigal composer took as his theme a verse or short lyric, and wove out of the meanings and shades of meaning he could find in the words a pattern of music for several voices, each of which had its melody running, so to speak, horizontally with occasional vertical concords. None of Shakespeare's verses has been identified in the collections of madrigals, though these borrow their texts from other notable Elizabethan poets such as Sidney, Spenser, Sir Walter Raleigh, Greene, Constable, Samuel

From Francis Pilkington's *First Book of Songs of Ayres* (1605), reprinted and edited by E. H. Fellowes (Stainer & Bell). An original copy of the songbook is in the Henry E. Huntington Library, San Marino, California.

Daniel, Michael Drayton, Thomas Middleton, Thomas Campian, Ben Jonson, and George Wither. The verses chosen as a rule are epigrammatic, but rhyme was not always indispensable. Free verse is used by William Byrd in "A Caroll for Christmas Day"—a translation from the Latin hymn, "Hodie Christus natus est":

> This day Christ was born.
> This day our Saviour did appear.
> This day the Angels sing in earth,
> The Archangels are glad.
> This day the just rejoice, saying
> Glory be to God on high. Alleluia.

The madrigal is the musical elaboration of an existing poem, which may indeed have been originally written to another melody. Thus, for instance, Thomas Bateson composed a madrigal on a poem which Sidney expressly states was written to an Italian tune, "Non credo giu che":

> The nightingale, as soon as April bringeth
> Unto her rested sense a perfect waking,
> While late bare earth, proud of new clothing, springeth,
> Sings out her woes, a thorn her song-book making,
> And mournfully bewailing,
> Her throat in tunes expresseth
> What grief her breast oppresseth.

While the madrigal had its followers among certain of the more skilled musicians, the lute - song or song with instrumental accompaniment had perhaps more general acceptance, even in musical Italy, judging by the following extracts from Castiglione's celebrated manual:

COUNT LEWIS OF CANOSSA. I am not pleased with the Courtier if he be not also a musician and, beside his understanding and cunning upon the book, have skill in like manner on sundry instruments. . . .

SIR FREDERICK FREGOSA. Methink pricksong is a fair music, so it be done upon the book surely and after a good sort. But to sing to the lute is much better, because all the sweetness consisteth in one alone—and beside every little error is soon perceived, which happeneth not in singing with company, for one beareth out another. But singing to the lute with the ditty is more pleasant than the rest, for it addeth to the words such a grace and strength that it is a great wonder.

The lutenist had more direct influence on lyrical verse than the madrigal composer, as the melody may in a number of cases have been written either before the words or in immediate collaboration with the poet.

CHAPTER X

Lutenist poets and composers—Thomas Campian—Measured Music—John Dowland
—Captain Tobias Hume.

CONTEMPORARY with Shakespeare was Thomas Campian, a dilettante student of law and doctor of physic, who moved, however, in a separate orbit from the actor - playwright, although they had points of contact among the musicians. Campian, who is credited with the authorship of one hundred and eighteen "ayres" or songs for the lute, seems to have been satisfied at first to let other musicians set his verses, but practice in composition gave him confidence, for he later published his own music for some of the lyrics that others had already set, in addition to songs that were entirely his own. These other musicians were Robert Jones, John Cooper or Coperario, Thomas Morley, John Dowland, Philip Rosseter, Francis Pilkington, Richard Alison, Nicholas Laniere and Alfonso Ferrabosco. With some at least of these his friendship must have been quite intimate. For Dowland he wrote two Latin epigrams, one as preface to the *First Book of Songs or Ayres* (1597).

Although his lyrics are essentially written for music, it is curious to note that Campian was resurrected from oblivion after more than two centuries by a critic and publisher (A. H. Bullen), who is described by W. B. Yeats as "a fine scholar in poetry who hates all music but that of poetry, and knows of no instrument that does not fill him with rage and misery." While one cannot but be grateful for this resurrection, the printing of the words apart from the music has misled a host of scribes into thinking that the words should be considered divorced from the music. Instance of this is J. C. Squire, who in the preface to *Songs from the Elizabethans* says pontifically:

> We think we know a song when we see one, but there must be and are borderland cases. An extreme instance is Campian's poem beginning:
>
> > "When thou must home to shades of underground,
> > And there arrived, a new admired guest,
> > The beautous spirits do engirt thee round,
> > White Iope, blithe Helen and the rest."
>
> When we first read that, it certainly does not appear to us to be a song. Yet Rosseter set it to music with the author's assent, and published it as a song.

Such criticism condemns itself, for Rosseter credits the music to Campian himself. The setting is essentially that of a musician, for the musical rhythm does not slavishly follow the verbal rhythm, although they run concurrently.

When thou must home to shades of under-
ground,
And there arrived a new admired guest,
The beauteous spirits do ingirt thee round,
White Iope, blithe Helen and the rest,
To hear the stories of thy finished love
From that smooth tongue whose music
hell can move.

Then wilt thou speak of banquetting
delights,
Of masks and revels which sweet youth
did make,
Of tourneys and great challenges of knights,
And all these triumphs for thy beauty's
sake.
When thou hast told these honours done
to thee,
Then tell, O tell how thou didst murder me.

From Rosseter's *Book of Ayres* (1601). Cf. E. H. Fellowes's edition of *Thomas Campian* (Stainer & Bell). An original copy of the songbook is in the Henry E. Huntington Library, San Marino, California.

"In these English Ayres," says Campian, "I have chiefly aimed to couple my words lovingly together, which would be much to do for him who had not power over *both*." As an instance of Campian's skill in the union of words and music take his oft-quoted, but too seldom sung, "There is a garden in her face":

There is a garden in her face
Where roses and white lilies grow;
A heavenly paradise is that place,
Wherein all pleasant fruits do flow.
There cherries grow that none may buy
Till "cherry-ripe" themselves do cry.

Those cherries fairly do enclose
Of orient pearl a double row,
Which when her lovely laughter shows
They look like rosebuds filled with snow.
Yet them nor peers nor prince can buy
Till "cherry-ripe" themselves do cry.

Her eyes like angels watch them still;
Her brows like bended bows do stand,

From Thomas Campian's *Fourth Book of Ayres* from *Elizabethan Love Songs*, Frederick Keel (reprinted by permission of Boosey & Co. Ltd.).

Threatening with piercing frowns to kill
All that attempt with eye or hand
Those sacred cherries to come nigh,
Till "cherry-ripe" themselves do cry.

The echo of this "Cherry Ripe" in Herrick's equally famous lyric is all the more significant when we remember that in the lutenist, Nicholas Laniere, Campian and Herrick had a mutual friend.

Campian seems to have spent some time in France, and perhaps studied medicine at a French university. His song, "Come let us sound with melody the praises," is written in "la musique mesurée à l'antique" propounded by the poet Baïf in conjunction with the musician Thibaut de Courville in their "Académie de Poésie et de Musique" founded in 1571 to revive what was presumed to be the ancient Greek and Latin method of composing measured verse *pour y accommoder le chant pareillement mesuré selon l'art métrique.* In this song the verses are written in sapphics, and by themselves seem crude, but when sung in conjunction with Campian's own music have a definite charm. The notes of the melody are long to short according to the metrical value of the syllables.

Come let us sound with melody the praises
Of the kings' King, th' Omnipotent
    Creator,
Author of number, that hath all the world in
    Harmony framèd.

Heaven is his throne, perpetually shining,
His divine power and glory thence he
    thunders,
One in all, and all still in one abiding,
    Both Father and Son.

Thomas Campian, *Songs from Rosseter's Book of Ayres* (1601), reprinted and edited by E. H. Fellowes (Stainer & Bell); marked as to quantity by the author. An original copy of the songbook is in the Henry E. Huntington Library, San Marino, California.

Although Campian makes no acknowledgment of his debt to Baïf or his disciples, most of whose works were deliberately retained in manuscript, he may well have come across the "measured music" of Baïf's follower, Claude le Jeune, as le Jeune's compositions in this form were published between 1585 and 1610. Gabriel Harvey, who led the movement to introduce quantitative metre into English poetry, was a purely literary pedant, and unlike Campian did not accompany his metrical experiments with music. Indeed this song seems to stand alone in English music. Campian's knowledge of Baïf seems to be further evidenced by his masques, which offer interesting parallels to those of the French classicists. The madrigal composers who took an existing verse and laboured to find music which should express every shade of meaning in that verse did not find much sympathy from Campian, who was quite willing to write new words to an existing tune. In an address, "To the Reader," prefaced to Rosseter's *Book of Ayres*, he says:

There are some, who to appear the more deep and singular in their judgment, will admit no music but that which is long, intricate, bated with fugue, chained with syncopation, and where the nature of every word is precisely expressed in the note, like the old exploded action in comedies, when if they did pronounce *Memini* they would point to the hinder part of their heads, if *Video* put their finger in their eye. But such childish observing of words is altogether ridiculous, and we ought to maintain as well in notes as in action a manly carriage, gracing no word but that which is eminent and emphatical.

As illustration of the simplicity of Campian's melody and the perfection with which words fit the music, three of his most familiar songs are here given:

I care not for these ladies that must be wooed and prayed;
Give me kind Amaryllis, the wanton country maid.
Nature Art disdaineth; her beauty is her own.
Her when we court and kiss, she cries: "Forsooth, let go!"
But when we come where comfort is, she never will say no.

If I love Amaryllis, she gives me fruit and flowers;
But if we love these ladies, we must give golden showers.
Give them gold that sell love, give me the nut-brown lass
Who, when we court and kiss, she cries: "Forsooth, let go!"
But when we come where comfort is, she never will say no.

Thomas Campian, *Songs from Rosseter's Book of Ayres* (1601), reprinted and edited by E. H. Fellowes (Stainer & Bell). An original copy of the songbook is in the Henry E. Huntington Library, San Marino, California.

In the next song we have the serenade theme which appears in so many French lyrics of the sixteenth century and survives quite frequently in the *chanson populaire* of French Canada:

Sommeilles-tu, ma petite Nanon?
Veux-tu ouvrir la porte à ton mignon?
N'entends-tu pas, minuit est sonné?
Secrètement reçois ton bien-aimé.

Shall I come, sweet love, to thee
When the evening beams are set?
Shall I not excluded be?
Will you find no feigned let?
Let me not, for pity, more
Tell the long hours at your door.

Who can tell what thief or foe
In the covert of the night
For his prey will work my woe,
Or through wicked foul despite?
So may I die unredressed
Ere my long love be possessed.

Thomas Campian's *Third Book of Ayres*
(1617). From *Elizabethan Love Songs*,
Frederick Keel (reprinted by permission of
Boosey & Co. Ltd.). Cf. also *English
Melodies* (J. M. Dent & Sons Ltd.).

The following lyric enshrines the fairy theme which captured the fancy of so many of the Elizabethans—Spenser, Sidney, Lyly, Peele, Shakespeare, and Ben Jonson, and had its obituary written by Bishop Corbet.

Thrice toss these oaken ashes in the air,
Thrice sit thou mute in this enchanted
   chair:
Then thrice three times tie up this true-
   love's knot
And murmur soft, "She will, or she
   will not."

.   .   .   .

Then come, you fairies, dance with me a
   round;
Melt her hard heart with your melodious
   sound.
In vain are all the charms I can devise;
She hath an art to break them with her eyes.

Thomas Campian, *Third Book of Ayres*
(1617). From *Elizabethan Love Songs*,
Frederick Keel (reprinted by permission of
Boosey & Co. Ltd.)

One more lyric from Campian illustrates the value of studying the music as well as the words, the rhythm of the melody removing any suspicion of monotony which might be entertained through reading the words alone. As John Davies of Hereford said,

   Never did Lyrics' more than happy strains
   (Strained out of Art by nature, so with ease,)
   So purely hit the moods and various veins
   Of Music and her hearers as do these.

Fair, if you expect admiring,
Sweet, if you provoke desiring,
Grace, dear love, with kind requiting.
Fond, but if thy sight be blindness,
False, if thou affect unkindness,
Fly both love and love's delighting.
Then when hope is lost and love is
    scornèd,
I'll bury my desires
And quench the fires
That ever yet in vain have burned.

Fates, if you rule lovers' fortune;
Stars, if men your powers importune,
Yield relief by your relenting.
Time, if sorrow be not endless,
Hope made vain, and Pity friendless,
Help to ease my long lamenting.
But if griefs remain still unredressèd,
I'll fly to her again and sue
For pity to renew
My hopes distressèd.

Next to Thomas Campian in the number of lyrics he set to lute music stands John Dowland, celebrated for his skill in playing and singing as well as for his compositions. In the *Passionate Pilgrim* there is a sonnet by Richard Barnfield once attributed to Shakespeare.

Thomas Campian, *Songs from Rosseter's Book of Ayres* (1601), reprinted and edited by E. H. Fellowes (Stainer & Bell). An original copy of the songbook is in the Henry E. Huntington Library, San Marino, California.

To His Friend Master R. L. in Praise of Music and Poetry

If music and sweet poetry agree,
As they must needs (the sister and the brother),
Then must the love be great twixt thee and me,
Because thou lov'st the one, and I the other.
Dowland to thee is dear; whose heavenly touch
Upon the lute doth ravish human sense:
Spenser to me; whose deep conceit is such,
As passing all conceit, needs no defence.
Thou lov'st to hear the sweet melodious sound
That Phœbus' lute (the Queen of Music) makes:
And I in deep delight am chiefly drowned
When as himself to singing he betakes.
    One God is God of both (as poets feign),
    One knight loves both, and both in thee remain.

So many of the anonymous lyrics found in the music books of the lutenists have been identified with other authors that there has been a tendency to consider these musicians as using only words supplied to them. Yet if Thomas Campian, a graduate of Cambridge, could write music as well as poetry, why should not John Dowland, a graduate of Oxford, write poetry as well as music? In certain cases we know that Dowland arranged the verses of others, but until this is proved of all, he may be given credit for at least some of his lyrics. One poet, known to have written the words for one of Dowland's ayres, is Fulke Greville, Lord Brooke, friend of Sir Philip Sidney.

Away with these self-loving lads
Whom Cupid's arrow never glads!
Away, poor souls, that sigh and weep
In love of those that lie and sleep!
For Cupid is a meadow god
And forceth none to kiss the rod.

God Cupid's shaft, like destiny,
Doth either good or ill decree.
Desert is born out of his bow,
Reward upon his foot doth go.
What fools are they that have not known
That love likes no law but his own.

From Dowland's *First Book of Ayres* (1597). Melody as in *Elizabethan Love Songs*, Frederick Keel (reprinted by permission of Boosey & Co. Ltd.)

The interest of Dowland's ayres depends as much on skilful harmony as on the melody, and his own interpretation as an admirable singer added no doubt to the charm of his settings, but in every case the tune is closely wedded to the words. One song in which the rhythm of words and music is so intimate that one cannot think of them apart is:

Come again!
Sweet love doth now invite
Thy graces that refrain
To do me due delight,
To see, to hear, to touch, to kiss, to die
With thee again in sweetest sympathy.

Come again!
That I may cease to mourn
Through thy unkind disdain,
For now, left and forlorn,
I sit, I sigh, I weep, I faint, I die
In deadly pain and endless misery.

John Dowland's *First Book of Ayres* (1597). Cf. *Reliquary of English Song* (G. Schirmer). An original copy of the songbook is in the Henry E. Huntingdon Library, San Marino, California.

H

Happily married also are melody and words of the Pedlar's song:

Fine knacks for ladies, cheap, choice, brave
　　and new.
Good pennyworths, but money cannot
　　move.
I keep a fair but for the fair to view;
A beggar may be liberal of love.
Though all my wares be trash, the heart
　　is true.
　　　　The heart is true!

Great gifts are guiles and look for gifts
　　again;
My trifles come as treasures from my mind.
It is a precious jewel to be plain;
Sometimes in shell the Orient's pearls we
　　find;
Of others take a sheaf, of me a grain.
　　　　Of me a grain!

Among those whom no belated
iconoclast has yet risen to deprive of
his twofold birthright as poet and composer remains Captain Tobias Hume,
John Dowland's *Second Book of Ayres* (1600.)
Cf. *Fifty Songs from Dowland*, edited by E. H.
Fellowes (Stainer & Bell). An original copy of
the songbook is in the Henry E. Huntington
Library, San Marino, California.

author of what many consider as perfect a lyric as the Elizabethan age
produced. While his output was small, it was, none the less, fired with
genius.

Fain would I change that note
To which fond love hath charmed me,
Long, long to sing by rote,
Fancying that that harmed me.
Yet when this thought doth come,
Love is the perfect sum
Of all delight,
I have no other choice
Either for pen or voice
To sing or write.

O Love, they wrong thee much
That say thy sweet is bitter,
When thy ripe fruit is such,
As nothing can be sweeter.
Fair house of joy and bliss,
Where truest pleasure is,
I do adore thee:
I know thee what thou art,
I serve thee with my heart
And fall before thee.

From *Ayres French, Polish, and others together*, by Tobias Hume (1605). Facsimile in
Reliquary of English Song (G. Schirmer).

CHAPTER XI

Shakespeare and music—Widespread knowledge of vocal and instrumental music in Elizabethan times—Shakespeare's use of old ballads—Mad songs—Scotch ballads and tunes introduced with James I—French influence on Scottish music—Collections of drinking songs, rounds and catches accessible to Shakespeare—Shakespeare songs set by Morley, Robert Jones, Ford.

AUGUSTINE PHILLIPS, Shakespeare's fellow actor, played "the base viall, citherne, bandore, and flute." Richard Cowley and John Sinkler were two members of the company of Lord Strange's men who, at the time of the production of *Love's Labour's Lost* (1592), were classed as "musicians," and in 1597 there is a record of a singing-boy in the company of Chamberlain's men to which Shakespeare was attached. Every theatre had in its employ musicians to play between the acts, the divisions between which were marked on the script by the stage manager as "Musicke." But it was not only in the theatre that Shakespeare heard music. Every time he visited the barber to have his beard trimmed, he might hear the lute or cittern played—the instruments hanging handy on the wall for any one to use. If he went to his shoemaker, he would hear the song of the apprentices, just as those who, as Thomas Deloney says, in *The Gentle Craft*—"passing up and down Westminster, did many times hear the shoemakers' journeymen singing, whose sweet voices and pleasant songs were so pleasing that it caused them to stay about the door to hearken thereto." The men of that craft had concluded "that what journeymen soever . . . that cannot sound the trumpet or play upon the flute, and bear his part in a three man's song and readily reckon up his tools in rhyme . . . shall forfeit and pay a bottle of wine or be reckoned for a colt."

"The Cobbler's Song," quoted in *The Shoemaker's Holiday*, was "Cold's the wind and wet's the rain." This, as Chappell has shown, fits an old tune known as "The Cobbler's Jig."

Cold's the wind and wet's the rain;
Saint Hugh be our good speed!
Ill is the weather that bringeth no gain,
Nor helps good hearts in need.
Hey down a down, hey down a down,
Hey derry derry down a down,
Ho! well done,
To me let come,
Ring compass gentle joy.

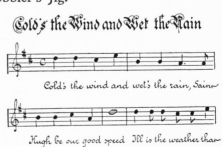

99

Troll the bowl, the jolly nutbrown bowl,
And here, kind mate, to thee!
Let 's sing a dirge for Saint Hugh's soul
And down it merrily.
Hey down a down, hey down a down
Hey derry derry down a down,
Ho! well done,
To me let come,
Ring compass gentle joy.

Tune from a Dutch collection of English
Songs, published 1622. Cf. Chappell's *Popular
Music of the Olden Time*.

In the street other journeymen sang their wares.　If Richard Deering's
Fancy *The Cries of London* may be trusted, Shakespeare would have heard
the cooper introducing his cry with the strains of his favourite tune:
"Heartsease."

A cooper I am and have been long,
And hooping is my trade;
And married I am to as pretty wench
As ever God hath made—
Have ye work for a cooper?

Tune "Heartsease."　Cf. Chapter V., pp. 46, 47.

Every inn at that time had its musicians, and the tavern was the natural
haunt of the Elizabethan actor and playwright.　The early plays were
staged in the courtyards of inns such as the "Cross-keys" in Gracechurch
Street and the "Belle Sauvage" in Ludgate Hill.　Scripts of plays were
discussed in tavern parlours.　When the plague or a desire for change
took Shakespeare's company into the provinces, the inns were their natural
resort, and *Henry VI* (Part I, Act II, sc. i) shows Shakespeare's familiarity
with the early morning life in the courtyard of an inn.　The "Crown" Inn

was his favourite hostel at Oxford. At the inns the guest "while he eats, he should be offered music, which he may freely take or refuse; and if he be solitary, the musicians will give him the good-day with music in the morning" (Fynes-Morison, *Itinerary*, 1617). In Deloney's *Jack of Newbury*, when some of the characters enter an inn "they had not sitten long, but in comes a noise of musicians in tawny coats who (putting off their caps) asked if they would have any music." The tavern in London most closely associated with Shakespeare's memory was of course the "Mermaid," meeting-place of the great wits of the day. Among those wits there were musicians such as Thomas Weelkes, who celebrates the resort in one of his "Airs or Fantastic Spirits":

> The Ape, the Monkey and Baboon did meet,
> And breaking of their fast in Friday Street,
> Two of them sware together solemnly
> In their three natures was a sympathy.

At St. Paul's,

> An open house, haunted with great resort,
> Long service mixed with musical disport.

Here Shakespeare may well have gone to evensong to hear his friend, Thomas Morley, play the organ and to listen to the finest choir in London. Thence he might stroll on to hear the city waits who played on Sunday evenings at the Royal Exchange.

The presentation of his plays at a court so musical as that of Queen Elizabeth accounts for the songs in *A Midsummer Night's Dream*, written to the queen's taste. During the Christmas and Twelfth Night festivities from 1595 to 1606, the Chamberlain's men presented fifty-one plays at Court, and between 1603 and 1616 there were one hundred and eighty-seven performances at Court by the company of which Shakespeare was a member.

In his caricatures of foppish courtiers, Ben Jonson indicates the taste for music in these circles. Fastidious Brisk, supposed to represent John Lyly, sings and plays the viol in *Every Man Out of His Humour* (1599). Hedon, the courtier in *Cynthia's Revels* (1601) who is generally identified as John Marston, has a "musician seen at his lodgings a-mornings," and both Hedon and Amorphus sing ditties of their own composing to the lyra. Amorphus, another musical courtier, boasts,

> Do you not observe how excellently the ditty is affected in every place? That I do not marry a word of short quantity to a long note? Nor an ascending syllable to a descending tone? Besides upon the word "best" there, you see how I do enter with an odd minim, and drive it through the brief; which no intelligent musician, I know, but will affirm it to be very rare, extraordinary and pleasing.

John Marston is caricatured again as the courtier Crispinus in Ben Jonson's *The Poetaster* (1602), where he both plays the viol and sings.

It is no wonder, therefore, that musical allusions are found in close upon five hundred passages in Shakespeare's plays. Take, for instance, the lute lesson in *The Taming of the Shrew* (Act III, scene i):

> "Gamut" I am, the ground of all accord,
> "A re," to plead Hortensio's passion;
> "B mi," Bianca, take him for thy lord.
> "C fa ut," that loves with all affection;
> "D sol re," one clef, two notes have I;
> "E la mi," show pity, or I die.

Shakespeare's philosophy of music is perhaps best stated in *The Merchant of Venice*:

> The man that hath not music in his heart
> Nor is not moved with concord of sweet sounds
> Is fit for treasons, strategems and spoils.

It was not only vocal music that rang in Elizabethan England. Michael Drayton, who like his friend Shakespeare came to London from Warwickshire, wrote in *Poly-Olbion*, his rhyming gazetteer (1613):

> The English that repined to be delayed so long,
> All quickly at the hint as if with one consent,
> Strook up at once and sung each to the instrument;
> (Of sundry sorts there were, as the musician likes)
> On which the practiced hand with perfect'st fingering strikes,
> Whereby their right of skill might liveliest be expressed.
> The trembling lute some touch, some strain the viol best,
> In settes which there were seen, the Music wondrous choice.
> Some likewise there affect the Gamba with the voice,
> To show that England could variety afford.
> Some that delight to touch the sterner wiry chord,
> The Cithron, the Pandore, and the Theorbo strike;
> The Gittern and the Kit the wandering fiddlers like.
> So there were some again, in this their learned strife,
> Loud instruments that loved, the Cornet and the Fife,
> The Hoboy, Sackbut deep, Recorder and the Flute,
> Even from the shrillest Shawm unto the Cornemute,
> Some blow the bagpipe up, that plays the country round,
> The Tabor and the Pipe some take delight to sound.

Shakespeare's use of song links him not with the sophisticated madrigal, but with popular ballad tunes, or with "ayres" suited to the accompaniment of a lute. Like the Duke in *Twelfth Night*, he evidently liked a song "old and plain" such as

> The spinsters and the knitters in the sun
> And the free maids that weave their threads with bones
> Do use to chant it.

When his company went on tour, Shakespeare would hear along the country roads the songs he may have remembered from his boyhood's days:

> How heartily the poorest swain doth please himself and flutter his breast with whistlings and singings. These, with a light heart make their heart go lighter, and while they use the solace of their natural instruments, both quicken themselves and encourage forward their over-laboured horse.—DR. JOHN CASE, *Praise of Music*. Oxford, 1586.

Hence it was that Justice Shallow "sang the tunes he heard the carmen whistle."

Ballad-singers were familiar figures at Temple Bar, and Autolycus was to be met at every fair. Henry Chettle, in *Kind Heart's Dream* (1592), brings up the ghost of Anthony Munday who complains of the bawdry surreptitiously printed and distributed by licentious ballad-mongers:

> There be a company of idle youths—in every corner of cities and market towns of the realm, singing and selling of ballads—to the profanation of God's name—When I was liked there was no thought of that idle upstart generation of ballad-singers—they have no better matter but the lascivious undersongs of "Watkin's Ale," the "Carman's Whistle," "Chopping Knives" and "Friar Foxtail."

Puttenham in his *Arte of English Poesie* talks of the "small and popular musics sung by these Catabanqui (or common rhymers) upon benches and barrels'-heads, or else by blind harpers or such-like tavern minstrels that give a fit of mirth for a groat."

As a boy, Shakespeare no doubt formed one of the crowd that trooped from all the countryside to witness what could be seen of the entertainment provided by the Earl of Leicester at Kenilworth for Queen Elizabeth, and there he would have listened with mouth agape to the minstrel described by Laneham whose

> harp in good grace depended upon him—After three lowly courtesies, cleared his voice with a hem and a reach and spat out withal—tempered a string or two with his wrest (tuning key), and after a little warbling on his harp for a prelude, came forth with a solemn song, warranted for story out of King Arthur's Acts.

Autolycus in *The Winter's Tale* was certainly drawn from the life.

SERVANT. O master, if you did but hear the pedlar at the door, you would never dance again after a tabor and pipe; no, the bagpipe could not move you; he sings several tunes faster than you'll tell money; he utters them as he had eaten ballads and all men's ears grew to his tunes.

CLOWN. He could never come better; he shall come in. I love a ballad but even too well, if it be doleful matter merrily set down, or a very pleasant thing indeed and sung lamentably.

SERVANT. He hath songs for man and woman, of all sizes; no milliner can so fit his customers with gloves; he has the prettiest love-songs for maids; so without bawdry, which is strange; with such delicate burthens of dildos and fadings, "jump her and thump her"; and where some stretch-mouthed rascal would, as it were, mean mischief and break a foul gap into the matter, he makes the maid to answer, "Whoop, do me no harm, good man."

Two of the ballads mentioned by Autolycus seem to have come down to us, the first of which "Whoop! Do me no harm, good man," is claimed by Dr. Grattan Flood as being sung to an Irish tune "Paddy Whack," The "fadings" mentioned by the servant are identified by the same authority as tunes for the *Rinnce Fada*, a country dance "longways for as many as will" where the dancers are ranged in two rows.

The sweet pretty Jinny sat on a hill
Where Johnny the swain her see;
He tun'd his quill and sang to her still,
Whoop! Jinny come down to me.
But she sang, but she sang, but she sang
    to him,
      O do no harm to me;
      So there on the hill
      She sang to him still,
      Whoop, do me no harm, good man!

Words from *Westminster Drollery* (1672). Tune discovered by Rimbault. Quoted in *Seventeenth Century Songs*, edited by Sir Frederick Bridge (Novello & Co. Ltd.), who gives another tune in his *Shakespearean Music* (J. M. Dent & Sons, Ltd).

Jog on, jog on the footpath way,
And merrily hent the stile-a:
Your merry heart goes all the day,
Your sad tires in a mile-a.

Your paltry moneybags of gold
What need have we to stare for,
When little or nothing soon is told,
And we have the less to care for?

Cast away care, let sorrow cease,
A fig for melancholy!
Let's laugh and sing, or, if you please,
We'll frolic with sweet Dolly.

Autolycus sings only the first verse. The second and third with the continuing melody are taken from Playford's *Musical Companion.*

Tune "Hanskin" in *Queen Elizabeth's Virginal Book.* Cf. Chappell's *Popular Music of the Olden Time.*

The lyrics sung by this entertaining ballad-monger may have been set to music by some lutenist, whose melodies so far have not been discovered. More fortune has attended the songs in *Twelfth Night*, where three ballads, a catch, and a song, "O Mistress Mine," have been preserved.

Of the ballads mentioned in Act II, sc. iii, Peg o' Ramsay's tune was found in a manuscript of Dr. John Bull, organist of the Chapel Royal in

Shakespeare's day, and also appears in William Ballet's *Lute Book* (1594) preserved in the library of Trinity College, Dublin—evidence sufficient to Dr. Grattan Flood that it was an Irish tune:

Bonny Peg o' Ramsay that any man may see,
And bonny was her face with a fair freckled eye;
Neat is her body made, and she hath good skill,
And round are her bonny arms that work well at the mill.
With a hey trolodel, hey trolodel, hey trolodel lill,
Bonny Peg o' Ramsay that works well at the mill.

Words from *Wit and Mirth, or Pills to Purge Melancholy* (1707). Tune from a manuscript by Dr. John Bull. Cf. Chappell's *Popular Music of the Olden Time.*

The music of the other two ballads, "Three merry men be we," and "Hey Robin, Jolly Robin," has already been given in Chapter V.

"The Gravedigger's Song" is sung in *Hamlet* from "I loathe that I did love," to the tune of "Now Ponder Well," or "The Children in the Wood," our old friend of the pantomimes, which dates at any rate from 1595, instead of to the tune favoured by the original poet, the Earl of Surrey:

THE CHILDREN IN THE WOOD

Now ponder well, you parents dear,
The words which I shall write;
A doleful story you shall hear
In time brought forth to light:
A gentleman of good account,
In Norfolk lived of late,
Whose wealth and riches did surmount
Most men of his estate.

[*Dies and leaves the care of his children to his brother, the wicked "Uncle."*]

Their parents being dead and gone,
The children home he takes,
And brings them home unto his house
And much of them he makes.
He had not kept these pretty babes
A twelvemonth and a day
But for their wealth he did devise
To make them both away.

Entered at Stationers' Hall, 1595. Ritson's *Ancient Songs and Ballads.* Tune from *Wit and Mirth* (1707). Cf. Chappell's *Popular Music of the Olden Time.*

In *Much Ado About Nothing*, Beatrice mentions the "Sick Tune," which served its turn for quite a number of ballads.

It befell at Martinmas,
When weather waxed cold,
Captain Carr said to his men,
"We must go take a hold."

Sick, sick and very, very sick
And sick and like to die;
The sickest night that I abode,
Good Lord, have mercy on me.

From Ritson's *Ancient Songs*. Tune from
Anthony Holborne's *Cittharn Schoole* (1597).
Quoted in Chappell's *Popular Music of the
Olden Time*.

Thomas Nashe in *Summer's Last Will and Testament* (1592) has a verse to this tune:

Sick, sick, and very sick
And sick and for the time;
For Harvest your master is
Abused without reason or rhyme.

Reference has already been made to other ballad tunes with which Shakespeare was clearly familiar: "Green Sleeves," "Fortune My Foe," "Heartsease," "Hanskin" ("Jog on, Jog on"), "Light o' Love," and "Calen o Casture Me."

The three snatches of song sung by Ophelia in her madness are strung together from old ballads. The tunes traditionally sung to the first and third of these may not have been their original melodies. The second is sung to the tune of "Who list to lead a soldier's life," mentioned by Peele in his *Edward III* (1593).

I

How should I your true love know
From another one?
By his cockle hat and staff
And his silver shoon.

He is dead and gone, lady,
He is dead and gone;
At his head a grass-green turf,
At his heels a stone.

White his shroud as the mountain snow,
Larded with sweet flowers,
Which bewept to the grave did go
With true-love showers.

II

Good morrow, 'tis Saint Valentine's day
All in the morning betime,
And I a maid at your window
To be your Valentine.

Then up he rose and donn'd his clothes,
And dupp'd the chamber door;
Let in the maid, that out a maid
Never departed more.

III

And will he not come again,
And will he not come again?
No, no he is dead,
Go to thy death-bed,
He never will come again.

His beard was as white as snow,
All flaxen was his poll;
He is gone, he is gone,
And we cast away moan—
God ha' mercy on his soul!

For tunes, cf. Chappell's *Popular
Music of the Olden Time.*

How deep felt was the sympathy and understanding of Shakespeare
for old ballads is indicated by the dialogue in *Othello* leading up to Desdemona's singing of the "Willow Song":

> My mother had a maid call'd Barbara;
> She was in love: and he she loved proved mad
> And did forsake her; she had a song of "willow";
> An old thing 'twas, but it express'd her fortune,
> And she died singing it: that song to-night
> Will not go from my mind; I have much to do
> But to go hang my head all at one side
> And sing it like poor Barbara.

A little later follows the song itself:

A poor soul sat sighing by a sycamore tree,
Sing willow, willow, willow!
With his hand upon his bosom and his head
    upon his knee.
Oh, willow, willow, willow, willow,
Oh, willow, willow, willow, willow, shall
    be my garland.

Sing all a green willow, willow. willow,
willow!
Ah me! the green willow shall be my garland

The fresh streams ran by her, and murmur'd
her moans;
Sing willow, willow, willow!
Her soft tears fell from her and soften'd the
stones;
Oh, willow, etc.

I call'd my love false love; but what said
he then?
Sing willow, willow, willow!
If I court moe women, you 'll couch with
moe men,
Oh, willow, etc.

Tune in Thomas Dallis's *Lute Book* (1583),
and in British Museum Add. MSS. 15117—
the latter of which is reproduced in facsimile
in *Shakespeare's Music in the Plays and
Early Operas*, by Sir Frederick Bridge
(J. M. Dent & Sons, Ltd.).

The union of the crowns by the accession of James VI of Scotland as
James I of England brought with it an incursion of needy Scots into London
in the wake of their king. With them, no doubt, came Scottish ballads
and ballad tunes, one of which may been have that sung by Iago in *Othello*,
the first play written by Shakespeare as member of the Company of His
Majesty's Servants established by King James. Iago's anglicized version
runs:

King Stephen was a worthy peer,
His breeches cost him but a crown;
He held them sixpence all too dear,
With that he called the tailor "lown."
He was a wight of high renown,
And thou are but of low degree:
'Tis pride that pulls the country down;
Then take thine auld cloak about thee.

The Scotch original quoted in Allan
Ramsay's *Tea Table Miscellany*, reads

In winter when the rain rain'd cauld
An' frost and snaw on ilka hill,
An' Boreas with his blasts sae bald,
Was threat'ning a' our kye to kill,
Then Bell, my wife, wha loves na strife,
She said to me right hastily,
"Get up, guidman, save Cromie's life
And tak your auld cloak about ye."

Tune from *Scottish Songs prior to Burns*,
edited by Robert Chambers (W. & R.
Chambers).

There is another reference to this song in *The Tempest* (Act IV, scene i,) where Trinculo says, "O King Stephano! O peer! O worthy Stephano! look what a wardrobe here is for thee!"

The Scots were as a nation just as musical as the English, their music being enriched, first by Celtic Highland melodies, and secondly by the "Auld Alliance" with France—the Scots College in Paris having given, ever since the fourteenth century, a continental education to the youth of the north. Part-singing flourished in Scotland before the period usually identified with the English madrigal. In the memoirs of Sir James Melville, we read that "Mary Queen of Scots had three valets who sang three parts, and she wanted a person to sing a bass or fourth part. David Rizzio, who had come to France with the ambassador of Savoy, was recommended as one fit to make the fourth in concert, and thus he was drawn in to sing sometimes with the rest; and afterwards, when her French secretary retired himself to France, this David obtained the said office."

Darnley, father of James VI, was "skilled in the art of music, dancing, and playing on instruments." At midnight, before his murder "his chamberchild begged him to play while a psalm was being sung, but his hand, he replied, was 'out for the lute.'" Mary Queen of Scots, his wife, played and sang French rather than Scots tunes. As for the Scottish people themselves, James VI in 1579 passed a statute requiring the local authorities to keep up existing song schools and encouraged the establishment of others.

From *Pammelia* (1609).

The melody of Iago's drinking song, "And let me the canakin clink," has not been preserved, but we have other drinking songs of the time which Shakespeare must have known, even before 1609 when he could pick up the printed collections *Pammelia* and *Deuteromelia*, sold at The Spread Eagle, at the great north door of Paul's, or At the Sign of the White Lion in Paul's churchyard. From *Pammelia* comes the catch:

Troll, troll, troll the bowl to me and I will troll the same again to thee,
Begin now, hold in now, for we must merry be as you see; be lusty
So must we—O it is a brave thing for to pass away the spring with mirth and joy to sing—
Tan tan tan tara tan tan tall a flaunt, brave boys, what joy is this to see, when friends
do well agree.

Grumio in *The Taming of the Shrew* plays on the first line of the catch which we find in *Pammelia*:

Jack, boy, ho, boy, news!
The cat is in the well,
Let us sing now for her knell,
Ding, dong, ding, dong, bell.

From *Deuteromelia*, the collection which contains our friend of the nursery, "Three Blind Mice," we get the music to which Sir Andrew, Sir Toby, and the Clown, sing a catch in *Twelfth Night*:

Hold thy peace and I prithee hold thy peace;
Thou knave, hold thy peace, thou knave,
Thou knave!

"Catches," says the introduction to *Pammelia*, "are consonant to all ordinary musical capacity—good art in all for the more musical—sweet harmony mixed with much variety." At Stratford-on-Avon there is a chair in which tradition says Shakespeare sat at the tavern and joined in the singing. In London there were, no doubt, many such chairs, for the poet was "good company" just like those waits in Beaumont and Fletcher's *The Coxcomb*—"good sober gentlemen who were

like careful members of the city
Drawing in diligent ale and singing catches.

"What shall he have that killed the deer?" is a song in *As You Like It,* of which one old setting has been preserved:

What shall he have that killed the deer?—His leather skin and horns to wear.
Then sing him home.—[*The rest shall bear this burthen.*]
Take thou no scorn to wear the horn; it was a crest ere thou wast born:
Thy father's father wore it—And thy father bore it:
The horn, the horn, the lusty horn, is not a thing to laugh to scorn.

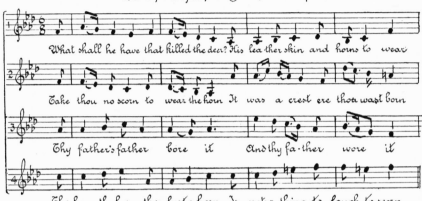

Catch arranged by John Hilton.   From Playford's *Musical Companion* (1672).   Quoted in
Rimbault's *Rounds, Catches and Canons of England.*
(In the singing version the words "wore" and "bore" are transposed.)

A drinking song which Shakespeare may very well have known is printed in Ravenscroft's third collection, entitled *Melismata* (1611):

Toss the pot, toss the pot, let us be merry,
And drink till our cheeks be as red as a
    cherry.
We take no thought, we have no care,
For still we spend and never spare
Till of all money our purse is bare,
We ever toss the pot!

From *Melismata* (1611).

Thomas Morley, composer of madrigals as well as songs for the lute, was a Gentleman of the Chapel Royal from 1592 till his death in 1602. He was a neighbour of Shakespeare in St. Peter's Bishopgate, and two of his settings of Shakespeare's songs have been preserved. He was modest enough to say that he was but a beginner in composition for the lute, and did it in his vacation time, yet there was no apology needed for songs so enchanting as his setting of "It was a lover and his lass." The second line came, no doubt, from Italy, a country with whose music Morley was intimately familiar.

It was a lover and his lass,
With a hey and a ho and a hey nonnino,
That o'er the green cornfield did pass
In the spring time,
The only pretty ring time,
When birds do sing,
Hey ding a ding a ding,
Sweet lovers love the spring.

This carol they began that hour,
With a hey and a ho and a hey nonnino,
How that life was but a flower
In the spring time, etc.

Between the acres of the rye,
With a hey and a ho and hey nonnino,
These pretty country folks would lie
In the spring time, etc.

And therefore take the present time,
With a hey and a ho and a hey nonnino,
For love is crowned with the prime
In the spring time, etc.

From Thomas Morley's *First Book of Ayres* (1600). Cf. *The English Ayre*, Peter Warlock (Oxford University Press).

Twelfth Night was written in the same year as *As You Like It* (1599) for production at Court, and Morley's connection with the Chapel Royal made his collaboration all the more natural. A traditional setting of "O Mistress Mine" is frequently credited to him, and William Byrd also used this melody for the virginals, but some recent experts are inclined to disassociate this tune from these words. However that may be, both the tune and the words are enchanting, so why not leave them contentedly married?

O mistress mine, where are you roaming?
O, stay and hear; your true love's coming,
That can sing both high and low.
Trip no further, pretty sweeting;
Journeys end in lovers meeting,
Every wise man's son doth know.

What is love? 'tis not hereafter;
Present mirth hath present laughter;
What's to come is still unsure.
In delay there lies no plenty;
Then come kiss me, sweet and twenty,
Youth's a stuff will not endure.

Melody from W. Byrd's arrangement in
Queen Elizabeth's Virginal Book. Cf. *English
Melodies* (J. M. Dent & Sons Ltd.).

In the same collection of Ayres (1600) as was published "It was a lover and his lass," may be found another altogether charming lyric overlooked in the anthologies, but resurrected by Arnold Dolmetsch, in his *Select English Songs and Dialogues of the 16th and 17th Centuries.*

What if my mistress now will needs incon-
    stant be?
Wilt thou be then so false in love as well
    as she?
No, no, such falsehood flee though women
    faithless be.

My mistress frowns and swears that now I
    love her not,
The change she finds is that which my
    despair begot.
Despair which is my lot since she all faith
    forgot.

If she doth change she must not be in-
    constancy,
For while she doth profess to take such
    liberty
Herself she will untie and yet fast bound
    am I.

Which if I find, my heart some otherwhere
    shall dwell,
For loving not to be loved, it is a hell;
Since so my hap befell I bid my love fare-
    well.

Tune from Thomas Morley's *First Book of
Ayres* (1600). Quoted in Arnold Dolmetsch's
Select English Songs and Dialogues. (Reprinted
by permission of Boosey & Co. Ltd.).

Michael Drayton wrote of Morley:

Such was old Orpheus' cunning
That senseless things drew near him
And herds of beasts to hear him;

The stork, the stone, the ox, the ass came running!
Morley! but this enchanting
To thee, to be music-god is wanting,
And yet thou needst not fear him.
Draw thou the shepherds and the bonny lasses;
And envy him not storks, stones, oxen, asses.

Morley published in 1597 a *Plaine and Easie Introduction to Practicall Musick*, with advice to song composers, in which he urges the musician to closely follow and interpret the words:

In no composition shall you prove admirable except you put on, and possess yourself wholly with that vein wherein you compose, so that you must in your music be wavering like the wind; sometimes grave and staid, otherwhile effeminate. . . . If you would have your music signify hardness, cruelty or other such effects, you must cause the parts proceed in their motions by whole notes, sharp thirds, sharp sixes and such like; you may also use cadences bound with the fourth and seventh, which being in long notes will exasperate the harmony; but when you would express a lamentable passion, then must you use motions proceeding by half notes, flat thirds and flat sixes, which of their nature are sweet, specially being taken in the true time and natural air with discretion and judgement. Also if the subject be light, you must cause your music go in motions, which carry with them a celerity or quickness of time, as minims, crotchets and quavers; if it be lamentable, the note must go in slow and heavy motions, as semi-breves, breves and such-like. Moreover you must have a care that when your manner signifieth ascending, high, heaven and such-like, you make your music ascend, and by the contrary, when your ditty speaketh of descending, lowness, depth, hell, and such-like, you must make the music descend. . . . We must also take heed of separating any part of a word from another by a rest, as some dunces have not scrupled to do, which is one of the greatest absurdities which I have seen committed in the dittying of music—you may set a crotchet or minim rest above a comma or colon in the ditty, but a larger rest than that of a minim you may not make till the sentence be perfect. . . . Also when you would express sighs, you may use the crotchet or minim rest at the most. Lastly you must not make a close (especially a full close) till the sense of the words be perfect so that keeping these rules you shall have a perfect agreement, and as it were, an harmonical concert betwixt the matter and the music, and likewise you shall be perfectly understood of the auditor what you sing, which is one of the highest degrees of praise which a musician in dittying can attain unto or wish for.

Morley was a publisher as well as a singer, composer, and writer on music. One of his publications was *The Triumphs of Oriana*, a collection of madrigals in honour of Queen Elizabeth, which links him with the family of John Milton, for it contains a contribution from the elder John Milton, the musician and father of the poet.

Morley did not slavishly follow the words of any verse he might be setting, but sought above all to make it singable, introducing particularly in the canzonets exclamations and refrains which add a life and movement to his settings.

In *Twelfth Night* Sir Toby sings a snatch from a song by Robert Jones which was published about the same time as the production of the play.

Farewell dear love, since thou wilt needs
    be gone,
Mine eyes do show my life is almost done.
Nay I will never die
So long as I can spy,
There be many mo'
Tho' that she do go,
There be many mo'e, I fear not.
Why then let her go, I care not!

Farewell, farewell, since this I find is true,
I will not spend my life in wooing you;
But I will seek elsewhere
If I may find love there.
Shall I bid her go?
What an if I do?
Shall I bid her go and spare not?
O no, no, no, no, I dare not.

Tune from Robert Jones's *First Book
of Songs and Ayres* (1600).

Robert Jones was a lutenist and composer of considerable skill who in 1610 was director of the Children of the Queen's Revels, organized by Philip Rosseter to produce plays at Court—their productions included Ben Jonson's *Epicœne*, and Fletcher's *The Coxcomb, Cupid's Revenge,* and *The Scornful Lady*. Another of his songs which attained much popularity was his setting of Sir Walter Raleigh's "Now what is Love":

Now what is Love, I pray thee tell?
It is that fountain and that well
Where pleasures and repentance dwell.
It is perhaps that saucing bell
That tolls all into heaven or hell.
And this is Love, as I hear tell.

Now what is Love, I pray thee say?
It is a work on holy day.
It is December matched with May,
When lusty blood in fresh array
Hear ten months after of their play.
And this is Love, as I hear say.

Now what is Love, I pray thee fain?
It is a sunshine mixed with rain.
It is a gentle pleasing pain;
A flower that dies and springs again.
It is a No that would full fain.
And this is Love, as I hear sayen.

Tune from Robert Jones's *Second Book of Songs and Ayres* (1601). Reprinted from *English Ayres*, transcribed and edited by Peter Warlock and Philip Wilson, by permission of the Oxford University Press.

Thomas Ford is another contemporary lutenist and song-writer whom we have reason to associate with Shakespeare's music. Ford was in the service of Prince Henry, and the quality of the lyrics with which his melodies are identified indicates that either he was himself a happy poet, or that he had friends among good writers. Best known of his songs are: "Since first I saw your face," and "There is a lady sweet and kind":

Since first I saw your face I resolved
To honour and renown ye.
If now I be disdained I wish
My heart had never known ye.
What, I that loved and you that liked,
Shall we begin to wrangle?
No, no, no, my heart is fast
And cannot disentangle.

If I admire or praise you too much,
That fault you may forgive me.
Or if my hands had strayed but a touch,
Then justly you might leave me.
I asked you leave, you bade me love,
Is 't now a time to chide me?
No, no, no, I 'll love you still
What fortune e'er betide me.

The sun whose beams most glorious are
Rejecteth no beholder;
And your sweet beauty past compare
Made my poor eyes the bolder.
Where Beauty moves and Wit delights
And signs of kindness bind me,
There, O there, where'er I go,
I leave my heart behind me.

Thomas Ford, *Airs to the Lute from Musicke of Sundrie Kinds* (1607), reprinted and edited by E. H. Fellowes (Stainer & Bell). An original copy of the songbook is in the British Museum.

The song "There is a lady sweet and kind" is perhaps better known to the setting of Edward Purcell, but Ford's original music is coming back to its proper recognition.

There is a lady sweet and kind,
Was never face so pleased my mind;
I did but see her passing by,
And yet I love her till I die.

Her gesture, motion, and her smiles,
Her wit, her voice my heart beguiles,
Beguiles my heart, I know not why,
And yet I love her till I die.

Thomas Ford, *Airs to the Lute*. Cf. edition of E. H. Fellowes (Stainer & Bell). An original copy of the songbook is in the British Museum.

Cupid is winged and doth range,
Her country so my love doth change;
But change she earth, or change she sky,
Yet will I love her till I die.

Ford's connection with Shakespeare
is evidenced in his setting for three
voices of "Sigh no more, ladies."
While this cannot have been used for
the original production of *As You
Like It*, it may very well have served
at any revival in the early seventeenth century, particularly a revival
at Court.

Sigh no more, ladies,
Sigh no more,
Men were deceivers ever.
One foot in sea
And one on shore.
To one thing constant never.
Then sigh not so,
But let them go,
And be you blithe and bonny,
Converting all
Your sighs of woe
Into hey nonny nonny.

Sing no more ditties,
Sing no more
Of dumps so dull and heavy.
The fraud of men
Was ever so
Since summer first was leafy.
Then sigh not so
But let them go
And be you blithe and bonny.
Converting all
Your sighs of woe
Into hey nonny nonny.

Setting by Thomas Ford from a MS. in the
library of Christ Church, Oxford, by permission
of the Governing Body, transcribed for this book
by Harold Eustace Key.

CHAPTER XII

Shakespeare and music (*continued*)—Robert Johnson—Music in *The Tempest, The Winter's Tale*—John Wilson—Ballads and songs in Fletcher's and Middleton's plays.

The Tempest was produced at Court in 1611, and suggests the influence of the masques produced by Ben Jonson, whom we know to have been Shakespeare's friend.   Indeed some go so far as to find definite indication that he had seen the *Masque of Blackness*, the *Masque of Beauty*, and *Hymenaei*, conceiving from these his pageantry of seascape and aerial musicians.   Robert Johnson, who has been identified with the traditional music of at least two of the songs in *The Tempest*, appears in the accounts for Ben Jonson's masque of *Love Freed From Ignorance and Folly* as receiving £5 "for setting the song to the lutes."   Johnson was in the service of Prince Henry and was a musician after any poet's heart, for he is quoted by Walter Porter, a later musician, as saying "marry the notes and words well together."   What more natural that in conversation Shakespeare should have obtained some ideas as to the use of the songs in this masque-like play from the musician who was to set the songs? The best of the boy-actors had by this time been absorbed into Shakespeare's company, so that he had no lack of singers.

Ariel is the very spirit of music, particularly the dance music of the pipe and tabor.   His first song is on a country-dance rhythm:

> Come unto these yellow sands
> And then take hands:
> Curtsey'd when you have and kiss'd
> The wild waves whist:
> Foot it featly here and there,
> And sweet sp'rites, the burthen bear:
> Hark, hark!
> *Burthen* (*dispersedly*) Bow-wow!
> The watchdogs bark—
> *Burthen* (*dispersedly*) Bow-wow!
> Hark, hark! I hear
> The strain of strutting chanticleer
> Cry "Cock a-diddle-dow!"

Enticing Caliban and his drunken crew, Ariel says:

> Then I beat my tabor;
> At which, like unback'd colts, they prick'd their ears,

Advanced their eyelids, lifted up their noses
As they smelt music; so I charmed their ears,
That calf-like they my lowing followed.

One of the tunes played by Ariel was that of a catch that Caliban would sing:

Flout 'em and scout 'em,
And scout 'em and flout 'em,
Thought is free.

First of the two songs set by Johnson, of which the music has been preserved is:

Full fathom five thy father lies;
Of his bones are coral made;
Those are pearls that were his eyes;
Nothing of him that doth fade
But doth suffer a sea-change
Into something rich and strange.
Sea-nymphs hourly ring his knell:
Burthen. Ding-dong!
Hark! now I hear them—Ding-dong, bell!

The song itself emerges from an atmosphere of music. Ferdinand introduces it and rounds it off by saying:

This music crept by me upon the waters,
Allaying both their fury and my passion
With its sweet air; I thence have follow'd it,
Or it hath drawn me rather? But 'tis gone.
No, it begins again. . . .
The ditty does remember my drown'd
    father.
This is no mortal business, nor no sound
That the earth owes.

From John Wilson's *Cheerful Ayres and Ballads.* Cf. *Songs from Shakespeare,* edited by Sir Frederick Bridge (Novello & Co. Ltd.).

The lyric sung by Ariel as he helps to attire Prospero was surely written for the music that we have with it:

Where the bee sucks, there suck I;
In a cowslip's bell I lie:
There I couch when owls do cry.
On the bat's back I do fly
After summer merrily.
Merrily, merrily shall I live now
Under the blossom that hangs on the bough.

The entry in the records of the Office of the Revels as regards the production of the play reads:

By the Kings Players: Hallomas nyght was presented att Whithall before yᵉ Kings Maᵗⁱᵉ a play called the Tempest.

From John Wilson's *Cheerful Ayres and Ballads.* Facsimile of music is given in *Shakespeare Music in the Early Plays and Operas,* edited by Sir Frederick Bridge (J. M. Dent & Sons Ltd.).

Four days later, on the 5th of November the King's Players presented another of Shakespeare's plays rich in music—*The Winter's Tale,* or as it is termed in the records, "Yᵉ winters nightes Tayle." This appears to have been already played at the Globe Theatre in the preceding May. It introduces some of the current features of the masque such as "The dance of satyrs," and was well suited to the same company of players as *The Tempest.* The ballads and snatches of popular song in *The Winter's Tale* have already been touched upon, but one song sung by Autolycus introduces us to a singer and composer of more than ordinary interest: Jack Wilson, a boy actor who appears to have sung the song "Sigh no more, ladies" in an early production of *Much Ado About Nothing,* and is generally identified with the John Wilson whose own songs are among the most celebrated of this century. "Lawn as white as driven snow" appears in the *Cheerful Ayres and Ballads,* first composed for a single voice and since set for three voices, published in 1659 by John Playford for Dr. John Wilson (1594–1673) who, in these days of precocious singing-boys was none too young at seventeen to have written the song in question; since only two years later (1613) he was commissioned to write the music for *The Masque of Flowers*, presented by the Gentlemen of Gray's Inn at the Banqueting Hall, Whitehall:

Lawn as white as driven snow;
Gloves as sweet as damask roses;
Bugle bracelet, necklace amber,
Golden coifs and stomachers,
Pins and poking-sticks of steel,
Come, buy of me, come, come buy, come buy;
Come buy!

Cypress black as e'er was crow:
Masks for faces and for noses:
Perfume for a lady's chamber:
For my lads to give their dears:
What maids lack from head to heel.
Buy, lads, or else your lasses cry:

From John Wilson's *Cheerful Ayres and Ballads* (1659). Cf. *Fifty Shakespeare Songs*, edited by Charles Vincent (Oliver Ditson Company).

Some have maintained that Wilson may have merely arranged for three voices a song which someone else (possibly Robert Johnson) originally set for one, but there is a notable similarity between this song and the coney-skin pedlar song in Fletcher's *The Beggar's Bush*:

Bring out your coney-skins, maids, to me
And hold them fair that I may see;
Grey, black and blue; for the smaller skins
I'll give you bracelets, laces, pins,
And here for your whole coney
Here's ready money.
Come, gentle Joan, do thou begin
With thy black coney coney-skin,
And Mary and Joan will follow
With their silver-haired skins and yellow;
The white coney-skin I will not lay by,
For though it be faint, it is fair to the eye.

The grey it is worn, but yet for my money,
Give me the bonny, bonny black coney.
Come away, fair maids, your skins will decay,
Come and take money, maids, put your wares away,
Ha' ye any coney skins here to sell?

Melody from D'Urfey's *Wit and Mirth*.

John Wilson was a close friend of two brother musicians who will be dealt with later, William and Henry Lawes, and according to one story got mixed up with them in a tavern brawl. He is the "curious Wilson," mentioned in Herrick's poem on Henry Lawes, who himself wrote of Wilson:

> From long experience and acquaintance, I
> Could tell the world thy known integrity
> Unto thy friends; thy true and honest heart,
> Ev'n mind, good nature, all but thy great art
> Which I but dully understand.

John Wilson was a favourite with Charles I, and according to Antony à Wood "played on the lute with such skill as gave the king great satisfaction, who generally leaned on his shoulder during his performance." Charles himself, according to Playford, "could play his part exactly well on the Bass-Viol, especially of those incomparable Phantasies of Mr. Coperario to the Organ."

A lyric attributed to Shakespeare though not found in his plays appears with John Wilson's music in Playford's *Select Ayres*:

From the fair Lavinian shore
I your markets come to store;
Muse not though so far I dwell,
And come here my wares to sell:
Such is the sacred hunger of gold.
Then come to my pack,
While I cry,
"What d'ye lack,
What d'ye buy?"
For here it is to be sold.

I have beauty, honour, grace,
Fortune, favour, time and place,
And what else thou wouldst request,
E'en the thing thou lik'st the best.
First let me have a touch of thy gold;
Then come to me, lad,
Thou shalt have
What thy dad
Never gave
For here it is to be sold.

Brit. Mus. Add, MSS. 11608, fol. 66b.
Playford's *Select Ayres* (1659). Cf. *English Melodies* (J. M. Dent & Sons Ltd.).

Another lyric sometimes ascribed to Shakespeare as it appears in the 1640 edition of *Measure for Measure* appears with Wilson's setting in Playford's *Select Musical Ayres and Dialogues*. This lyric, however, has also been credited to John Fletcher as it was sung with an additional verse in *The Bloody Brother*, a play on which Fletcher collaborated with Ben Jonson and Nathaniel Field (1613). The lyric in question is a paraphrase from the Latin, and Shakespeare was no classical scholar.

Take, O take those lips away,
That so sweetly were forsworn,
And those eyes, the break of day,
Lights that do mislead the morn:
But my kisses bring again,
Seals of love, but seal'd in vain.

Hide, O hide those hills of snow
Which thy frozen bosom bears,
On whose tops the pinks that grow
Are of those that April wears;
But first set my poor heart free,
Bound in those icy chains by thee.

Melody from Playford's *Select Music Ayres and Dialogues* (1653). Quoted in *English Melodies* (J. M. Dent & Sons Ltd.).

Wilson is identified with the music of another song more certainly ascribed to Fletcher, and appearing in *The Beggar's Bush* (1615), Act II, sc. i, "Cast our caps and cares away." The song version reads, "Cast your caps and cares away."

From Wilson's *Cheerful Ayres* (1660), also Playford's *Musical Companion* (1673). Cf. *English Melodies* (J. M. Dent & Sons Ltd.).

Cast our caps and cares away: this is Beggars' Holy-day,
At the crowning of our King, thus we ever dance and sing.
In the world look out and see: where 's so happy a Prince as he?
Where the nation lives so free, and so merry as do we?
Be it peace or be it war, here at liberty we are,
And enjoy our ease and rest; to the field we are not prest;
Nor are called into the Town, to be troubled with the Gown.
Hang all officers we cry, and the Magistrate too, by;
When the Subsidie's encreast, we are not a penny sest.
Nor will any go to Law, with a Beggar for a straw.
All which happiness he brags, he doth owe unto his rags.

Robert Johnson, who graduated in music at Oxford in 1604, was a favourite song-writer for the stage of James the First's day. In addition to music for Shakespeare's songs, he is credited with the songs and incidental music in Chapman's *Masque for the Middle Temple and Lincoln's Inn* (1613), where the performers included such outstanding musicians as John Dowland and his son Robert, Philip Rosseter, and Thomas Ford.

In Ben Jonson's masque *Love Freed from Ignorance and Folly*, Robert Johnson received payment for "setting the song to the lute," and he is further associated with Ben Jonson as the composer of the music for the masque of *The Gipsies Metamorphosed* (1621). For John Fletcher's *Valentinian* (1615) Johnson wrote the setting of the song "Care-charming Sleep":

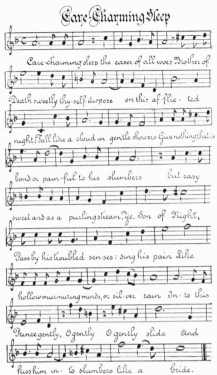

Care-charming Sleep, thou easer of all woes,
Brother to Death, sweetly thyself dispose
On this afflicted prince; fall like a cloud
In gentle showers; give nothing that is loud,
Or painful to his slumbers; easy, sweet,
And as a purling stream, thou son of Night,
Pass by his troubled senses; sing his pain,
Like hollow murmuring wind or silver rain;
Into this prince gently, oh, gently slide,
And kiss him into slumbers like a bride.

(The literary version has several verbal differences from that of the song).

Melody from Col. Probert's MS. and Brit. Mus. 11608, Quoted in *Songs and Lyrics from the plays of Beaumont and Fletcher, with contemporary Musical Settings*," edited by E. H. Fellowes (Frederick Etchells and Hugh Macdonald—The Haslewood Books, 192 Church Street, London, 1928).

The simplicity and charm of this composer are heard in a song, seemingly based on a ballad, "As I walked forth to take the air":

As I walked forth one summer's day
To view the meadows green and gay,
A pleasant bower I espied
Standing fast by the river's side;
And in't a maiden I heard cry:
"Alas, alas! there's none e'er loved as I."

Then round the meadow did she walk
Catching each flower did she walk,
Such flowers as in the meadows grew,
The deadman's thumb, an herb all blue;
And as she pulled them, still cried she:
"Alas, alas, there's none e'er loved as I."

When she had filled her apron full
Of such green things as she could cull,
The green things served her for her bed,
The flowers were pillows for her head;
Then down she lay'd her, ne'er word more did speak,
Alas, alas! with love her heart did break.

Melody from Playford's *Ayres and Dialogues* (1659). Cf. *English Melodies* (J. M. Dent & Sons Ltd.).

There are ninety-two songs cited in Fletcher's plays, surely sufficient indication that he was in close contact with musicians—a contact which explains the essentially singable quality of his verse. He was, moreover, steeped in the ballad music of his day—over seventy snatches from contemporary ballads are sung by characters in *The Knight of the Burning Pestle, The Little French Lawyer, Wit without Money, Bonduca, The Loyal Subject, The Woman's Price, Monsieur Thomas, The Maid in The Mill,* and *Two Noble Kinsmen.* The tunes of "Green Sleeves," "Fortune My Foe," and "The Spanish Pavan" are mentioned, and in *The Chances,* the victim of an operation has "John Dory" sung to him as an anæsthetic.

ANTONIO.   I 'll have John Dory
                For to that tune I will be opened.
                Give me some drink—Have you stopt
                The leaks well, surgeon?
                All will run out else.

SURGEON.   Fear not.

ANTONIO.   Sit down, gentlemen—
                And now advance your plasters.

As it fell on a holiday,
And upon a holy tide-a,
John Dory bought him an ambling nag
To Paris for to ride-a.

And when John Dory to Paris was come
A little before the gate-a,
John Dory was fitted, the porter was witted
To let him in thereat-a.

The first man that John Dory did meet
Was good King John of France-a;
John Dory could well of his courtesie,
But fell down in a trance-a.

Deuteromelia (1609). Cf. Chappell's *Popular Music of the Olden Time,* and the introduction to *English Melodies* (J. M. Dent & Sons Ltd.).

A pardon, a pardon, my liege and king,
For my merry men and me-a;
And all the churls in merry England,
I'll bring them bound to thee-a, etc.

In *The Pilgrim,* and *The Knight of the Burning Pestle,* verses are sung from the old ballad of "The Knight and the Shepherd's Daughter," and "Fair Margaret and Sweet William" is quoted in *The Knight of the Burning Pestle.* This delightful comedy and *Monsieur Thomas,* both played by children's companies, are treasuries of old song:

There was a shepherd's daughter
Came tripping on the way,
And there by chance a knight she met
Which caused her to stay.

Good morrow to you, beauteous maid,
These words pronounced he;
O I shall die this day, he said,
If I've not my will of thee.

.   .   .   .   .

He set her on a milkwhite steed,
And himself upon a gray;
He hung a bugle about his neck
And so they rode away.

Words from Percy's *Reliques.* Melody from Playford's *Dancing Master.* Cf. Chappell's *Popular Music of the Olden Time.*

As it fell out on a long summer's day
Two lovers they sat on a hill;
They sat together that long summer's day
And could not take their fill.

.   .   .   .   .

You are no love for me, Margaret,
I am no love for you.

When all was grown to dark midnight
And all men fast asleep,
In came Margaret's grisly ghost
And stood at William's feet.

Melody from Watt's *Musical Miscellany* (1729). Cf. Chappell's *Popular Music of the Olden Time.*

Thomas Middleton is another playwright of this period who makes rich use of song, *Blurt Master Constable,* written for the Children of

Paul's (1602), brought him in touch with singers at the outset of his stage career, and we find him uniting numerous other plays for children's companies. Forty-seven songs are quoted in his collected works, several to ballad tunes, such as "Cupid is Venus' only joy" in *A Chaste Maid in Cheapside*, written to a Welsh air. Ravenscroft's setting of "Love for such a cherry lip" is transcribed in the next chapter. Two dance songs appear in *The Spanish Gipsy*, a play in which Rowley collaborated.

Trip it, gipsies, trip it fine,
Show tricks and lofty capers;
At threading needles we repine,
And leaping over rapiers:
Pindy-pandy rascal toys!
We scorn cutting purses;
Though we live by making noise,
For cheating none can curse us.

Over high ways, over low,
And over stones and gravel,
Though we trip it on the toe,
And thus for silver travel;
Though our dances waste our backs,
At night fat capons mend them,
Eggs well brewed in buttered sack,
Our wenches say befriend them.

Melody from *Queen Elizabeth's Virginal Book*.
Cf. Chappell's *Popular Music of the Olden Time*.

Come, follow your leader, follow,
Our convoy be Mars and Apollo!
The van comes brave up here;
(*Answer*) As hotly comes the rear;
Chorus:
    Our knackers are the fifes and drums,
    Sa, sa, the gipsies' army comes.

Horsemen we need not fear,
There's none but footmen here;
The horse sure charge without,
Or if they wheel about,
    Our knackers are the shot that fly,
    Pit-a-pat rattling in the sky.

Melody entitled "The Spanish Gipsy," from Playford's *Dancing Master*. Cf. Chappell's *Popular Music of the Olden Time*.

CHAPTER XIII

Use of boy-actors' voices in Elizabethan plays—Plays produced by children's companies—Collections of popular songs, *Pammelia* and *Deuteromelia*.

THE prevalence of songs in Elizabethan plays was due partly to the engagement of boy actors by the companies to play the female roles. English boys of the period were trained to sing in church choirs, and a playwright so practical as Shakespeare naturally used their singing talent. In *As You Like It*, two pages sang "It was a lover and his lass." Boys dressed as fairies sang "Fie on sinful fantasy" in *The Merry Wives of Windsor*, and the fairies who sang "You spotted snakes with double tongue" in *A Midsummer Night's Dream* were boys. "Come, thou monarch of the vine" in *Antony and Cleopatra* is stated in the text as sung by a boy. Ariel in *The Tempest*, whose voice was entrusted with three of Shakespeare's loveliest songs: "Come unto .these yellow sands," "Full fathom five," and "Where the bee sucks," may have been a boy, though it is possible that the singer was a tenor, originally one of the boy-actors of the Chapel Royal or St. Paul's, who were absorbed into Burbage's company in the year 1608. Ophelia with her mad songs; Desdemona in *Othello* with her Willow song, were roles suited to singing boy-actors.

Between the years 1600 and 1607, two companies of boy-actors produced a number of plays in which the songs they were so fitted to sing were introduced—the Children of Paul's and the Blackfriars Children who were in fact the Children of the Chapel Royal. James Burbage in 1597 had built the Blackfriars Theatre in the best residential district of London, but was forbidden to use this as a public playhouse by the Privy Council, owing to the objections of the neighbouring landlords. There was less objection to an exclusive theatre in which the actors were the Queen's own Chapel Children, and so a series of plays largely interspersed with music delighted audiences which were probably more select than those of the older theatres. In Ben Jonson's *Cynthia's Revels*, produced in 1600, eight of the boy-actors had their songs to sing, one being the celebrated

HYMN TO DIANA

Queen and huntress, chaste and fair,
Now the sun is laid to sleep,
Seated in thy silver chair,
State in wonted manner keep;
Hesperus entreats thy light,
Goddess excellently bright.

The melody is lost, but the stage directions state that "music accompanied" these words. Nathaniel Giles was Master of the chapel at this time and may have composed the music for this and for Ben Jonson's *The Poetaster* (1602).

The library of Christ Church, Oxford, preserves the manuscript of a song by this Nathaniel Giles, with words that have found their way into several anthologies, and music that surely deserves resurrection on this page:

Melody from Nathaniel Giles, Christ Church, Oxford, MS. I, 5, 49, by permission of the Governing Body. Transcribed for this book by Harold Eustace Key.

Hey nonny no!
Men are fools that wish to die.
Is't not fine to dance and sing
When the bells of death do ring?
Is't not fine to swim in wine
And turn upon the toe
And sing hey nonny no
When the winds do blow
And the seas do flow?
Hey nonny no!

One madrigal composer with whom Ben Jonson seems to have at this time collaborated is Henry Youll, whose canzonet for three voices to one of the songs for this play has been preserved:

> Slow, slow, fresh fount, keep time with my salt tears;
>   Yet slower, yet! oh, faintly, gentle springs;
> List to the heavy part the music bears,
>   Woe weeps out her division when she sings.

Salathiel Pavy, one of the boy-actors in *Cynthia's Revels*, died two years later, and in a touching epitaph Ben Jonson commemorated his virtues:

> Weep with me, all you that read
>   This little story,
> And know, for whom a tear you shed
>   Death's self is sorry.

'Twas a child that so did thrive
In grace and feature
As heaven and nature seem'd to strive
Which owned the creature.

The plays produced by this Children's Company were preceded by concerts. The Duke of Stettin-Pomerania, who attended a performance at the Blackfriars Theatre in 1602, wrote:

For a whole hour preceding the play one listens to delightful instrumental music on organs, lutes, pandorins, mandolins, violins and flutes; as indeed on this occasion when a boy sang *cum voce tremulo* so charmingly to the accompaniment of a bass-violin that unless possibly the Nuns at Milan excelled him, we had not heard his equal on our journey.

In *Epicœne, or The Silent Woman,* written for the Children of the Revels to the Queen (1609), Ben Jonson has a famous paraphrase from the Latin verse of Jean Bonnefons. (This Children's Company was under the direction of two lutenist composers, Philip Rosseter and Robert Joncs, and one old setting, perhaps the original of this notable song in this play, has been preserved.)

From Playford's *Select Ayres and Dialogues* (1669), where it appears anonymously with the title "On a Proud Lady."

Still to be neat, still to be dress'd
As you were going to a feast;
Still to be powder'd, still perfumed,
Lady, it is to be presumed,
Though art's hid causes are not found,
All is not sweet, all is not sound.

Give me a look, give me a face,
That makes simplicity a grace;
Robes loosely flowing, hair as free,
Such sweet neglect more taketh me
Than all the adulteries of art;
They strike mine eyes, but not my heart.

Another company was founded by the Children of Paul's, who made a little theatre out of the singing school, appealing with more sophisticated plays to select audiences. To quote from one of their plays ascribed to John Marston:

I saw the children of Paul's last night. . . .
I' faith, I like the audience that frequented there
With much applause. A man shall not be choked
With the stench of garlic, nor be pasted
To the barmy jacket of a beer-brewer.

Thomas Ravenscroft (1585–1633), who was a chorister at St. Paul's at the date of their first production—*Maid's Metamorphosis* in 1601—

appears to have himself written the
music for two of the songs, so that
this may have been a schoolboy
production.

> By the moon we sport and play,
> With the night begins our day;
> As we frisk the dew doth fall,
> Trip it, little urchins all,
> Lightly as the little bee
> Two by two and three by three,
> And about go we.

Another of the songs in the *Maid's
Metamorphosis* was written by John
Bennett, an admirable composer of
madrigals, but otherwise unknown.
In the libretto of this play, John Lyly
may have had a hand.

Ravenscroft, in his *Melismata*,
prints the music written by Edmund
Pearce, Master of the Choristers at
St. Paul's, for a song described as
Italian, in Middleton's *Blurt, Master
Constable*, another of the productions
of this Children's Company.

Love for such a cherry lip
Would be glad to pawn his arrows;
Venus here to take a sip
Would sell her doves and teams of sparrows.
But they shall not so;
Hey nonny, nonny no.
None but I this lip must owe,
Hey nonny, nonny no.

Did Jove see this wanton eye,
Ganymede must wait no longer;
Phœbe here one night to lie
Would change her face and look much
    younger.
But they shall not so;
Hey nonny, nonny no.
None but I this lip must owe;
Hey nonny, nonny no.

Thomas Ravenscroft made several
collections of popular songs, two

Ravenscroft's *Melismata* (1611).

Ravenscroft's *Melismata* (1611).

of which, *Pammelia* and *Deuteromelia*, were published in 1609. John Fletcher either knew Ravenscroft or was familiar with these collections, judging from his use of certain songs in *The Knight of the Burning Pestle,* written for the Blackfriars Children at a date which some put at 1606–7, and others at 1611. The second of these, *Deuteromelia,* contains songs popular at the "King's Head," a tavern in Cheapside, famous for its musical company. One need not be surprised at finding a chorister of St. Paul's interested in drinking songs. In his *Microcosmography* John Earle wrote in 1628:

> The Common Singing Men in cathedral churches are a bad society, and yet a company of good fellows, that roar deep in the church, deeper in the tavern. . . . Their pastime or recreation is prayers, their exercise drinking, yet herein so religiously conducted that they serve God oftest when they are drunk. . . . Their skill in melody makes them the better companions abroad, and their anthems abler to sing catches.

Merrythought, in *The Knight of the Burning Pestle,* has three snatches of song from *Pammelia.* "Who can sing a merrier note" comes, with a little variation, from the catch "Sing we now merrily":

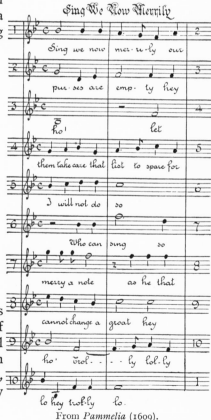

Sing we now merrily
Our purses are empty, hey ho!
Let them take care
That list to spare,
For I will not do so.
Who can sing so merry a note
As he that cannot change a groat?
Hey ho! trolly, lolly lo, hey trolly lo!

Pammelia is described as "Musick's Miscellanie: or Mixed Varietie of Pleasant Roundelais and delightful Catches of 3, 4, 5, 6, 7, 8, 9, 10 Parts in one. None so ordinarie as musical, None so musical as not to all, very pleasing and acceptable."

From *Pammelia* (1609).

Then comes another catch, "Ho, ho! Nobody at home!" with a slight difference in the words from those printed in the song book:

MERRYTHOUGHT:

> Let's have a catch, boys;
> Follow me, come. [*They sing.*
> Ho, ho!
> Nobody at home!
> Meat nor drink nor
> Money have I none.
> Fill the pot, Eedy,
> Never more need I.

Knight of the Burning Pestle,
Act IV, sc. v.

From *Pammelia* (1609).

The line quoted by Merrythought, "Troll the black bowl to me," is taken by Chappell as a snatch from another song in *Pammelia*, "Now peace be with old Simeon":

> Now peace be with old Simeon,
> For he made cans for many a one,
> And a good old man was he,
> And Jenkin was his journeyman,
> And he could tipple of every can,
> And thus said he to me,
> "To whom drink'st thou?"
> "Sir knave, to you."
> Then hey, ho! jolly Jenkin,
> I spy a knave in drinking,
> Come, troll the bowl to me.

Merrythought introduces this by saying, "Give me a man that when he goes to hanging cries, 'Troll the black bowl to me!'"

From *Pammelia* (1609).

Another drinking song of which Merrythought quotes four lines is found in *Deuteromelia*:

Of all the birds that ever I see,
The owl is the fairest in her degree;
For all the day long she sits in a tree,
And when the night comes, away flies she:
To whit, to whoo!
To whom drink'st thou?
Sir knave, to you . . .
This song is well sung, I make you a vow,
And he is a knave that drinketh now:
Nose, nose, jolly red nose!
And who gave thee that jolly red nose?
Cinnamon, ginger, nutmeg and cloves,
And that gave me my jolly red nose.

Deuteromelia is described as "The Second Part of Musick's Melodie or Melodious Musicke of Pleasant Roundelais; K. H. Mirth, or Freemen's Songs and such delightful catches. 'Qui canere potest, canat.' Catch that catch can. 'Ut Melos, sic Cor melos afficit et reficit.'"

From *Deuteromelia* (1609).

Yet another of Merrythought's snatches comes from one of John Dowland's ayres, "Wilt thou, unkind, thus reave me?":

Wilt thou, unkind, thus reave me
Of my heart, of my heart, and leave me?
Farewell! Farewell!
But yet or ere I part, O cruel!
Kiss me, kiss me, sweet my jewel.

Hope by disdain grows cheerless,
Fear doth love, love doth fear beauty
    peerless.

Farewell! Farewell!
But yet or ere I part, O cruel!
Kiss me, kiss me, sweet my jewel!

Yet be thou mindful ever,
Heat from fire, fire from heat none can
    sever.
Farewell! Farewell!
But yet I part, O cruel!
Kiss me, kiss me, sweet my jewel.

Melody from John Dowland's *First Book
of Songs or Ayres* (1597), edited by E. H.
Fellowes (Stainer and Bell). An original
copy of the songbook is in the Henry E.
Huntington Library, San Marino, California.

Fletcher was evidently as familiar as Shakespeare with the ballad tunes of his day, and Merrythought of *The Knight of the Burning Pestle* would have been a good customer of Autolycus of *The Winter's Tale.*

In Dyce's edition of Beaumont and Fletcher's plays (and Fletcher is generally conceded to have been the most lyrical of the partners) snatches are sung of seventy-three ballads, sufficient evidence that ballad tunes were running in Fletcher's head. One in particular, "Go from my window, go," appears in three different plays. This was a song popular in the time of Henry VIII, and was adapted to sacred words for the use of the Scottish Reformers by John Wedderburn in his *Gude and Godlie Ballates,* whose version is here quoted:

Who is at my window? Who, who?
Go from my window, go, go!
Who calls there, so like a stranger?
Go from my window, go!

Lord, I am here, ane wretched mortal
That for Thy mercy does cry and call
Unto Thee, my Lord Celestial,
So who is at my window, who?

Melody in *A New Book of Tablature* (1596)
Cf. Chappell's *Popular Music of the Olden Time.*

The ballads referred to in Fletcher's play include several of Scottish origin, indicating the incursion of Scottish culture with the Scots King James, an incursion which was satirized in *Eastward Ho* (1605) by Ben Jonson, Chapman, and Marston. Merrythought in Act II, scene viii sings an evidently Scottish ballad:

She cares not for her daddy, nor
She cares not for her mammy,
For she is, she is, she is, she is
The Lord of Lowgave's lassy.

In the same scene Citizen George calls on the musicians to play "Baloo," the tune of the song known as "Lady Anne Bothwell's Lament":

Baloo, my babe, lie still and sleep!
It grieves me sair to see thee weep:
If thou be silent, I'll be glad,
Thy moaning makes my heart full sad.
Baloo, my boy, thy mother's joy,
Thy father breeds me great annoy.
Baloo, my babe, lie still and sleep,
It grieves me sair to see thee weep.

Baloo, my darling, sleep awhile,
And when thou wakest, sweetly smile;
But smile not as thy father did,
To cozen maids, may God forbid!
For in thine eye his look I see,
The tempting look that ruined me.

Baloo, my babe, thy father's fled,
When he the thriftless son has played;
Of vows and oaths forgetful, he
Preferred the wars to thee and me:
But now perhaps thy curse and mine
Makes him eat acorns with the swine.

Baloo

Baloo, my boy, lie still and sleep, It grieves me
sair to hear thee weep: If thou'lt be
si-lent I'll be glad, Thy mourning
makes my heart full sad. Baloo, my
boy, thy mo-ther's joy, Thy father
bred me great an-noy. Baloo my
dear, lie still and sleep, It grieves me
sair to hear thee weep.

Melody from Johnson's *Musical Museum.* Cf.
Scottish Songs prior to Burns (W. & R. Chambers).

Another song with melody by an unknown composer is sung in *The Captain*, as well as in *The Knight of the Burning Pestle*:

"Tell me, dearest, what is love?"
"'Tis a lightning from above,
'Tis an arrow, 'tis a fire,
'Tis a boy they call desire,
'Tis a grave
Gapes to have
Those poor fools who long to prove."

The second verse in *The Knight of the Burning Pestle* runs as follows:

"Tell me more, are women true?"
"Some love change, and so do you."
"Are they fair and never kind?"
"Yes, when men turn with the wind."
"Are they froward?"
"Ever toward,
Those that love, to love anew."

Tell Me, Dearest, What Is Love?

Tell me, dearest, what is love?
'Tis a light-ning from a-bove
'Tis an ar-row, 'tis a fire
'Tis a boy they call De-sire
'Tis a grave Gapes to have
These poor fools that long to prove.

Melody from J. Stafford Smith's *Musica Antiqua.*

The special talents of these child actors were naturally employed when possible, hence the introduction of masques into so many of the plays they produced. There are masques in Chapman's *The Gentleman Usher* and *The Tragedy of Biron,* in Marston's *Antonio and Mellida, The Dutch Courtezan,* and *Histriomastix,* in four of Middleton's plays, in Ben Jonson's *Cynthia's Revels,* in Beaumont and Fletcher's *The Coxcomb* and *The False One.* If these companies of child actors had been employed only to produce plays suited to their musical talent, the output of lyrics might have been still greater. The playwrights, however, drew them into a vortex of satirical comedies which resulted in the suppression of the two leading companies. With the approval of King James, the Blackfriars Company was dissolved, and in 1608 the best of the young talent (which, by the way, in any case was growing older) was absorbed into Shakespeare's Company of His Majesty's Servants. This accounts for the introduction of a masque and of songs into Beaumont and Fletcher's *The Maid's Tragedy* played by the King's Men in 1609, and in Shakespeare's own three last plays, *Cymbeline, The Winter's Tale,* and *The Tempest.*

Aspasia in *The Maid's Tragedy* sings this lovely lyric:

> Lay a garland on my hearse
> Of the dismal yew;
> Maidens, willow-branches bear;
> Say I died true.
> My love was false, but I was firm
> From my hour of birth:
> Upon my buried body lie
> Lightly, gentle earth.

CHAPTER XIV

Masques under the Stuarts—Ben Jonson—Alfonso Ferrabosco—Music and Masques—
Nicholas Laniere—Traditional tunes—Ballad and dance tunes—"Joan's Ale
is New."

ANNE OF DENMARK, consort of James the First, had a passion for masques
and pageantry, and though masques were no new thing in English Court
life, they were developed under the Stuarts to a high splendour. For the
settings and costumes Inigo Jones was the master architect, and Alfonso
Ferrabosco, Thomas Campian, the choir-masters of the Chapel Royal,
Nicholas Laniere, and lutenists, such as Robert Johnson, John Coperario or
Cooper, John and Robert Dowland, Philip Rosseter and Thomas Ford,
provided admirable music. Thomas Lupo was one of the violinist-com-
posers named, and Thomas Giles was the chief director of dances. The
libretto and often the whole conception of the masque offered an opportunity to the lyric poet, and in this sphere Ben Jonson was especially
prolific. Other librettists were Thomas Campian, Samuel Daniel, George
Chapman, Francis Beaumont, Ford, Thomas Dekker, Thomas Middleton,
William Browne, James Shirley.

The accounts for Ben Jonson's masque *Love Freed from Ignorance and
Folly*, produced at Court for the Queen, February 1611, are illuminating:

REWARDS TO THE PERSONS IMPLOYED IN THE MASKE

Imprimis, to Mr. Benjamin Johnson for his invention	£40
Item, to Mr. Inigo Jones, for his paynes & invention	40
Item, to Mr. Alfonso, for making the songes	20
Item, to Mr. Johnson, for setting the song to the lutes	5
Item, to Thomas Lupo, for setting the dances to the violins	5
Item, to Mr. Confesse, for teaching all the dances	50
Item, to Mr. Bocken, for teaching the ladies the footing of two dances	20
Item, to the 12 Musicions that were preestes, that songe & played	24
Item, to the 12 other lutes that suplied, and with flutes	12
Item, to the 10 violencas that continually practized to the Queen	20
Item, to four more that were added to the Maske	4
Item, to 15 musitions that played to the pages and fooles	20
Item, to 13 hoboyes and sackbutts	10
Item, to 5 boyes, that is 3 Graces, Sphynks & Cupid	10
Item, to the 12 fooles that danced	12
	£292

The music employed in these masques was both vocal and instrumental:
the songs being mostly part-songs or madrigals for two to six voices, or

even for whole choirs.   Campian in his *Description of a Masque in Honour of Lord Hayes* (1607), tells what was required on that occasion.

This Chorus was in a manner of an echo seconded by the Cornets, then by the consort of ten (musicians with bass and mean lutes, a bandora, a double sackbut and a harpsicord, with two treble violins) then by the consort of twelve (nine violins and three lutes) and by a double chorus of voices standing on either side, the one against the other, bearing five voices apiece, and sometime every chorus was heard severally, sometimes mixed, but in the end all together; which kind of harmony so distinguished by the place, and by the several nature of the instruments, and changeable conveyance of the song, and performed by so many excellent masters as were actors in that music (their number in all amounting to forty-two voices and instruments) could not but yield great satisfaction to the hearers.

Later on, in his description he says, "All this time of procession the six cornets and six chapel voices sung a solemn motet of six parts made upon these words:

> With spotless minds now mount we to the tree
> Of single chastity . . . "

In masques thus made to order, one cannot expect to find poetry of high quality, yet there are at times lyrics of considerable charm.

Martin Peerson, who was Master of the Children at St. Paul's, wrote the music for Ben Jonson's *Entertainment of the King and Queen* on May Day, 1604, at the house of Sir William Cornwallis at Highgate.   The metre shows where Herrick came from:

> See, O see, who comes here a-maying?
> The Master of the Ocean
> And his sweet beauteous Orian.
> Why left we off our playing?
> On them to gaze
> That gods as well as men amaze.
> Up, nightingale and sing
> Jug, jug, jug, jug.
> Lark, raise thy note and wing.
> All birds their music bring.
> Robin, linnet, thrush,
> Record on every bush
> The welcome of the King and Queen.

No. 24 in Martin Peerson's *Private Musique
containing Songs of 4, 5 and 6 parts.*

Ben Jonson as a Westminster schoolboy had had music drummed into him.   He collaborated in particular with two musicians—Alfonso Ferrabosco and Nicholas Laniere.   Alfonso Ferrabosco wrote music for at least seven of Jonson's masques:

The Masque of Blackness (1605), which cost £3000 to produce.
The Masque of Lord Haddington's Marriage (*Hymenaei*, 1606).
Hue and Cry After Cupid (1608).

Masque of Beauty (1607).
Masque of Queens (1609).
Masque of Oberon (1611).
Love Freed From Ignorance and Folly (1611).

Alfonso Ferrabosco, whom Jonson calls "my loved Alfonso," was musical instructor to Prince Henry, King James's short-lived heir, and was English-born, though of an Italian father. His song-music tends to be sophisticated, and yet on that account may have been appropriate to the words for which it was written, words full of classical allusions appreciated only by a highly educated Court circle.

Ben Jonson paid this tribute to Ferrabosco: "Mastering all the spirits of music; to whose judicial care, and as absolute performance, were committed all those difficulties both of song and otherwise. Wherein, what his merit made to the soul of our invention, would ask to be expressed in tunes no less ravishing than his."

This admiration of the poet for the musician is further expressed in Ben Jonson's epigram on Ferrabosco's *Book of Ayres*, published in 1609:

> To urge, my loved Alfonso, that bold fame
> Of building towns and making wild beasts tame
> Which music had, or speak her own effects,
> That she removeth cares, sadness ejects,
> Declineth anger, persuades clemency,
> Doth sweeten mirth and heighten piety,
> And is to a body, often, ill inclined,
> No less a sovereign care than to the mind;
> T'allege that greatest men were not ashamed,
> Of old, even by her practice to be famed;
> To say indeed she were the soul of heaven,
> That the eighth sphere, no less than planets seven,
> Moved by her order, and the ninth, more high,
> Including all, were thence called harmony;
> I yet had uttered nothing on thy part
> When these were but the praises of the art;
> But when I have said the proofs of all these be
> Shed in thy songs; 'tis true: but short of thee.

Ben Jonson was not alone in his admiration of this musician. Thomas Campian, his fellow composer, wrote this preface to Ferrabosco's *Ayres*:

> Music's master and the offspring
> Of rich music's father,
> Old Alfonso's image living,
> These fair flowers you gather,
> Scatter through the British soil;
> Give thy fame free wing,
> And gain the merit of thy toil.
> We whose loves affect to praise thee
> Beyond thine own deserts can never raise thee.

Volpone, written for the King's Men in 1605, has a song which appears in these *Ayres*:

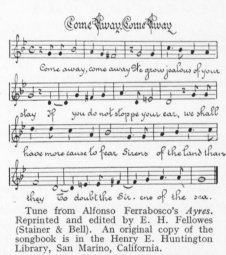

Come, my Celia, let us prove,
While we can, the sports of love;
Time will not be ours for ever,
He at length our good will sever.
Spend not then his gifts in vain;
Suns that set may rise again,
But if once we lose this light
'Tis with us perpetual night.
Why should we defer our joys?
Fame and rumour are but toys.
Cannot we delude the eyes
Of a few poor household spies?

. . . . .

'Tis no sin love's fruits to steal;
But the sweet thefts to reveal.
To be taken, to be seen,
These have crimes accounted been.

Tune from Alfonso Ferrabosco's *Ayres* (1609). Transcribed and edited by Peter Warlock and Philip Wilson in *English Ayres*. Re-transcribed by permission of the publishers, Enoch & Sons (1927) Ltd., Boosey and Co., Inc., U.S.A. and Canada. Oxford University Press (for all other countries).

Another song by Ben Jonson in this collection appears also in the *Masque of Blackness,* where it is described as a "Charm sung by a tenor voice":

Come away, come away,
We grow jealous of your stay;
If you do not stop your ear,
We shall have more cause to fear
Syrens of the land, than they
To doubt the Syrens of the sea.

Tune from Alfonso Ferrabosco's *Ayres.* Reprinted and edited by E. H. Fellowes (Stainer & Bell). An original copy of the songbook is in the Henry E. Huntington Library, San Marino, California.

In the description of the *Masque of Queens,* a masque which Swinburne described as "one of the typically splendid monuments or trophies of English literature," we read that the masquers "danced the measures almost to the space of an hour; when to give them rest, from the music which attended the chariots, by that most excellent tenor voice and exact singer, Her Majesty's servant, Master Jo Allin, this ditty was sung:

When all the ages of the earth
Were crowned but in this famous birth;
And that when they would boast their store
Of worthy queens, they knew no more,
How happier is that age, can give
A Queen in whom they all do live!"

Text from the reprint in the Carisbrooke Library (George Routledge & Sons).

The masque concluded with another song, "whose notes (as the former) were the work and honour of my excellent friend, Alfonso Ferrabosco."

In this masque, presented on Twelfth Night, 1609, the queen herself took part.

Melody from Alfonso Ferrabosco's *Ayres* (1609), reprinted and edited by E. H. Fellowes (Stainer & Bell). An original copy of the songbook is in the Henry E. Huntington Library, San Marino, California.

In the *Masque of Love Restored*, played in January 1612 by Gentlemen the King's Servants, there is this dainty lyric:

CUPID'S SONG

O how came Love, that is himself a fire,
    To be so cold?
Yes, tyrant Money quencheth all desire,
    Or makes it old.
But here are beauties will revive
Love's youth, and keep his heat alive:
    As often as the torch here dies
    He need but light it at fresh eyes.
Joy, joy the more; for in all courts,
If Love be cold, so are his sports.

A manuscript in the British Museum contains a song now ascribed to Alfonso Ferrabosco of which the words are Ben Jonson's, and appear both in his play *The Devil is an Ass* and in *Underwoods*.

In the latter publication Jonson collected some of his poems which had other than dramatic value. To this lyric he prefaced another verse, an addition which might be explained on the theory that the poet liked the melody enough to write this other verse under its inspiration. The lyric in the play reads:

Have you seen but a white lily grow
Before rude hands had touched it?
Have you marked but the fall of the snow
Before the earth hath smutched it?
Have you felt the wool of beaver
Or swan's down ever?
Or have smelt of the bud of the briar
Or the nard in the fire,
Or have tasted the bag of the bee?
O so white, O so so soft, O so sweet,
So sweet is she!

In *Underwoods* the following verse is prefixed:

See the chariot at hand here of Love
Wherein my Lady rideth!
Each that draws is a swan or a dove,
And well the car Love guideth.
As she goes, all hearts do duty
Unto her beauty;
And enamoured do wish, so they might
But enjoy such a sight,
That they still were to run by her side,
Through swords, through seas, whither she,
Whither she would ride.

Brit. Mus. Add. MS., fol. 15117, fol. 17b.
Facsimile in *Reliquary of English Song*, edited by Frank Hunter Potter (G. Schirmer). Cf. *English Melodies* (J. M. Dent & Sons Ltd.), note on p. 41.

This song must have been known to Sir John Suckling, who has an ironical lyric evidently written to the same tune:

Hast thou seen the down in the air
When wanton blasts have tossed it?
Or the ship on the sea
When ruder winds have crossed it?
Hast thou marked the crocodile's weeping;
Or the fox's sleeping?
Or hast viewed the peacock in his pride,
Or the dove by his bride
When he courts for his lechery?
O so fickle, O so vain, O so false,
So false is she!

Alfonso Ferrabosco died in 1627, a note in the royal accounts stating that he enjoyed "four places, a musician's place in general, a composer's place, a violl's place, and an instructor's place to the prince in the art of music."

The name of Nicholas Laniere, another musician associated with Ben Jonson, appears first in the accounts of the Queen's Musick for 1560 as "one of the flutes," and recurs regularly thereafter till 1618. This, however, was probably not the Nicholas Laniere who set songs for Ben Jonson and Robert Herrick, but was his uncle of the same name. Our Laniere was the son of John Laniere, "one of the sackbuts" in the royal orchestra, born in 1588, attached to the household of Prince Henry, and appointed Master of the King's Musick in 1626 with the classification of being "for the lutes and voices." An artist as well as a musician, he painted the portrait of himself now hanging at Oxford, and was sent by King Charles to Italy to purchase pictures for the Royal collection. The son of a Huguenot settled in England, he was a singer as well as composer, performing in Campian's *Masque of Squires* (1613), on St. Stephen's Night, in celebration of the wedding of Robert, Earl of Somerset, with Lady Frances Howard. For this he also wrote one of the songs, others being written by the lutenist John Cooper or Coperario.

The new Italian fashion of recitative, from which the modern operatic form resulted, was used by Laniere in composing the music for Ben Jonson's libretto of *The Vision of Delight* (1617), a masque in which Prince Charles himself took part. In this Delight sings:

STILO RECITATIVO

Let us play and dance and sing,
Let us now turn every sort
Of the pleasures of the Spring
To the graces of a court,
From air, from cloud. from dreams, from toys,
To sounds, to sense, to love, to joys;
Let your shows be new, as strange,
Let them oft and sweetly vary;
Let them haste so to their change,
As the seers may not tarry
Too long to expect the pleasing'st sight
Doth take away from the delight.

This is followed later on by a song evidently written in the old style with chorus:

NIGHT'S SONG

Break, Phant'sie, from thy cave of cloud
And spread thy purple wings;
Now all thy figures are allowed,
And various shapes of things;
Create of airy forms a stream
It must have blood and nought of phlegm,
And though it be a waking dream,

Chorus.

Yet let it like an odour rise
To all the senses here,
And fall like sleep upon their eyes
Or music in their ear.

For Ben Jonson's masque *Lovers Made Men* (*Masque of Lethe*, 1617), Laniere not only wrote the music, but sang, and also painted the scenery.

John Playford in his *Select Ayres* gives the setting by Laniere of a song from Ben Jonson's *The Sad Shepherd*:

Though I am young and cannot tell
Either what Love or Death is well,
And then again I have been told
Love wounds with heat, and Death with
  cold;
Yet I have heard they both bear darts
And both do aim at human hearts;
So that I fear they do but bring
Extremes to touch, and mean one thing.

In this singing version, the fifth and sixth lines are transposed with the third and fourth.

Playford's *Select Ayres* (1653).

Ben Jonson's interest in music finds corroboration in his preface to Edward Filmer's *French Court Airs* (1629):

> What charming peals are these
> That while they bind the senses do so please!
> They are the marriage rites
> Of two, the choicest pair, of Man's delights,
> Music and Poesy!
> French air and English verse here wedded be.

> Who did this knot compose
> Again hath brought the Lily to the Rose;
> And with their chained dance
> Re-celebrates the joyful Match with France.
> They are a School to win
> The fair French Daughter to learn English in;
> And, graced with her Song,
> To make the language sweet upon her tongue.

Robert Johnson is said to have written the music for *The Gipsies Metamorphosed*, a masque which so delighted King James that it was performed three times. This masque incorporates a ballad which was enormously popular:

Cocklorrel would needs have the devil his
   guest
And bade him into the Peak for dinner,
Where never the fiend had such a feast
Provided him yet at the charge of a sinner.

Six pickled tailors sliced and cut,
Sempsters and tirewomen fit for his palate;
With feathermen and perfumers put
Some twelve in a charger to make a grand
   salad.

The jowl of a jailor served for a fish,
A constable soused with vinegar by;
Two aldermen lobsters asleep in a dish,
A deputy tart, a churchwarden pie.

Tune from Playford's *Dancing Master*. Quoted
in Chappell's *Popular Music of the Olden Time*.

That Jonson was not averse to writing with a tune in his head has
already been evidenced in the case of his "Christmas Carol," written to
the melody of the Huguenot Battle Hymn. The metre of this carol
appears again in his masque *Chloridia*:

> Come forth, come forth, the gentle Spring,
> To carry the glad news I bring
> To earth our common mother.
> It is decreed by all the Gods
> That heaven of earth shall have no odds,
> But one shall love another.

Another interesting case is that of the ballad tune or tunes identified
with a poem credited to Sir Walter Raleigh, "As at noon Dulcina rested":

As at noon Dulcina rested
In her sweet and shady bower,
Came a shepherd and requested
In her lap to sleep an hour,
But from her look
A wound he took
So deep, that for a further boon
The nymph he prays,
Whereto she says,
"Forego me now, come to me soon."

But in vain she did conjure him
To depart her presence so;
Having a thousand tongues to allure him
And but one to bid him go:
Where lips invite
And eyes delight,
And cheeks, as fresh as rose in June,
Persuade delay,
What boots she say
"Forego me now, come to me soon."

These tunes are also identified with a lyric ascribed to Ben Jonson.

From Oberon in fairyland,
The king of ghosts and shadows there,
Mad Robin I, at his command
Am sent to view the night-sports here.
What revel rout
Is kept about
In every corner where I go,
I will o'ersee
And merry be,
And make good sport, with ho, ho, ho!

More swift then lightning can I fly
About this airy welkin soon,
And in a minute's space descry
Each thing that's done below the moon.
There's not a hag
Or ghost shall wag
Or cry "'Ware Goblins!" where I go,
But Robin I
Their feats will spy
And send them home with ho, ho, ho!

Yet, now and then, the maids to please,
At midnight I card up their wool;
And while they sleep and take their ease,
With wheel to threads their flax I pull.
I grind at mill
Their malt up still;
I dress their hemp, I spin their tow;
If any wake
And would me take
I wend me laughing, ho, ho, ho!

Brit. Mus. Add. MSS. 24665, fol. 35b. Quoted in *English Melodies* (J. M. Dent & Sons Ltd.).

From Chappell's *Popular Music of the Olden Time*. Quoted in *English Melodies* (J. M. Dent & Sons Ltd.).

The ballad singer was a familiar figure in these days, and it was only fitting that one should play his part in *Bartholomew Fair*. Nightingale, the ballad singer, has a sheaf of songs to suit all tastes, including one on St. George that "O did break the dragon's heart." This has been identified by Chappell as the following:

> Why should we boast of Arthur and his knights,
> Knowing well how many men have endured fights?
> For besides King Arthur and Lancelot du Lake,
> Or Sir Tristram de Lionel that fought for ladies' sake,
> Read in old histories and there you shall see
> How St. George the Dragon made to flee.
> Saint George he was for England, St. Denis was for France,
> Sing *Honi soit qui mal y pense.*

From a black-letter ballad in the Pepys Collection "imprinted at London 1612"—reprinted in Percy's *Reliques* as "Why do ye boast," etc.

Tune from Chappell's *Popular Music of the Olden Time.*

When Nightingale comes to sing a ballad himself, he sings it to a country dance tune, "Packington's Pound":

> My masters and friends and good people
>   draw near,
> And look to your purses, for that I do say;
> And though little money in them you do
>   bear,
> It costs more to get than to lose in a day.

You oft have been told,
Both the young and the old,
And bidden beware of the cutpurse so bold,
Then if you take heed not, free me from the curse
Who both give you warning, for, and the cutpurse.
Youth, youth, thou hadst better been starved by thy nurse
Than live to be hanged for cutting a purse.

It hath been upbraided to men of my trade
That oftentimes we are the cause of this crime;
Alack and for pity, why should it be said?
As if they regarded or places or time!
Examples have been
Of some that were seen
In Westminster Hall, yea the pleaders between;
Then why should the judges be free from this curse,
More than my poor self for cutting the purse?
Youth, youth, thou hadst better been starv'd by thy nurse
Than live to be hanged for cutting a purse.

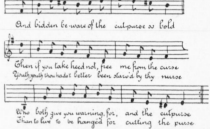

Tune from Playford's *Musical Companion*. Quoted in Chappell's *Popular Music of the Olden Time*.

Although Nightingale is shown in none too favourable a light, Ben Jonson like his friend Bishop Corbet dearly loved a ballad, and one can well believe Addison's saying of him that "he would rather have been the author of Chevy Chase than of all his own works." In his *Tale of a Tub* Jonson brings in Father Rosin, Chief Minstrel of Highgate, and refers to three popular dance tunes, all connected with ballads—"Tom Tiler," "The Jolly Joiner," and "The Jovial Tinker." As to the last named, Jonson may well have known the "Ballet intituled 'Joan's ale is new'" entered on the books of the Stationer's Company in 1594, and sung to this tune:

There was a jovial tinker
Who was a good ale drinker;
He never was a shrinker,
Believe me this is true.
And he came from the Weald of Kent
When all his money was gone and spent,
Which made him look like a Jack-a-Lent,
And Joan's ale is new.

The tinker he did settle
Most like a man of mettle,
And vow'd to pawn his kettle;
Now mark what did ensue.
His neighbours they flock in apace
To see Tom Tinker's comely face,
Ahere they drank soundly for a space,
And Joan's ale is new.

The cobbler and the broom-man
Came up into the room, man,
And said they would drink for boon, man,
Let each one take his due!
But when the liquor good they found,
They cast their caps upon the ground,
And so the tinker he drank round,
And Joan's ale is new.

Tune from *Pills to Purge Melancholy* (1707).
Quoted in Chappell's *Popular Music of the Olden Time*.

CHAPTER XV

John Donne—Donne and Dowland—George Wither—Wither and Music—Orlando Gibbons—"Sleep, Baby, Sleep."

THE stage had no monopoly of lyrical interest, any more than the masque. Bishop Corbet, John Donne, and George Wither are three contemporaries of Ben Jonson identified rather with religion than with the drama.   Bishop Corbet, with whom Jonson stayed during a visit to Oxford in 1619, had sung "John Dory" in his youth, and by his own account

> could chaunt
> "Chevy" and "Arthur" and "The Siege of Gaunt."

Aubrey in his *Brief Lives* says of Corbet:

After he was Doctor of Divinity, he sang ballads at the Cross at Abingdon on a market day.   He and some of his comrades were at the tavern by the Cross.   The ballad-singer complained he had no custom, he could not put off his ballads.   The jolly doctor puts off his gown and puts on the ballad-singer's leathern jacket, and being a handsome man and had a rare full voice, he presently vended a great many, and had a great audience.

Corbet's song, "Farewell rewards and fairies," is cited as "to be sung or whistled to the tune "The Meadow Brow":

Farewell, rewards and fairies!
Good housewives now may say;
For now foul sluts in dairies
Do fare as well as they.
And though they sweep their hearths no less
Than maids were wont to do;
Yet who, of late, for cleanliness
Finds sixpence in her shoe?

. . . . . .

At morning and at evening both
You merry were and glad,
So little care of sleep or sloth
These pretty ladies had.
When Tom home came from labour
Or Ciss to milking rose,
Then merrily, merrily went their tabour
And nimbly went their toes.

Farewell Rewards and Fairies

Tune from Robinson's *Schoole of Musicke* (1603).   Quoted as "Walking in a Country Town" in Chappell's *Popular Music of the Olden Time*.

John Donne, who was born in the same year as Ben Jonson (1573), went to Oxford at the age of eleven, studying at Hart Hall for five impressionable years before migrating to Cambridge.   According to Jonson, he had "written all his best pieces ere he was twenty-five years old," and Izaac Walton says that most of his secular verse was composed before his twentieth year.   This would include:

Go and catch a falling star,
Get with child a mandrake root;
Tell me where all past times are,
Or who cleft the devil's foot.
Teach me to hear mermaids singing
Or to keep off envy's stinging,
And find
What wind
Serves to advance an honest mind.

If thou beest borne to strange sights,
Things invisible to see,
Ride ten thousand days and nights
Till age snow white hairs on thee.
Thou, when thou return'st, will tell me
All strange wonders that befell thee,
And swear
No where
Lives a woman true and fair.

Tune from Egerton MS. 2013. Cf. *Poems of John Donne*, edited by H. J. C. Grierson (Oxford University Press).

Three of Donne's songs are specifically stated to have been "made to certain ayres which were made before."   One of these is:

Send back my long stray'd eyes to me
Which O! too long have dwelt on thee; (*bis*)
But if from you they 've learnt such ill
To sweetly smile
And then beguile,
Keep the deceivers, keep them still.

This singing version differs from the version printed in Donne's *Songs and Sonets*, which reads:

Send home my long-stray'd eyes to me,
Which Oh! too long have dwelt on thee;
Yet since there they have learn'd such ill,
Such forc'd fashions,
And such passions,
That they be
Made by thee
Fit for no good sight, keep them still.

Tune from Ritson's *English Songs* (1783).

Another of Donne's songs set to an old tune is his fishing song "The Bait," written to the same melody as Christopher Marlowe's "Come live with me and be my love." This melody was clearly also in Herrick's mind when he wrote his "Live, live with me and thou shalt see," which for purpose of comparison is printed as the third line below the music, the first line being the original verse of Marlowe:

Come live with me

Come live with me   and be my love. And
Come live with me   and be my love, And
Live, live with me,   and thou shalt see   The

we will all the   pleasures prove That
we will some new   pleasures prove Of
pleasures I'll pre- pare for thee What

hills and val-leys. dale and field, And
gol-den sands and crys-tal brooks With
sweets the coun-try can af-ford Shall

all the crag-gy mountains yield
silk-en lines and sil-ver hooks.
bless thy bed and bless thy board.

Tune from W. Corkine's *Second Book of Ayres* (1612), as transcribed in Chappell's *Popular Music of the Olden Time*. Cf. also *English Melodies* (J. M. Dent & Sons Ltd.).

The Bait: by John Donne

Come live with me and be my love,
And we will some new pleasure prove
Of golden sands, and crystal brooks,
With silken lines and silver hooks.

There will the river whispering run
Warm'd by thy eyes, more than the sun.
And there th' enamour'd fish will stay,
Begging themselves they may betray.

When thou wilt swim in that live bath,
Each fish, which every channel hath,
Will amorously to thee swim,
Gladder to catch thee than thou him.

Come Live with Me: by Marlowe

Come, live with me and be my love,
And we will all the pleasures prove
That hills and valleys, dale and field,
And all the craggy mountains yield.

There will we sit upon the rocks
And see the shepherds feed their flocks
By shallow rivers, to whose falls
Melodious birds sing madrigals.

There will I make thee beds of roses,
And a thousand fragrant posies,
A cap of flowers and a kirtle
Embroider'd all with leaves of myrtle.

Live, Live with Me: by Herrick

Live, live with me and thou shalt see
The pleasures I 'll prepare for thee;
What sweets the country can afford
Shall bless thy bed and bless thy board.

The soft sweet moss shall be thy bed
With crawling woodbine overspread;
By which the silver-shedding streams
Shall gently melt thee into dreams.

.   .   .   .

Where thou shalt sit, and Redbreast by
For meat shall give thee melody.
I'll give thee chains and carcanets
Of primroses and violets.

Donne was evidently familiar with John Dowland's ayres, for his lyric "Break of Day" is an obvious sequence to Dowland's "Sweet, stay awhile":

Sweet, stay awhile. Why will you rise?
The light you see comes from your eyes.
The day breaks not, it is my heart
To think that you and I must part.
O stay, or else my joys must die
And perish in their infancy.

Dear, let me die in this fair breast,
Far sweeter than the Phoenix' nest.
Love, raise desire by his sweet charms
Within this circle of thine arms.
O stay, and let thy kisses cherish
Mine infant joys that else must perish.

Donne's answer runs:

'Tis true 'tis day; what though it be?
O wilt thou therefore rise from me?
Why should we rise because 'tis light?
Did we lie down because 'twas night?
Love, which in spite of darkness brought
    us hither,
Should in despite of light keep us together.

Tune from *A Pilgrim's Solace* by John Dowland (1612), reprinted and edited by E. H. Fellowes (Stainer & Bell). An original copy of the songbook is in the Henry E. Huntington Library, San Marino, California.

Donne may indeed have supplied Dowland with the words for his ayre, for at a later date, a variation of the Dowland version is associated with his name, and printed as to be sung to a tune arranged by Giles Farnaby for the *Queen Elizabeth's Virginal Book* as a "Loth to Depart."

Lie near, my dear, why dost thou rise?
The light that shines comes from thine eyes.
'Tis not the day breaks, but my heart,
To think that thou and I must part.

The third of Donne's songs admitted by him as written to a tune is also a parting song—the melody of which has not yet been identified.

Sweetest love, I do not go
For weariness of thee,
Nor in the hope the world can show
A fitter love for me,
But since that I
Must die at last, 'tis best
To use myself in jest,
Thus by feigned deaths to die.

Tune from *Queen Elizabeth's Virginal Book*, arranged by Giles Farnaby. Quoted in Chappell's *Popular Music of the Olden Time*.

As Dean of St. Paul's, Donne could not fail to have been affected by the music of his great choir. Izaac Walton tells how the dean had his "Hymn to God the Father" set to a "grave and solemn tune, and to be often sung to the organ by the choristers of St. Paul's Church in his own hearing, especially at the evening service; and at his return from his customary devotions in that place did occasionally say to a friend: 'The words of this hymn have restored me to the same thoughts of joy that possessed my soul in my sickness when I composed it. And O the power of church-music! That harmony added to it has raised the affections of my heart.' "

The setting to which he refers was probably that composed by John Hilton, organist of St. Margaret's Church, Westminster:

Wilt Thou forgive that sin where I begun,
Which was my sin though it were done
    before?
Wilt Thou forgive that sin through which
    I run
And do run still, though still I do deplore?
When Thou hast done, Thou hast not done,
For I have more.

Wilt Thou forgive that sin by which I won
Others to sin and made my sin their door?
Wilt Thou forgive that sin which I did shun
A year or two, but wallow'd in a score?
When Thou hast done, etc.

I have a sin of fear that when I've spun
My last thread, I shall perish on the shore;
Swear by Thyself that at my death Thy Son
Shall shine as he shines now and heretofore,
And having done that, Thou hast done.
I fear no more.

Tune by John Hilton. Quoted in *Poems of John Donne*, edited by H. J. C. Grierson (Oxford University Press).

One song connects John Donne with Alfonso Ferrabosco, although Donne's name is not attached to the music in Ferrabosco's volume of *Ayres* (1609). The literary version as printed in Donne's *Songs and Sonets* differs slightly from the singing version:

So, so, break off this last lamenting kiss
Which sucks two souls and vapours both
    away.
Turn, thou ghost, that way, and let me turn
    this,
And let ourselves benight our happiest day.
We ask none leave to love; nor will we owe
Any so cheap a death as saying "Go."

Go, and if that word have not quite kill'd
   thee,
Ease me with death by bidding me go too.
Or, if it have, let my word work on me,
And a just office on a murderer do.
Except it be too late to kill me so,
Being double dead, going, and bidding go.

George Wither (1585–1667) who passed his student years at Oxford in the musical atmosphere of Magdalen, clearly regarded the lyric as verse

Printed with original harmony in Alfonso Ferrabosco's *Ayres*, reprinted and edited by E. H. Fellowes (Stainer & Bell). An original copy of the songbook is in the Henry E. Huntington Library, San Marino, California.

composed to a melody, for in his tract *The Scholar's Purgatory*, defending his metrical versions of scripture, he draws attention to "how many differences must be observed between lyric verse and that which is composed for reading only." In both his *Hymns and Songs of the Church* (1623) and his *Haleluiah* (1641), he definitely specifies the tune to which his verses should be sung, while the music of at least one of his secular verses has been preserved. The most famous "Shall I wasting in despair," seems to have been written to an older ballad tune, "The Young Man's Opinion":

Shall I wasting in despair
Die because a woman's fair?
Or make pale my cheeks with care
'Cause another's rosy are?
Be she fairer than the day
Or the flowery meads in May,
If she think not well of me,
What care I how fair she be?

Shall my heart be grieved or pined
'Cause I see a woman kind?
Or a well disposed nature
Joined with a lovely feature?
Be she meeker, kinder than
Turtle dove or pelican;
If she be not so to me,
What care I how kind she be?

Great or good or kind or fair,
I will ne'er the more despair;
If she love me, this believe,
I will die ere she shall grieve;
If she slight me when I woo,
I can scorn and let her go;
For if she be not for me,
What care I for whom she be?

From Wither's *Mistress of
   Philarete* (1622).

Tune from Ritson's *English Songs* (1783).
(The singing version of the words differs slightly from the literary version.)

Other ballad tunes are quoted as suitable for his religious lyrics, such as:
"In sad and ashy weeds":

In sad and ashy weeds
I sigh, I groan, I pine, I mourn,
My oaten yellow reeds
I all to jet and ebon turn,
My wat'ry eyes
Like winter's skies
My furrow'd cheeks o'erflow;
All heav'n know why
Men mourn as I!
And who can blame my woe?

Wither's Hymn 57 (*Halleluiah*)

Why live I muddling here
In base and fruitless works employed,
As if I knew not where
A better life might be enjoyed?
Since I have fought
And have been taught
The noblest things to know;
Why should I still
Retain a will
To spend more time below?

Tune transcribed by Hawkins from a MS. volume of virginal music. Quoted in Chappell's *Popular Music of the Olden Time*.

There is the lilt of the lute in the ditty dating from Wither's Oxford days, "I loved a lass, a fair one"—the tune has been forgotten:

I loved a lass, a fair one,
As fair as e'er was seen;
She was indeed a rare one,
Another Sheba Queen.
But, fool as then I was,
I thought she loved me too;
But now, alas! sh'as left me,
Falero, lero, loo!

. . . .

In summer time to Medley
My love and I would go;
The boatman there stood ready
My love and I to row.
For cream there would we call,
For cakes and for prunes too;
But now, alas! sh'as left me,
Falero, lero, loo!

. . . .

And as abroad we walked,
As lovers' fashion is,
Oft as we sweetly talked
The sun would steal a kiss;

The wind upon her lips
Likewise most sweetly blew;
But now, alas! sh'as left me,
Falero, lero, loo!

The musical refrain is used again with happy touch in Wither's
"Christmas Carol," which might possibly have been written to the tune
of "Green Sleeves."

Rank misers now do sparing shun,
Their hall of music soundeth;
And dogs thence with whole shoulders run,
So all things here aboundeth.
The country folk themselves advance,
For Crowdy-mutton 's come out of France,
And Jack shall pipe, and Jill shall dance,
And all the town be merry.

Ned Swash hath fetched his bands from pawn,
And all his best apparel;
Brisk Nell hath bought a ruff of lawn
With droppings of the barrel.
And those that hardly all the year
Had bread to eat or rags to wear,
Will both have clothes and dainty fare
And all the day be merry.

As he left youth behind, Wither grew pious, moralizing over everything.
One of his *Haleluiah* hymns is inscribed:

FOR A MUSICIAN

Many musicians are more out of order than their instruments; such as are so, may
by singing this Ode become reprovers of their own untuneable affections: they who are
better tempered are hereby remembered what music is most acceptable to God, and
most profitable to themselves.

1. What helps it those
   Who shall in song have found
   Well to compose
   Of disagreeing notes,
   By artful choice,
   A sweetly pleasing sound,
   To fit their voice,
   And their melodious throats?
   What helps it them
   That they this cunning know,
   If most condemn
   The way in which they go?

2. What will he gain
   By touching well his lute
   Who shall disdain
   A grave advice to hear?

What from the sounds
Of organ, fife or lute,
To him redounds
Who doth no sin forbear?
A mean respect,
By tuning strings he hath,
Who doth neglect
A rectifièd path.

3. Therefore, O Lord,
So tunèd let me be
Unto Thy word,
And thy ten-stringèd law,
That in each part
I may thereto agree,
And feel my heart
Inspired with loving awe;
He sings and plays
The songs which best Thou lovest
Who does and says
The things which Thou approvest.

In the dedication to the *Hymnes and Songs of the Church* Wither wrote:

I have also laboured to suit them to the nature of the subject, and the common people's capacities, without regard to catching the vain blasts of opinion. The same also hath been the aim of Master Orlando Gibbons (your Majesty's servant and one of the Gentlemen of your honourable Chapel) in fitting them with tunes; for he hath chosen to make his music agreeable to the matter, and what the common apprehension can best admit, rather than to the curious fancies of the time.

The first canticle illustrates the simple type of melody set by Orlando Gibbons, and thus praised by Wither, whose own translations are above the common run of his time:

Come kiss me with those lips of thine,
For better are thy loves than wine,
And as the poured ointments be
Such is the savour of thy name,
And for the sweetness of the same
The virgins are in love with thee.

These are the opening verses of the Song of Solomon, the prose version reading:

Let him kiss me with the kisses of his mouth; for thy love is better than wine. Because of the savour of thy good ointments thy name is as ointment poured forth, therefore do the virgins love thee.

Hymnes and Songs of the Church (1623). Tune by Orlando Gibbons, reprinted in *Tudor Church Music* (Oxford University Press).

The sixth canticle is another metrical version from the Song of Solomon happily fitted to Orlando Gibbons's music:

Arise thou north wind from the north,
And from the south thou south wind blow;
Upon my garden breath ye forth
That so my spices (there that grow)
From thence abundantly may flow;
And to thy garden come, my dear,
To eat thy fruits of pleasure there.

This is the sixteenth verse of the fourth chapter, and reads in prose:

Awake, O north wind; and come, thou south; blow upon my garden, that the spices thereof may flow out. Let my beloved come into his garden, and eat his pleasant fruits.

Hymns and Songs of the Church (1623). Tune by Orlando Gibbons, reprinted in *Tudor Church Music* (Oxford University Press).

Orlando Gibbons, who was organist of the Chapel Royal (1604–23) till he became organist at Westminster Abbey, wrote seventeen published settings for Wither's sacred songs, one of which may still be found in most hymnals under the title of "Angels," though the rhythm has sometimes been changed to suit some verses by Charles Wesley. The words of Wither's original hymn explain the title:

Thus Angels sang, and thus sing we,
To God on high all glory be.
Let Him on earth His peace bestow
And unto men His favour show.

Hymns and Songs of the Church (1623). Tune by Orlando Gibbons, reprinted in *Tudor Church Music* (Oxford University Press).

Yet all the tunes for Wither's hymns were not specially set. He expressly states in a preface

To the Reader

That such as have skill, and are delighted with music, may have the more variety, to stir up the soon cloyed affections, these Hymns are fitted with many new tunes: nevertheless all (but some few of them) may be sung to such tunes as have been heretofore in use, For the benefit, therefore, of those who have no experience in music, I have here set down which songs they be, and to what old tunes they may be sung.

M

So, too, in his *Haleluiah, or Britain's Remembrancer,* he says in the dedication:

So innumerable are the foolish and profane Songs now delighted in (to the dishonour of our Language and Religion) that Haleluiahs and pious Meditations are almost out of use and fashion; yet, not in private only; but at our public Feasts and civil meetings also, scurrilous and obscene Songs are impudently sung, without respecting the reverend Presence of Matrons, Virgins, Magistrates or Divines."

To the reader, he adds:

As in the language, so in the sorts of verse I have affected plainness, that I might the more profit those who need such helps: this I have done also, that they may be sung to the common Tunes of the Psalms, and such other as are well known; to which I have directed my reader, not to confine him to such Tunes; but that he may have those, until he may be provided of such as may be more proper; which perchance may by some devout Musician be hereafter prepared.

HYMN I

Come, oh come, in pious lays
Sound we God-Almighty's praise,
Hither bring in one consent
Heart and Voice and Instrument.
Music add of every kind;
Sound the trump, the cornet wind,
Strike the viol, touch the lute,
Let not tongue nor string be mute.

.   .   .   .   .

Come ye sons of human race
In this chorus take a place;
And amid this mortal throng
Be you masters of the song.
Angels and supernal powers,
Be the noblest tenor yours;
Let in praise of God, the sound
Run a never-ending round;
   That our song of praise may be
   Everlasting as is He.
From Earth's vast and hollow womb
Music's deepest bass may come;
Seas and floods from shore to shore
Shall their counter-tenors roar.
To this consort (when we sing)
Whistling winds your descants bring,
That our songs may ever climb
All the bounds of place and time,
   And ascend from Sphere to Sphere
   To the great Almighty's ear.

Most of the poems are prefaced by phrases such as "Sing this as the 133rd Psalm," or "Sing this as the Paternoster."

With all his piety, Wither retained his sense of humour, as is evidenced in his Hymn 28, in Part III of his *Haleluiah*:

For a Widower or Widow delivered from a troublesome yokefellow (Because deliverance from a troublesome yokefellow is a benefit neither to be despised nor indiscreetly rejoiced in; this hymn teacheth with what moderation, with what tenderness of heart, and with what desire we should be affected in such cases).

Sing this as "The Lamentation":

Rejoice not without fear, my heart,
That thou by death's impartial stroke
Discharged from thy partner art,
And freed from an unequal yoke;
Yea, though by means of this divorce
Thou mayst escape much discontent,
Yet both with pity and remorse
Consider well of this event.

Tune of "The Lamentation," from Este's *The Whole Book of Psalms* (1592).

Hymn 50, which is the lovely lullaby "Sleep, baby, sleep, what ails my dear?" has the following comment:

Nurses usually sing their children asleep, and through want of pertinent matter, they oft make use of unprofitable (if not worse) songs. This was therefore prepared, that it might help acquaint them and their nurse-children with the loving care and kindness of their Heavenly Father.

Although the tune is not specified in this case, the context and metre indicate that the tune Wither intended was "The Paternoster," which was Luther's "Vater Unser," and is the Old 112th, an exquisite melody admirably suited to these words:

Sleep, baby, sleep! What ails my dear,
What ails my darling thus to cry?
Be still, my child, and lend thine ear
To hear me sing thy lullaby.
My pretty lamb, forbear to weep;
Be still, my dear! Sweet baby, sleep.

·   ·   ·   ·   ·

When God-with-us was dwelling here
In little babes He took delight;
Such innocents as thou, my dear,
Are ever precious in His sight.
Sweet baby, then forbear to weep;
Be still, my babe! Sweet baby, sleep!

.   .   .   .   .

A little infant once was He;
And, strength in weakness, then was laid
Upon His Virgin Mother's knee
That power to thee might be conveyed.
Sweet baby, then forbear to weep;
Be still, my babe! Sweet baby, sleep!

.   .   .   .   .

The King of Kings when He was born
Had not so much for outward ease;
By Him such dressings were not worn,
Nor such like swaddling-clothes as these.
Sweet baby, then forbear to weep;
Be still, my babe! Sweet baby, sleep.

Within a manger lodged thy Lord,
Where oxen lay and asses fed;
Warm rooms we do to thee afford,
An easy cradle for thy bed.
Sweet baby, then forbear to weep;
Be still, my babe! Sweet baby, sleep!

Sleep.Baby.Sleep!

Sleep ba--by sleep! What ails my dear
What ails my dar-ling thus to cry
Be still, my child, and lend thine ear
To hear me sing thy lullaby.
My pretty lamb, for-bear to weep
Be still, my dear, sweet ba-by, sleep!

Early seventeenth century tune for the Paternoster which was Luther's "Vater Unser."

CHAPTER XVI

Robert Herrick—Nicholas Laniere—Henry and William Lawes—"To Anthea"—
Herrick and country dance tunes.

ROBERT HERRICK (1591–1674), like his poetical father, Ben Jonson, is said
to have attended Westminster School, where singing occupied two hours
of the week's calendar. Singing was evidently one form of music in which
Herrick took particular delight:

> Rare is the voice itself; but when we sing
> To th' lute or viol, then 'tis ravishing.

Of Julia, his favourite mistress, he says:

> When I thy singing next shall hear
> I 'll wish I might turn all to ear,
> To drink in notes and numbers; such
> As blessed souls can't hear too much;
> Then melted down, there let me lie
> Entranced and lost confusedly;
> And by thy music stricken mute,
> Die, and be turned into a lute.

Various references to lute and viol indicate that Herrick played both
instruments and sang "to the tension of a string." That he wrote some
at least of his lyrics with a tune in his head has already been seen in the
case of "Live, live with me and thou shalt see," clearly written to the
melody of Marlowe's "Come live with me and be my love." Again,
the "Mad Maid's Song" is an obvious re-writing of Ophelia's "Good-
morrow, 'tis Saint Valentine's Day":

Good morrow to the day so fair,
Good morning, Sir, to you:
Good morrow to mine own torn hair
Bedabbled with the dew.

Good morning to this primrose too;
Good morrow to each maid,
That will with flowers the tomb bestrew
Wherein my love is laid.

Ah woe is me, woe, woe is me,
Alack and welladay!
For pity, Sir, find out that bee
Which bore my love away.

165

I 'll seek him in your bonnet brave;
I 'll seek him in your eyes;
Nay, now I think th'ave made his grave
I' th' bed of strawberries.

No record has been left of any tune for "The Cobbler's Catch," but the thought at once recurs to the melody which Chappell calls "The Cobbler's Jig," the three men's song sung to Saint Hugh, patron of shoemakers, both in Dekker's *The Shoemaker's Holiday*, and in Ben Jonson's *The Case is Altered*:

Cold 's the wind and wet 's the rain;
Saint Hugh be our good speed!
Ill is the weather that brings no gain,
Nor helps good hearts in need.

(See Chapter xi, p. 99.)

The first part of this melody be can sung in canon, and this gives us the catch which Herrick probably had in mind to sing:

Come sit we by the fire's side,
And roundly drink we here,
Till that we see our cheeks ale-dyed
And noses tann'd with beer.

One has only to consult the collections of Ravenscroft entitled *Pammelia, Deuteromelia, Melismata*, to realize how many of the popular songs of the time were sung as catches.

Returning from Cambridge to London in 1620, Herrick enjoyed many happy hours in the company of Ben Jonson and of his musical friends— Nicholas Laniere, John Wilson, Jacques Gaultier, the court lutenist, John Parsons, organist at Westminster Cathedral, whose daughters, Dorothy and Thomasin, became Herrick's close friends, and above all, Henry Lawes, "the most excellent composer of his Lyrics," and his brother, "the rare musician," William Lawes. To Henry Lawes he wrote:

Touch but thy lyre (my Harrie) and I hear
From thee some raptures of the rare Gotier.
Then if thy voice commingle with the string
I hear in thee rare Laniere to sing,
Or curious Wilson. Tell me, canst thou be
Less than Apollo, that usurp'st such three?
Three unto whom the whole world give applause;
Yet their three praises praise but one, that 's Lawes.

Nicholas Laniere wrote the setting for one of the daintiest lyrics of Herrick's *Hesperides*:

White though ye be; yet, Lilies, know
From the first ye were not so;
 But I 'll tell ye
 What befell ye;
Cupid and his mother lay
In a cloud; while both did play,
He with his pretty finger pressed
The ruby niplet of her breast;
Out of the which, the cream of light,
 Like to a dew
 Fell down on you,
 And made ye white.

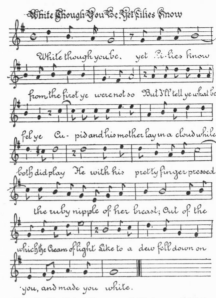

Playford's *Select Ayres and Dialogues* (1669).

From his country retreat in Devon, Herrick sent to Laniere the words for a musical *Pastoral upon the Birth of Prince Charles*, with this happy conclusion:

AMARILLIS. A garland for my gift shall be
Of flowers, ne'er sucked by th' thieving bee:
And all most sweet; yet all less sweet than he.

AMINTAS. And I will bear along with you
Leaves dropping down the honey'd dew,
With oaten pipe, as sweet as new.

MIRTILLO. And I a sheep-hook will bestow,
To have his little King-ship know,
As he is Prince, he 's shepherd too.

CHORUS. Come, let 's away, and quickly let 's be dressed,
And quickly give, *The swiftest grace is best.*
And when before him we have laid our treasures,
We 'll bless the babe, then back to country pleasures.

The influence of Ben Jonson's masque songs is evident in some of Herrick's metres, and he clearly felt that he was following in that master's footsteps; four poems in *Hesperides* are tributes to the older poet.

His Prayer to Ben Jonson

When I a verse shall make,
Know I have prayed thee,
For old Religion's sake,
Saint Ben to aid me.

Make the way smooth for me,
When I, thy Herrick,
Honouring thee, on my knee
Offer my Lyric.

Candles I'll give to thee,
And a new Altar;
And thou, Saint Ben, shalt be
Writ in my Psalter.

or that other,

An Ode for Him

Ah Ben!
Say how, or when
Shall we thy Guests
Meet at those Lyric Feasts,
Made at the *Sun*,
The *Dog*, the triple *Tunne*?
Where we such clusters had,
As made us nobly wild, not mad;
And yet each verse of thine
Out-did the meat, out-did the frolic wine.

It is said to have been on Ben Jonson's advice that Herrick had gone from his apprenticeship in Cheapside to Cambridge. While at Cambridge he may have made the acquaintance of Robert Ramsay, organist of Trinity College, for whose music he translated the *Dialogue betwixt Horace and Lydia* (1627):

HORACE. While, Lydia, I was lov'd of thee,
    Nor any was preferr'd 'fore me
    To hug thy whitest neck: Than I
    The Persian King liv'd not more happily.

LYDIA. While thou no other didst affect,
    Nor Cloe was of more respect;
    Then Lydia, far-fam'd Lydia,
    I flourish'd more than Roman Ilia.

HORACE. Now Thracian Cloe governs me,
    Skilful i' th' harp and melody:
    For whose affection, Lydia, I
    (So fate spares her) am well content to die.

.   .   .   .   .

His first dislike of exile in the country may well have been due to his separation from the happy company of musical friends. There were times, too, when he was not in the mood to sing

To His Friend, on the Untuneable Times

Play I could once; but, (gentle friend) you see
My harp hung up here on the willow tree.
Sing I could once; and bravely too inspire
(With luscious numbers) my melodious lyre,
. . . but (ah!) I know not how,
I feel in me this transmutation now.
Grief (my dear friend) has first my harp unstrung;
Withered my hand and palsy-struck my tongue.

The political troubles were also disturbing:

The Bad Season Makes the Poet Sad

.   .   .   .   .

Lost to all Music now; since everything
Puts on the semblance here of sorrowing.
Sick is the land to th' heart, and doth endure
More dangerous faintings by her desperate cure.

Herrick was an ardent Royalist, and had as little use for the Puritans as they had for him—they dispossessed him of his living in 1647. Yet his *Noble Numbers* testifies to his spiritual nature. These include *To God: an Anthem, sung in the Chapel at Whitehall, before the King*, and *A Christmas Carol, sung to the King in the Presence at Whitehall*, of which "The Musical Part was composed by M. Henry Lawes":

What sweeter music can we bring
Than a carol, for to sing
The birth of this our heavenly King?
Awake the voice! Awake the string!
Heart, ear and eye, and everything
Awake! the while the active finger
Runs division with the singer.

From the flourish they came to the song.

1. Dark and dull night, fly hence away,
    And give the honour to this day,
    That sees December turned to May.

2. If we may ask the reason, say;
    The why and wherefore all things here
    Seem like the springtime of the year?

.   .   .   .

Chorus. We see Him come, and know him ours,
Who with His sunshine and His showers,
Turns all the patient ground to flowers.

Although some later settings have replaced the original melodies in popular favour, the simple charm of the music written by William Lawes for Herrick's "Gather Ye Rosebuds" has surely won for it immortality. In comparing the words with the music in this and other songs of the period, it is frequently found that the singing version differs slightly from the purely literary version. That is our reason for printing both versions side by side without further explanation:

Gather ye rosebuds while ye may,
Old Time is still a-flying;
And this same flower that smiles to-day
To-morrow will be dying.

The glorious lamp of heaven, the sun,
The higher he's a getting,
The sooner will his race be run,
And nearer he's to setting.

That age is best which is the first,
When youth and blood are warmer;
But being spent, the worse and worst
Times still succeed the former.

Then be not coy, but use your time,
And while ye may, go marry;
For having lost but once your prime,
You may for ever tarry.

From *Hesperides*.

Tune and words from Playford's *Select Musical Ayres* (1652). Cf. *English Melodies*, (J. M. Dent & Sons Ltd.).

Both William Lawes and his younger brother Henry were Gentlemen of the Chapel Royal in Herrick's time. William was killed by a stray shot at the siege of Chester, and Herrick paid this tribute to his memory:

Should I not put on Blacks, when each one here
Comes with his cypress and devotes a tear?
Should I not grieve (my Lawes) when every lute,
Viol and voice is (by thy loss) struck mute?
Thy loss, brave man! whose numbers have been hurled
And no less praised than spread throughout the world.
Some have thee called Amphion; some of us
Named thee Terpander, or sweet Orpheus;
Some this, some that, but all in this agree,
Music had both her birth and death with thee.

Five collections of songs published in Herrick's own lifetime include the first two of the following settings by Henry Lawes, indicating their great popularity:

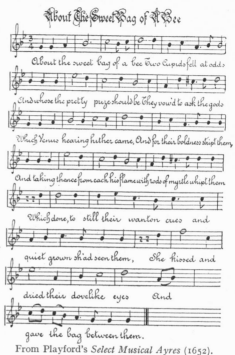

About the sweet bag of a bee,
Two Cupids fell at odds;
And whose the pretty prize should be
They vow'd to ask the Gods.

Which Venus hearing thither came,
And for their boldness stript them;
And taking thence from each his flame,
With rods of myrtle whipt them.

Which done, to still their wanton cries,
When quiet grown sh'ad seen them,
She kissed and wiped their dove-like eyes,
And gave the bag between them.

From *Hesperides.*

From Playford's *Select Musical Ayres* (1652).

It has of late years become the fashion to belittle the settings of Henry Lawes, but if any of the critics could compose anything one-half so delightful as the following, he would be more entitled to our respect. Mrs. Elizabeth Wheeler, the subject of this lyric, inspired at least two others from his pen:

Among the myrtles as I walkt,
Love and my sighs thus intertalkt;
Tell me, said I, in deep distress,
Where I may find my shepherdess.
Thou fool, said Love, knowst thou not
    this?
In everything that's sweet she is.
In yond' carnation go and seek,
There thou shalt find her lip and cheek.
In that enamel'd pansy by,
There thou shalt have her curious eye:
In bloom of peach and rose's bud,
There waves the streamer of her blood.
'Tis true, said I, and thereupon
I went to pluck them one by one.
To make of parts an union;
But on a sudden all were gone.

From *Hesperides.*

Tune and words from Playford's *Select Musical Ayres* (1652).

Another setting by Henry Lawes which was clearly much in favour is that of Herrick's "The Primrose":

Ask me why I send you here
This sweet Infanta of the year?
Ask me why I send to you
This Primrose thus bepearl'd with dew?
I will whisper to your ears,
The sweets of love are mixed with tears.

Ask me why this flower do's show
So yellow-green and sickly too?
Ask me why the stalk is weak
And bending (yet it doth not break)?
I will answer: "These discover
What fainting hopes are in a lover."

From *Hesperides*.

Tune and words from Henry Lawes *Ayres and Dialogues* (1653).

Most famous, perhaps, of all Herrick's songs is "To Anthea, who may command him anything." The original setting by Henry Lawes has been eclipsed in popularity by a modern composition, and yet there is a simple virility about the contemporary music which deserves its resurrection:

Bid me to live, and I will live
Thy Protestant to be;
Or bid me love and I will give
A loving heart to thee.

A heart as soft, a heart as kind,
A heart as sound and free,
As in the whole world thou canst find,
That heart I 'll give to thee.

Bid that heart stay, and it will stay
To honour thy decree;
Or bid it languish quite away,
And 't shall do so for thee.

Bid me to weep, and I will weep,
While I have eyes to see;
And having none, yet I will keep
A heart to weep for thee.

Bid me despair, and I 'll despair
Under that cypress tree;
Or bid me die, and I will dare
E'en death to die for thee.

Tune and words from Playford's *Select Musical Ayres* (1652).

Thou art my life, my love, my heart,
The very eyes of me,
And hast command of every part
To live and die for thee.

From *Hesperides.*

Henry Lawes is also named as composer of Herrick's *The New Year's Gift or Circumcisions Song, sung to the King in the Presence at Whitehall*:

Prepare for songs; He 's come, He 's come;
And be it sin here to be dumb,
And not with lutes to fill the room.

No composer is named, nor is the music preserved for

THE STAR SONG: A CAROL TO THE KING; SUNG AT WHITEHALL
(*Flourish of music*)

1.   Tell us, thou clear and heavenly tongue,
   Where is the Babe but lately sprung?
   Lies he the lily-banks among?

2.   Or say, if this new Birth of ours
   Sleeps, laid within some ark of flowers,
   Spangled with dew-light; thou canst clear
   All doubts and manifest the where.

3.   Declare to us, bright star, if we shall seek
   Him in the morning's blushing cheek,
   Or search the beds of spices through,
   To find him out?

STAR.   No, this ye need not do;
But only come and see Him rest
A princely Babe in 's mother's breast.

CHORUS.   He 's seen, He 's seen, why then a round,
Let 's kiss the sweet and holy ground;
And all rejoice that we have found
A King before conception crowned.

4.   Come then, come then, and let us bring
   Unto our pretty *Twelfth-Tide King*
   Each one his several offering.

CHORUS.   And when night comes, we 'll give Him wassailing;
And that His treble honours may be seen,
We 'll choose Him King, and make His Mother Queen.

From *Noble Numbers.*

Herrick's love of music is revealed in many verses, none more beautiful than those written with the lilt of a dance tune:

TO MUSIC, TO BECALM HIS FEVER

Charm me asleep, and melt me so
With thy delicious numbers;
That being ravished, hence I go
Away in easy slumbers.

Ease my sick head,
And make my bed,
Thou Power that canst sever
From me this ill;
And quickly still,
Though thou not kill
My fever.

Thou sweetly canst convert the same
From a consuming fire
Into a gentle-licking flame,
And make it thus expire.
Then make me weep
My pains asleep;
And give me such reposes,
That I, poor I
May think thereby,
I live and die
'Mongst roses.

Fall on me like a silent dew,
Or like those maiden showers,
Which, by the peep of day, do strew
A baptism o'er the flowers.
Melt, melt my pains
With thy soft strains;
That, having ease me given,
With full delight,
I leave this light,
And take my flight
For Heaven.　　*From Hesperides.*

The exile from London to a Devonshire parsonage which Herrick sometimes bemoans may have removed him from the boon company of court musicians, but it brought him into another company of country dance tunes which influenced many of his metres. One of these dance tunes, "Up Tails All," is actually prefaced as the title of a lyric which, however, has been expurgated from the Oxford standard edition, and therefore has been lost sight of. The metre, however, so exactly fits this tune that the kinship is unquestionable. Remembering the custom of the time to write ditties to a tune, one may not unfairly surmise that he had this tune running in his head when he wrote his other lyrics in this metre—for instance "Ceremonies for Christmas":

Begin with a kiss,
Go on too with this,
And thus, thus, thus let us smother
Our lips for a while,
But let 's not beguile
Our hope of one for the other.

CEREMONIES FOR CHRISTMAS

Come, bring with a noise,
My merry, merry boys,
The Christmas log to the firing;
While my good dame she
Bids ye all be free,
And drink to your hearts desiring.

Another country dance tune fitting another metre which Herrick sometimes used is "Pepper is Black," mentioned by Nashe in *Have with You to Saffron Walden*, written in 1594. An instance of this metre is "An Hymn to Love":

Tune from *Queen Elizabeth's Virginal Book*. Quoted in Chappell's *Popular Music of the Olden Time*.

AN HYMN TO LOVE

I will confess
With cheerfulness
Love is a thing so likes me,
That let her lay
On me all day,
I 'll kiss the hand that strikes me.

OF LOVE

I'll get me hence
Because no fence
Or fort that I can make here,
But Love by charms
Or else by arms
Will storm, or starving take here.

Tune from Playford's *Dancing Master*. Cf. Chappell's *Popular Music of the Olden Time*.

The lightness of Herrick's verse is due essentially to the ease with which it can be spoken or sung. One does not thereby have to maintain that his lyrics were always written to existing melodies. Some were written so that they might be sung if any one should set the music, and all were written by one who himself could sing. Herrick himself states his case in the epigram

UPON HIMSELF

Thou shalt not all die; for while love's fire shines
Upon his altar, men shall read thy lines;
And learned musicians shall to honour Herrick's
Fame, and his name, both set and sing his lyrics.

And again in one of the introductory verses to *Hesperides* he says:

In sober mornings do not thou rehearse
The holy incantation of a verse;
But when that men have both well drunk and fed,
Let my Enchantments then be sung, or read.

CHAPTER XVII

William and Henry Lawes—Settings by Henry Lawes of songs by Milton, Waller, Carew—Lovelace—Cavalier poets—Sir John Suckling—Cromwell and music— Martin Parker, "the Prelates' poet"—Francis Quarles—Marquis of Montrose.

BOTH William and Henry Lawes were pupils of John Cooper or Coperario, the English lutenist who had brought foreign graces back from Italy. Henry Lawes, however, much as he appreciated Italian songs, seems to have thought English words just as suitable for singing. In one of his prefaces he says:

And (I speak it freely once for all) that if English words which are fitted for song do not run smooth enough 'tis the fault either of the Composer or Singer. Our English is so stor'd with plenty of monosyllables (which, like small stones, fill up the chinks) that it hath great privilege over divers of its neighbours, and in some particulars (with reverence be it spoken) above the very Latin, which language we find overcharged with the letter S especially in "bus" and such hissing terminations."

To prove his case against the singing of Italian words, he wrote a burlesque song called "Tavola," the words of which are merely the titles of old Italian songs.

"I have often had it performed," says Sir Frederick Bridge, "and when sung in Italian it is listened to very stolidly, but when the English translation is given it creates much hilarity."

Here follows his translation:

TAVOLA

In that frozen heart . . . (*for one voice*).
Weep, my lady, weep, and if your eyes . . . (*for two voices*).
'Tis ever thus, even when you seem to save me,
Truly you scorn me
Unhappy, unbelieving . . .
Alas! Of splendour yet!
But why, oh why? from the pallid lips
And so my life . . . (*for three voices*).

Such a burlesque presupposes many an argument in tavern or elsewhere between poet and musician on the singable quality of English verse, and accounts for the popularity of Lawes with contemporary poets whose lyrics he so aptly set. In addition to Herrick, whose tribute has already been quoted, Edmund Waller, Richard Lovelace, Thomas Carew, Sir

John Suckling and John Milton found in him the ideal composer who made the music fit the words. Waller, for whom Lawes set the lyric "Go, Lovely Rose" wrote:

To Mr. Henry Lawes

(who had then newly set a song of mine in the year 1635)

Verse makes heroic virtue live,
But you can life to verses give.

. . . . .

You by the help of tune and time
Can make that song that was but rhyme.

. . . . .

As a church-window thick with paint
Lets in a light but dim and faint,
So others with division hide
The light of sense, the poet's pride.
But you alone may truly boast
That not a syllable is lost.

. . . . .

Let those who only warble long
And gargle in the throats a song,
Content themselves with Ut Re Mi,
Let words and sense be set by thee.

John Milton's tribute is even better known:

To Mr. H. Lawes on His Airs

Harry, whose tuneful and well-measured song
First taught our English music how to span
Words with just note and accent, not to scan
With Midas' ears, committing short and long,
Thy worth and skill exempts thee from the throng
With praise enough for envy to look wan;
To after age thou shalt be writ the man
That with smooth air couldst humour best our tongue.

Such unanimous approval from the foremost poets of the time makes it all the more desirable to study the melodies to which the lyrics are fitted, and such study soon reveals nuances of rhythm and accent which might escape those who only read with the eye. These nuances are sometimes lost in modern reprints of the music, with barring re-arranged to suit a later taste. The original pages of Playford's publications are the proper guide.

Waller's finest lyric has inspired innumerable composers, and yet the contemporary setting by Lawes still holds its own:

N

Go, lovely rose—
Tell her that wastes her time and me,
That now she knows,
When I resemble her to thee,
How sweet and fair she seems to be.

Tell her that 's young,
And shuns to have her graces spied,
That hadst thou sprung
In deserts where no men abide
Thou must have uncommended died.

Small is the worth
Of beauty from the light retired;
Bid her come forth,
Suffer herself to be desired,
And not blush so to be admired.

Then die—that she
The common fate of all things rare
May read in thee;
How small a part of time they share
That are so wondrous sweet and fair.

Playford's *Select Musical Ayres.*

Another, a truly enchanting setting, was made by Lawes for Waller's:

TO PHILLIS

Phillis, why should we delay
Pleasures shorter than the day?
Could we (which we never can)
Stretch our lives beyond their span,
Beauty like a shadow flies
And our youth before us dies.
Or would youth and beauty stay,
Love has wings and will away;
Love has swifter wings than time,
Change in love to heaven does climb.
Gods, that never change their state,
Vary oft their love and hate.
Phillis, to this truth we owe
All the love betwixt us two:
Let not you and I enquire
What has been our past desire;
On what shepherds you have smiled,
Or what nymphs I have beguiled.

Playford's *Select Musical Ayres* (1652).
Cf *Reliquary of English Song* (G. Schirmer).

In the chapter on dance tunes (Chapter VI, pp. 63–4), it was shown that Waller was inspired to write a lyric on a saraband rhythm. The interest that he took in the singing of his songs is indicated in several lyrics. Take for instance:

TO A LADY

SINGING A SONG OF HIS COMPOSING

Chloris, yourself you so excel,
When you vouchsafe to breathe my thought,
That like a spirit with this spell
Of mine own teaching I am caught.

That eagle's fate and mine are one,
Which, on the shaft that made him die,
Espied a feather of his own,
Wherewith he wont to soar so high.

Had Echo with so sweet a grace
Narcissus' loud complaints returned,
Not for reflection of his face,
But of his voice, the boy had burned.

From *Poems written upon Several Occasions.*

Tune and words from Henry Lawes, *Ayres and Dialogues* (1653). Cf. *Minstrelsy of England* (Augener Ltd.).

The lady in question may have been a Mrs. Arden, though one feels rather tempted to identify her with Lady Isabella Thynne. Aubrey in his account of Oxford, the seat of the Court during the Civil War, says:

Many times my lady Isabella Thynne would make her entry (into Trinity Garden) with a theorbo or lute played before her. I have heard her play on it in the grove myself, which she did rarely; for Mr. Edmund Waller hath in his poems for ever made her famous.

Here is the celebration of the lady:

OF MY LADY ISABELLA PLAYING ON THE LUTE

Such moving sounds from such a careless touch!
So unconcerned herself, and we so much!
What art is this, that with so little pains
Transports us thus and o'er our spirits reigns?
The trembling strings about her fingers crowd
And tell their joy for every kiss aloud.
Small force there needs to make them tremble so;
Touched by that hand who would not tremble too?

Yet another song in the same vein, and we can leave Waller:

SONG

While I listen to thy voice,
Chloris, I feel my life decay.
That powerful noise
Calls my fleeting soul away!
Oh, suppress that magic sound
Which destroys without a wound!

Peace, Chloris, peace, or singing die!
That together you and I
To Heaven may go;
For all we know
Of what the Bless'ed do above
Is that they sing, and that they love!

From *Poems written upon Several Occasions.*

Henry Lawes, *Ayres and Dialogues.* Cf.
Hullah's *English Songs* (Augener Ltd.).

In one of those polished songs so typical of the cavalier poets, Thomas
Carew (1598–1639) gives answer to Ben Jonson's "Have you seen but a
white lily grow," the song to which, as may be remembered, Suckling
also replied (p. 144):

Would you know what's soft ? I dare
Not bring you to the down or air;
Nor to stars to show what's bright,
Nor to snow to teach you white.

Nor if you would music hear
Call the orbs to take your ear;
Nor to please your sense bring forth
Bruised nard or what's more worth.

Or on food were your thoughts placed,
Bring you nectar for a taste.
Would you have all these in one,
Name my mistress, and 'tis done!

For Carew, Henry Lawes wrote the music for the lyrics in the masque

Caelum Britannicum, produced in 1634, and also settings for several other lyrics, of which the most remembered is:

He that loves a rosy cheek
Or a coral lip admires,
Or from star-like eyes doth seek
Fuel to maintain his fires,
As old Time makes these decay
So his flames must waste away.

But a smooth and steadfast mind,
Gentle thoughts and calm desires,
Hearts with equal love combin'd
Kindle never-dying fires:
Where these are not, I despise
Lovely cheeks or lips or eyes.

Celia now no tears can win
My resolv'd heart to return;
I have search'd my soul within,
And find naught but pride and scorn:
I have learnt those arts, and now
Can disdain as much as thou.
Some god in my revenge convey
That love to her I cast away.

From *Poems* (1640).

Henry Lawes, *Ayres and Dialogues* (1653). Quoted in *English Melodies* (J. M. Dent & Sons Ltd.).

Richard Lovelace has been compared to Sir Philip Sidney, and as a well-bred cavalier had the accomplishment of music. He was indeed modest about his skill in singing, if we can take as evidence his ironical poem:

To a Lady that Desired Me I would Bear my Part with Her in a Song

What, though 'tis said I have a voice;
I know 'tis but that hollow noise
Which (as it through my pipe doth speed)
Bitterns do carol through a reed;
In the same key with monkey's jigs,
Or dirges of proscribèd pigs,
Or the soft serenades above
In calm of night, when cats make love.

As the poem proceeds, he indicates his knowledge of the technique of music:

Yet can I music too; but such
As is beyond all voice or touch;

My mind can in fair order chime
Whilst my true heart still beats the time;
My soul so full of harmony
That it with all parts can agree;
If you wind up to the highest fret,
It shall descend an eight from it,
And when you shall vouchsafe to fall
Sixteen above you it shall call,
And yet so dis-assenting one,
They both shall meet an unison.

From *Lucasta* (1649).

Five at least of Lovelace's lyrics were set to music by Henry Lawes, the most remembered of which is that "To Amarantha, That she would dishevell her hair." The song versions do not strictly correspond to the literary versions.

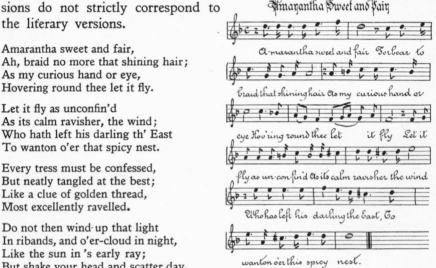

Amarantha sweet and fair,
Ah, braid no more that shining hair;
As my curious hand or eye,
Hovering round thee let it fly.

Let it fly as unconfin'd
As its calm ravisher, the wind;
Who hath left his darling th' East
To wanton o'er that spicy nest.

Every tress must be confessed,
But neatly tangled at the best;
Like a clue of golden thread,
Most excellently ravelled.

Do not then wind up that light
In ribands, and o'er-cloud in night,
Like the sun in 's early ray;
But shake your head and scatter day.

From *Lucasta* (1649).

Tune and words from Henry Lawes, *Ayres and Dialogues* (1653).

Although Lawes wrote most of the contemporary settings for Lovelace's lyrics, there were other musicians with whom the poet collaborated, and indeed the most celebrated of his songs "To Althea, from Prison" was set by John Wilson. Yet Lawes was no jealous artist, and paid this tribute to Wilson:

For this I know, and must say to thy praise,
That thou hast gone in music unknown ways,
Hast cut a path where there was none before,
Like Magellan traced an unknown shore.
Thou taught'st our language, first, to speak in time,
Gav'st the right accent and proportion.

When Love, with unconfinèd wings,
Hovers within my gates;
And my divine Althea brings
To whisper at the grates;
When I lie tangled in her hair
And fetter'd to her eye,
The birds that wanton in the air
Know no such liberty.

. . . . .

Stone walls do not a prison make,
Nor iron bars a cage;
Minds innocent and quiet take
That for a hermitage.
If I have freedom in my love,
And in my soul am free,
Angels alone that soar above
Enjoy such liberty.

From *Lucasta* (1649).

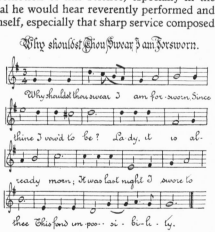

Tune and words from Playford's *Songs or Ballads for Three Voices* (1659). Originally set for one voice as stated in Wilson's *Cheerful Ayres* (1660).

The setting for Lovelace's lyric "The Scrutinie," ascribed to "Mr. Charles," carries with it a tradition that the composer was Charles I himself. In a manuscript of the British Museum (Add. MSS. 11608, fol. 25) the music of a song "Mark how the blissful morn" is also ascribed to King Charles, although Playford credits it to Nicholas Laniere. In his *Introduction to the Skill of Music*, Playford says of this tuneful monarch:

Nor was his late sacred majesty and blessed martyr, King Charles the First, behind any of his predecessors in the love and promotion of this science, especially in the service of Almighty God, and with much zeal he would hear reverently performed and often appointed the service and anthems himself, especially that sharp service composed by Dr. William Child, being by his knowledge in music a competent judge therein; and would play his part exactly well on the *bass-violl*, especially of those incomparable fancies of Mr. Coperario to the organ.

THE SCRUTINIE

Why should you swear I am forsworn,
Since thine I vow'd to be?
Lady, it is already morn,
And 'twas last night I swore to thee
That fond impossibility.

Have I not loved thee much and long,
A tedious twelve hours' space?
I must all other beauties wrong,
And rob thee of a new embrace,
Could I still dote upon thy face.

From *Lucasta* (1649).

Tune and words from Playford's *Select Musical Ayres* (1652). Cf. *Reliquary of English Song* (G. Schirmer).

John Laniere set the music, unfortunately lost, of that immortal lyric:

To Lucasta, Going to the Wars

Tell me not, sweet, I am unkind
That from the nunnery
Of thy chaste breast and quiet mind
To war and arms I fly.

True, a new mistress now I chase,
The first foe in the field;
And with a stronger faith embrace
A sword, a horse, a shield.

Yet this inconstancy is such
As thou too shall adore.
I could not love thee, dear, so much,
Loved I not honour more.

From *Lucasta* (1649).

Sir John Suckling (1609–41) enjoys the distinction among cavalier poets of having been made the subject of a ballad by a brother poet, Sir John Mennes. This was a lampoon on Suckling's ignominious retreat before the Scottish forces at Duns, and was fitted to the tune of the ballad of "John Dory" (cf. p. 126):

Sir John he got him an ambling nag,
To Scotland for to ride-a,
With a hundred horse more, all his own, he swore,
To guard him on every side-a.

No errant knight ever went to fight
With half so gay a bravado,
Had you seen but his look, you'd have sworn on a book
He'd have conquered a whole armada.

.   .   .   .   .   .

None liked him so well as his own colonell,
Who took him for John de Weart-a;
But when there were shows of gunning and blows,
My gallant was nothing so pert-a.

For when the Scots army came within sight,
And all prepared to fight-a,
He ran to his tent; they asked what he meant;
He swore he could not go right-a.

The colonell sent for him back agen,
To quarter him in the van-a;
But Sir John did swear he would not come there
To be killed the very first man-a.

From *Musarum Deliciae* (c. 1656).

Suckling's "Ballad upon a Wedding" runs to a tune which was favoured by many other ballad writers during the Great Rebellion. The rhythm indicates that the tune was originally a dance tune, probably that of a saraband, which at this period was being transformed into an English country dance (cf. pp. 63–4).

I tell thee, Dick, where I have been,
Where I the rarest things have seen,
O things beyond compare!
Such sights again cannot be found
In any place on English ground,
Be it at wake or fair.

At Charing Cross hard by the way
Where we (thou know'st) do sell our hay,
There is a house with stairs;
And there did I see coming down
Such folk as are not in our town,
Forty at least in pairs.

Tune from *A Choice Collection of 180 Loyal Songs* (1685). Quoted in Chappell's *Popular Music of the Olden Times.*

. . . . . .

From *Fragmenta Aurea* (1646).

Of the settings made for Suckling's lyrics by Henry Lawes, perhaps the happiest is:

I am confirmed a woman can
Love this or that or any man:
This day her love is melting hot,
To-morrow swears she knows you not.
Let her but a new object find,
And she is of another mind.
Then hang me, ladies, at your door,
If e'er I dote upon you more.

Yet still I'll love the fair one,—why?
For nothing but to please mine eye;
And so the fat and soft-skinn'd dame
I'll flatter to appease my flame,
For her that's musical I long,
When I am sad, to sing a song.
But hang me, ladies, at your door,
If e'er I dote upon you more.

From Playford's *Select Musical Ayres* (1652).

Aglaura was a play by Suckling produced in 1638 with all the lavish staging of a masque. In this was sung the celebrated "Why so pale and wan, fond lover?" of which Rimbault gives an old setting in his *Musical Illustrations of English Poetry*, but whether this was the contemporary setting has not been proved:

Why so pale and wan, fond lover?
Prithee, why so pale?
Will, when looking well won't move her,
Looking ill prevail?
Prithee, why so pale?

Why so dull and mute, young sinner?
Prithee, why so mute?
Will, when speaking well can't win her,
Saying nothing do 't?
Prithee, why so mute?

Quit, quit for shame; this will not move,
This cannot take her;
If of herself she will not love,
Nothing can make her!
The devil take her!

From *Aglaura* (c. 1638).

Rimbault, *Musical Illustrations of English Poetry.*

The popularity of Henry Lawes is indicated by a statement made by Aubrey in regard to Thomas Hobbes, the author of *Leviathan* (1588–1679):

He had always books of prick-song lying on his table—e.g. of H. Lawes, etc. Songs which at night, when he was a-bed and the doors made fast and was sure nobody heard him, he sang aloud (not that he had a very good voice) but for his health's sake; he did believe it did his lungs good and conduced much to prolong his life.

The most celebrated of the poetical alliances of Henry Lawes is that with John Milton, who may have known the composer first as a teacher of music. According to Aubrey, Milton "had a delicate tuneable voice, and had good skill. His father instructed him. He had an organ in his house; he played on that most." Next to the organ, singing was evidently his delight, for according to the same authority, when he was tutoring his sister's sons, "he made his nephews songsters and sing from the time they were with him."

Milton's father and grandfather were both musicians, and he himself shows his love of music in innumerable lines. He was just twenty when

he wrote the *Hymn on the Morning of Christ's Nativity* (1629), with the
stanza:

> Ring out, ye crystal spheres!
> Once bless our human ears
> If ye have power to touch our senses so;
> And let your silver chime
> Move in melodious time;
> And let the bass of heaven's deep organ blow;
> And with your ninefold harmony
> Make up full consort to the angelic symphony.

Three years later he wrote in *L'Allegro*:

> Lap me in soft Lydian airs,
> Married to immortal verse,
> Such as the meeting soul may pierce,
> In notes with many a winding bout
> Of linkèd sweetness long drawn out
> With wanton heed and giddy cunning,
> The melting voice through mazes running,
> Untwisting all the chains that tie
> The hidden soul of harmony.

Again in the same year in *Il Penseroso*:

> There let the pealing organ blow,
> To the full-voiced choir below
> In service high and anthems clear,
> As may with sweetness, through mine ear,
> Dissolve me into ecstasies,
> And bring all heaven before mine eyes.

The following year he wrote:

At a Solemn Music

> Blest pair of Sirens, pledges of Heaven's joy,
> Sphere-born harmonious sisters, Voice and Verse,
> Wed your divine sounds, and mixed power employ,
> Dead things with inbreathed sense able to pierce;
> And to our high-raised phantasy present
> That undisturbèd song of pure concent,
> Aye sung before the sapphire-coloured throne
> To Him that sits thereon,
> With saintly shout and solemn jubilee;
> Where the bright Seraphim in burning row
> Their loud uplifted angel-trumpets blow,
> And the Cherubic host in thousand quires
> Touch their immortal harps of golden wires,
> With those just Spirits that wear victorious palms,
> Hymns devout and holy psalms
> Singing everlastingly.

Henry Lawes now enters the scene as the composer of music for Milton's lyrics at the entertainment at Harefield for the Countess Dowager of Derby.   Of these the second shows considerable skill in song-writing:

SONG II

O'er the smooth enamelled green,
Where no print of step hath been,
Follow me, as I sing
And touch the warbled string;
Under the shady roof
Of branching elm star-proof
Follow me.

I will bring you where she sits
Clad in splendour as befits
Her deity.
Such a rural Queen
All Arcadia hath not seen.

In the following year (1634) Henry Lawes set the lyrics for two masques, one *Caelum Britannicum*, written by Thomas Carew, and produced at Court with scenery by Inigo Jones, the other *Comus* by John Milton, a family entertainment for the festivities at Ludlow Castle to celebrate the appointment of the Earl of Bridgewater as President of the Council of Wales and the Marches.   Lawes was instructor in music to the earl's children, and in this masque himself took the part of the Attendant Spirit, singing five of the songs.   One of these was the invocation song to Sabrina:

Sabrina fair,
Listen where thou art sitting
Under the glassy, cool, translucent wave,
In twisted braids of lilies knitting
The loose train of thy amber-dropping hair;
Listen for dear honour's sake,
Goddess of the silver lake,
Listen and save!

For harmonized version cf. *The Masque of Comus*, edited by Sir Frederick Bridge (Novello & Co. Ltd.).

It is not known who sang the answering song of Sabrina:

By the rushy fringèd bank,
Where grows the willow and the osier dank,
My sliding chariot stays,
Thick set with agate, and the azurn sheen
Of turkis blue, and emerald green,
That in the channel strays;
Whilst from off the waters fleet
Thus I set my printless feet
O'er the cowslip's velvet head,
That bends not as I tread.
Gentle swain, at thy request
I am here!

For harmonized version, cf. *The Masque of Comus*, edited by Sir Frederick Bridge (Novello & Co. Ltd.).

During Milton's visit to Italy in 1638, music was not forgotten, and three of his Latin epigrams are addressed to Leonora Baroni, the Roman singer, whom he heard at a reception held in the palace of the Cardinal Francesco Barberini. During all his later life, music was his chief recreation, and it was unquestionably this musical instinct that gave such sonorous quality to his verse.

The disturbing years leading up to the Great Rebellion diverted Milton from lyrical poetry to travel and pamphleteering, but in the stormiest circumstance he never lost his love for music. In the sonnet "To Mr. Lawrence," he writes:

What neat repast shall feaſt us, light and choice,
Of Attic taste, with wine, whence we may rise,
To hear the lute well touched, or artful voice
Warble immortal notes and Tuscan air?
He who of these delights can judge, and spare
To interpose them oft, is not unwise.

A charming picture is suggested in Anne Manning's novel, *Mary Powell*—extracts from the imaginary diary of Milton's first wife:

October, 1646.

At one we dine. My husband careth not to sitt over the wine; and hath noe sooner finished the Cheese and Pippins than he reverts to the Viol or Organ, and not onlie sings himself, but will make me sing too, although he sayth my Voice is better than my Eare. Never was there such a tunefulle Spiritt. . . .

From six to eight we are seldom without Friends. . . . If the guests chance to be musicalle, the Lute and Viol are brought forthe, to alternate with Roundelay and Madrigal: the old Man beating Time with his feeble Fingers, and now and then joining with his quavering Voice. (By the way, he hath not forgotten to this Hour my imputed crime of losing that song by Harry Lawes. . . .)

On Sabbaths . . . we have much Reading, Singing and Discoursing among ourselves. The Maids sing, Herbert sings, Olde Mr. Milton sings; and trulie with so much of it, I woulde sometimes as lief have them quiete.

The Roundheads were unsympathetic to music, but their proscription of this vicious indulgence was carried out in practice much as the prohibition of liquor is observed in the United States. Oliver Cromwell himself loved the organ, and when his Ironsides were smashing the pipes in Westminster Abbey, he had the organ transferred from Magdalen College Chapel in Oxford to Hampton Court Palace for his own entertainment. He engaged John Hingston, formerly in the service of Charles I, to instruct his daughters in music. Hingston had with him two boys, and according to Hawkins taught them to "sing with him Deering's Latin songs which Cromwell delighted to hear, and had often performed before him." According to the old newspapers (see Carlyle's *Letters and Speeches of Oliver Cromwell*):

Next Friday, Friday the 20th, which was Thanksgiving Day, the Honourable House, after hearing two sermons at Margaret's, Westminster, partook of a most princely entertainment, by invitation from his Highness, at Whitehall. After dinner his Highness withdrew to the Cockpit, and there entertained them with rare music, both of voices and instruments, till the evening; his Highness being very fond of music.

While the Ironsides might make official raids on instrumental music, they could not destroy the ballad, and this was used by the Royalist poets with famous skill. Martin Parker, nicknamed "The Prelates' Poet," was particularly effective. Using the old tune of "Green Sleeves," he wrote this "Exact Description of how his Majesty and his nobles went to the Parliament in 1640":

Come the merriest of the Nine　　　Unto the world to say and sing
And now unto my aid incline,　　　The praises of our royal king
I need a little aid of thine,　　　Who now this present hopeful spring
For now I have intent　　　　　　Hath called a Parliament.

What Ritson calls "the most famous and popular air ever heard of in this country" was Martin Parker's "When the King enjoys His Own Again":

What Booker can prognosticate
Concerning Kings or Kingdom's fate,
I think myself to be as wise
As he that gazeth on the skies.
My skill goes beyond the depths of a pond,
Or rivers in the greatest rain,
Whereby I can tell all things will be well
When the King enjoys his own again.

·   ·   ·   ·   ·

Though for a time we see Whitehall
With cobwebs hanging on the wall,
Instead of silk and silver brave
Which formerly it used to have,
With rich perfume in every room,
Delightful in that princely train,
Which again you shall see when the time it
   shall be
That the King enjoys his own again.

Tune in *Elizabeth Rogers's Virginal Book*.
Quoted in Chappell's *Popular Music of the
Olden Time*.

Martin Parker did not confine himself to political ballads. One of his happiest is "The Country Lass," written to the tune of "Stingo," or "Oil of Barley":

Although I am a country lass
A lofty mind I bear-a,
I think myself as good as those
That gay apparel wear-a.
My coat is made of comely gray,
Yet is my skin as soft-a,
As those that with the choicest wines
Do bathe their bodies oft-a.

What though I keep my father's sheep,
A thing that must be done-a,
A garland of the fairest flowers
Shall shroud me from the sun-a;
And when I see them feeding by,
Where grass and flowers spring-a,
Close by a crystal fountain side
I sit me down and sing-a.

Tune from Playford's *Dancing Master*
(1650). Quoted in Chappell's *Popular Music
of the Olden Time*.

Francis Quarles, another poet who sharpened his pen in the Royalist cause, used an old tune, "The Clean Contrary Way," for one of his most successful "Shepherd's Oracles":

Know this, my brethren, heav'n is clear,
And all the clouds are gone,
The righteous man shall flourish now;
Good days are coming on.
Then come, my brethren, and be glad,
And eke rejoice with me;
Lawn sleeves and rochets shall go down,
And hey, then up go we.

.   .   .   .   .

Whate'er the Popish hands have built,
Our hammers shall undo;
We'll break their pipes and burn their copes,
And pull down churches too;
We'll exercise within the grove
And teach beneath a tree;
We'll make a pulpit of a cask
And hey, then up go we.

Tune from Playford's *Dancing Master* (1686).
Words by Alexander Brome.

An earlier ballad to the same tune is that of "The Saint's Encouragement," by Alexander Brome:

Fight on, brave soldiers, for the cause,
Fear not the Cavaliers;
Their threat'nings are as senseless as
Our jealousies and fears.

'Tis you must perfect this great work
And all the Tories slay,
And make the King a glorious Saint
The clean contrary way.

One of the most celebrated of all the songs written during the Civil War was that of the Marquis of Montrose (1614–50) to an older ballad tune traced by Chappell to the time of James I, and claimed by Dr. Grattan Flood as an Irish harp melody.

My dear and only love, I pray
That little world of thee
Be govern'd by no other sway
But purest monarchy;
For if confusion have a part,
Which virtuous souls abhor,
I'll call a synod in thine heart,
And never love thee more.

Tune from John Gamble's MS. (1659). Quoted in Chappell's *Popular Music of the Olden Time.*

As Alexander I will reign,
And I will reign alone;
My thoughts did evermore disdain
A rival on my throne.
He either fears his fate too much,
Or his deserts are small,
Who dares not put it to the touch
To gain or lose it all.

And in the empire of my heart
Where I should solely be,
If others do pretend a part,
Or dare to share with me;
Or if committees thou erect,
Or go on such a score,
I'll smiling mock at my neglect,
And never love thee more.

But if no faithless action stain
Thy love and constant word,
I'll make thee famous by my pen
And glorious by my sword;
I'll serve thee in such noble ways
As ne'er was known before;
I'll deck and crown thy head with bays
And love thee more and more.

Montrose Lines, 1695.
Cf. *The Songs of Scotland prior to Burns*, edited
by Robert Chambers (W. & R. Chambers).

CHAPTER XVIII

Purcell—Dryden—Summing up.

ALTHOUGH the Restoration once more gave liberty to music, that music came back from its exile with a distinct penchant for foreign fashions, and though Purcell made a brave fight to retain the supremacy which English music had enjoyed in the days of Byrd and Orlando Gibbons, even he, so far at least as song-writing was concerned, inclined to give an operatic flair to perfectly simple lyrics, using the words as a peg for an aria. Take, for instance, his setting of Shakespeare's "Full Fathom Five," and compare it with that of Robert Johnson. Here is Purcell's libretto in cold print:

> Full fathom five thy father lies,
> Full fathom five thy father lies;
> Of his bones are cor—al made;
> Those are pearls that were his eyes,
> No—thing of him that doth fade,
> Full fathom five thy father lies,
> Full fathom five thy father lies,
> Of his bones are cor—al made
> Those are pearls that were his eyes,
> No—thing of him that doth fade
> But doth suffer, doth suffer a sea—change
> Into some—thing rich and strange;
> But doth suffer, doth suffer a sea—change
> Into some—thing rich and strange.
> Sea nymphs hourly ring his knell,
> Hark! now I hear them ding dong ding dong bell,
> Hark! now I hear them ding dong ding dong bell.
> Hark! now I hear them
> Hark! now I hear them,
> Hark! now I hear them
> Ding dong bell, ding ding dong bell, ding dong bell.

Dryden was a prolific dramatist, but the kind of drama he wrote did not offer the same opportunity for song as the pre-Commonwealth plays. His own theory was that songs should be used in a play only when supernatural beings or lunatics are introduced.

There are eight stage productions by Dryden for which Purcell composed the overtures and songs. "All these dusty plays," says Ernest Walker in his *History of English Music,* "with their scanty blossoms of poetry among acres of bombast, owe well-nigh all of whatever vitality they possess to the fact that Purcell wrote music for them."

Purcell wrote the music for Dryden's *Tyrannic Love* (produced in 1686), but the chief period of their collaboration seems to centre round the years 1690–2. By this time the Revolution of 1688 had forced Dryden, who had turned Catholic to engage the favour of the Stuart kings, to resign the post of poet laureate, and he was willing to adapt his muse to the melody of Purcell, though Purcell was little more than half his age (in 1691 he was sixty and Purcell was thirty-two). In the epistle dedicatory to *Amphitryon*, a play produced in 1690, Dryden writes:

What has been wanting on my part has been abundantly supplied by the Excellent Composition of Mr. Purcell; in whose Person we have at length found an Englishman equal with the best abroad. At least my Opinion of him has been such, since his happy and judicious Performances in the late Opera, and the Experiences I have had of him, in the setting of my three Songs for this Amphitryon: To all which, and particularly to the Composition of the Pastoral Dialogue, the numerous Quire of Fair Ladies gave so just an Applause on the Third Day.

In the Epistle Dedicatory to the libretto of the opera *King Arthur* (1691), Dryden goes still further:

There is nothing better, than what I intended, than the Musick; which has since arrived to a greater perfection in England, than ever formerly; especially passing through the artful hands of Mr. Purcell, who has composed it with so great a genius, that he has nothing to fear but an ignorant, ill-judging audience. But the numbers of poetry and vocal musick are sometimes so contrary, that in many places I have been obliged to cramp my Verses, and make them rugged to the Reader, that they may be harmonious to the Hearer; of which I have no reason to repent me, because these sorts of Entertainments are principally designed for the ear and the eye; and therefore, in reason, my art on this occasion ought to be subservient to his.

Purcell wrote the music for three of Dryden's plays in the following year, and Wheatley suggests that the friendship which grew up between the musician and the poet proved of practical value to the latter, for Purcell had an apartment in the clock tower of St. James's Palace, and "when Dryden was in danger of arrest for debt, he would take refuge there, where he could enjoy safety, and opportunity for exercise in the Palace Gardens."

In his dedication to the opera *The Prophetess*, Purcell says:

Musick and Poetry have ever been acknowledged sisters, which walking hand in hand support each other; as Poetry is the harmony of words, so Musick is that of notes; and as Poetry is a rise above Prose and Oratory, so is Musick the exaltation of Poetry. Both of them may excell apart, but surely they are most excellent when they are joined, because nothing is then wanting to either of their proportions; for thus they appear like wit and beauty in the same person.

The formality of English poetry in the eighteenth century, with its aping of French and Latin models in verse, was alien to a native lyrical mood. The opera was Italian, in spite of the opposition of Addison and Steele, until John Gay, with *The Beggar's Opera*, laughed it out of fashion, and then it was replaced not so much by English opera as by oratorio, the leading exponent of which was the German Handel.

Except for a few song-writers, English lyric poetry in this century was practically divorced from melody. For this, Alexander Pope, the critic who fancied himself a poet, was largely responsible. He himself was tone-deaf, and the century he dominated might almost be called the tone-deaf century, were it not for a few choice spirits like Robert Burns who save it from utter damnation.

That being so, I have decided to close this volume with the melodies associated with the cavalier poets, who sang what they wrote.

A last word.

Does it really concern us whether or not an Elizabethan or Stuart poet wrote his lyrics to dance music or psalter tunes? Personally I think it does, if only to suggest the thought that the sooner our present-day poets return to this musical tradition, the better. It is not an accident that the English lyric poets of the golden age of English literature were steeped in music, any more than it was an accident that Robert Burns should have written his lyrics always with a tune in his head. The poet who writes to a melody instinctively writes verses that come trippingly from the tongue, whereas the poet of the printed page is heavy with sibilants and successive consonants.

Burns was fortunate in choosing fine old folk-melodies to give a lilt to his verses. The sickly ballads of the Victorian Age could not inspire any but indifferent lyrics. The happiest results can only come when poets and music are good as well as friendly. But as Ezra Pound once said:

Poetry withers and dries out when it leaves music, or at least imagined music, too far behind it. Poets who are not interested in music are, or become, bad poets.

INDEX

INDEX

First Line or Title	Author	Composer, Tune, or Songbook	Page
About the sweet bag of a bee	R. Herrick	H. Lawes	171
A cooper I am		Heartsease	100
"A Geste of Robin Hood"			21
Ah! the sighs that come fro' my heart		W. Cornysshe	32
Alas, my love, ye do me wrong		Green Sleeves	53
All in a garden green		Gathering Peascods	51
Alma Redemptoris		Herman Contract	5
Although I am a country lass	M. Parker	Stingo	191
Amarantha sweet and fair	R. Lovelace	H. Lawes	182
Amidst the myrtles as I walk	R. Herrick	H. Lawes	171
And said, "Si ambulavero"	W. Langland		11
And will he not come again			107
Angelus ad Virginem			7
A poor soul sat sighing			107
Après avoir constamment attendu	T. Beza	"Huguenot Psalter"	72
Arise thou north wind from the north	G. Wither	O. Gibbons	161
As at noon Dulcina rested	W. Raleigh		147
As it fell on a holiday		John Dory	126
As it fell out on a long summer's day			127
As I walked forth		R. Johnson	125
As one without refuge		Row Well	45
As ye came from the holy land		Walsingham	47
Ask me why I send you here	R. Herrick	H. Lawes	172
Away with these self-loving lads	F. Greville	J. Dowland	97
Baloo, my babe			137
Beauty sat bathing	A. Munday	R. Jones	57
Begin with a kiss	R. Herrick	Up Tails All	174
Bid me but live	R. Herrick	H. Lawes	172
Blessed is he whose filthy stain	Sir P. Sidney	"Huguenot Psalter"	74
Blow thy horn, hunter		W. Cornysshe	30
Bonny Peg o' Ramsay		Peg o' Ramsay	105
Bring out your coney-skins	J. Fletcher	J. Wilson	122
Bring us in good ale			17
By a bank as I lay			29
By force I am fixed		Light o' Love	54
By the moon we sport and play		T. Ravenscroft	132
By the rushy fringed bank	J. Milton	H. Lawes	189
"Calen o Casture Me"			50
Care-charming Sleep	J. Fletcher	J. Wilson	125
Cast your caps and cares away	J. Fletcher	J. Wilson	124
"Chevy Chase"		Flying Fame	24
Chloris, yourself you so excel	E. Waller	H. Lawes	179

First Line or Title	Author	Composer, Tune, or Songbook	Page
"Clean Contrairy Way, The"	F. Quarles		192
"Cobbler's Catch, The"	R. Herrick	Cobbler's Jig	166
Cocklorrel must needs have the devil	Ben Jonson		147
Cold 's the wind and wet 's the rain	Dekker	Cobbler's Jig	99
Come again		J. Dowland	97
Come away, come away	Ben Jonson	A. Ferrabosco	142
Come bring with a noise	R. Herrick	Up Tails All	175
Come follow your leader, follow	Rowley	The Spanish Gipsy	128
Come kiss with me those lips of thine	G. Wither	O. Gibbons	160
Come let us sound with melody	T. Campian	T. Campian	93
Come live with me and be my love	Marlowe	W. Corkine	154
Come live with me and be my love	J. Donne	W. Corkine	154
Come, my Celia	Ben Jonson	A. Ferrabosco	142
Come sit we by the fire's side	R. Herrick	Cobbler's Jig	166
"Cooper's Song"		Heartsease	100
"Country Lass, The"	M. Parker	Stingo	191
Dare you haunt our hallow'd green		"Melismata"	79
"Doleful Lover, The"		Row well, ye mariners	45
Down-a-down	T. Lodge	F. Pilkington	89
Fain would I change that note		Tobias Hume	98
Fain would I have a pretty thing		Lusty Gallant	65
Fair, if you expect admiring	T. Campian	T. Campian	96
"Fair Margaret and Sweet William"			127
Farewell, adieu, that courtly life		Sellinger's Round	52
Farewell dear love		R. Jones	115
Farewell rewards and fairies	Bishop Corbet	Meadow Brow	152
Fight on, brave soldiers, for the cause	A. Brome	The Clean Contrary Way	192
Fine knacks for ladies		J. Dowland	98
"First Canticle, The"	G. Wither	O. Gibbons	160
Fortune my foe			49
"Frog Galliard, The"		J. Dowland	60
From Oberon in fairyland	Ben Jonson	Dulcina	148
From the fair Lavinian shore		J. Wilson	123
Full fathom five	Shakespeare	R. Johnson	119
Gather your rosebuds	R. Herrick	H. Lawes	170
"Geste of Robin Hood, A"			21
"Gipsies' Round, The"	Rowley		128
"Gipsy Song"	Rowley	The Spanish Gipsy	128
Go and catch a falling star	J. Donne		153
Go from my window, love, go			136
Go, lovely rose	E. Waller	H. Lawes	178
God prosper long our noble king		Flying Fame	24
Good morrow, 'tis Saint Valentine's day		Who list to lead a soldier's life	107
Good morrow to the day so fair	R. Herrick	Who list to lead a soldier's life	165
"Green Sleeves"		Green Sleeves	53
Have you seen but a white lily grow	Ben Jonson	A. Ferrabosco	144
"Heartsease"			46
He bare him up, he bare him down		The Three Ravens	19
Heave and ho, rumbelow			20

First Line or Title	Author	Composer, Tune, Songbook	Page
Henry our royal king		Lavolta	60
He that loves a rosy cheek	T. Carew	H. Lawes	181
Hey ho, nobody at home		"Pammelia"	134
Hey nonny no		N. Giles	130
Hey Robin, gentle Robin	T. Wyatt	W. Cornysshe	35
Hide, Absalon, thy giltë tresses clear	Chaucer	de Machault	3
His golden locks	G. Peele	J. Dowland	81
Hold thy peace		"Pammelia"	112
How can the tree	Lord Vaux		36
How should I your true love know			106
"Hunting of the Cheviot, The"			23
"Hymn for a Widower"	G. Wither	The Lamentation	163
"Hymn to God the Father, A"	J. Donne	J. Hilton	156
"Hymn to Love, An"	R. Herrick	Pepper is Black	175
I am confirmed a woman can	Sir J. Suckling	H. Lawes	185
I cannot eat but little meat		John Dory	46
I care not for these ladies	T. Campian	T. Campian	94
I come from heaven high	Wedderburn	Can ye sew cushions	39
If all the ages	Ben Jonson	A. Ferrabosco	143
If ever I marry		Turkeyloney	66
I'll get me hence	R. Herrick	Pepper is Black	175
I loathe that I did love	Earl of Surrey		36
In Nottingham there lives a jolly tanner		Hey down a down	50
In quorum manibus	Vulgate		10
In peascod time			22
In sad and ashy weeds			158
In winter when the rain rain'd cauld		Tak your auld cloak	108
I saw a sweet, seely sight	John Brackley		12
I sing the birth was born to-night	Ben Jonson	"Huguenot Psalter"	74
I tell thee, Dick	Sir J. Suckling		185
It befell at Martinmas		The Sick Tune	106
It was a lover and his lass	Shakespeare	T. Morley	112
It was a maid of my country	G. Peele	Donkin Dargason	80
I will confess	R. Herrick	Pepper is Black	64 & 175
Jack, boy, ho! boy		"Pammelia"	110
Joan's ale is new		The Jovial Tinker	150
Jog on, jog on		Hanskin	104
John Dory		John Dory	126
King Stephen was a worthy peer		Tak your auld cloak	108
"Knight and the Shepherd's Daughter, The"			127
Know this, my brethren, heav'n is clear	F. Quarles	The Clean Contrary Way	192
Lawn as white as driven snow	Shakespeare	J. Wilson	121
"Leather Bottel, The"			44
Lie near, my dear	J. Donne	Giles Farnaby	155
"Light o' Love"			54
Live, live with me and thou shalt see	R. Herrick	W. Corkine	154

First Line or Title	Author	Composer, Tune, or Songbook	Page
Look up my lords	W. Elderton	*Pepper is Black*	64
Lord, how do they increase	Sir P. Sidney	"Huguenot Psalter"	71
Love for such a cherry lip		Edmund Pearce	132
Lythe and listen, gentlemen			21
Matthew, Mark, Luke, and John			8
Move now with measured sound	T. Campian	T. Campian	61
My dear and only love	Marquis of Montrose		192
My little pretty one			37
My masters and friends and good people		*Packington's Pound*	149
Nowell, Nowell, Nowell			17
Now is the month of Maying		T. Morley	62
Now, O now, I needs must part		J. Dowland	60
Now ponder well			105
Now peace be with old Simeon		"Pammelia"	134
Now Robin, lend to me thy bow		"Pammelia"	67
Now well may we merthës make			13
Now what is Love	Sir W. Raleigh	R. Jones	115
Now would I fain some merthës make			18
O Death, rock me on sleep	Anne Boleyn		34
Of all the birds that ever I see		"Deuteromelia"	135
O mistress mine	Shakespeare		113
"Ophelia's Mad Songs" (3)			106–7
O Seigneur, que de gens	Clément Marot	"Huguenot Psalter"	71
Pastime with good company	Henry VIII	*Poor Man's Dump*	33
"Peg o' Ramsay"		*Peg o' Ramsay*	105
Phillis, why should we delay	E. Waller	H. Lawes	178
Placebo	John Skelton		26
"Psalm 3"	Sir P. Sidney	"Huguenot Psalter"	71
"Psalm 40"	Sir P. Sidney	"Huguenot Psalter"	72
Que Dieu se monstre seulement	T. Beza	"Huguenot Psalter"	73
Quoth John to Joan			80
Rejoice not without fear, my heart	G. Wither	*The Lamentation*	163
Rex gloriose Martyrum			7
Sabrina fair	J. Milton	H. Lawes	188
"St. George for England"			149
Send back my long-stray'd eyes	J. Donne		153
Shall I come, sweet love, to thee	T. Campian	T. Campian	95
Shall I go walk the woods so wild			30
Shall I wasting in despair	G. Wither	*The Young Man's Opinion*	157
"Sick Tune, The"			106
She makes good cheer	Ben Jonson	*Saraband*	64
Sigh no more, ladies	Shakespeare	T. Ford	117
Since first I saw your face		T. Ford	116
Sing care away, with sport and play		*Heartsease*	46
Sing we and chant it		T. Morley	86

First Line or Title	Author	Composer, Tune, or Songbook	Page
Sing we now merrily		"Pammelia"	133
"Sir Hugh"		Who list to lead a soldier's life	6
"Sixth Canticle, The"	G. Wither	O. Gibbons	161
Sleep, baby, sleep	G. Wither	Old 112th	163
So, so leave off	J. Donne	A. Ferrabosco	156
"Song of Angels, The"	G. Wither	O. Gibbons	161
"Spanish Lady, The"	T. Deloney		48
Still to be neat	Ben Jonson		131
Sweet, stay awhile		J. Dowland	155
Take, O take those lips away	J. Fletcher	J. Wilson	123
Tell, me, dearest, what is love	J. Fletcher		137
The hunt is up	Gray		31
"The Leather Bottle"			44
The little pretty nightingale			32
Then Robin Hood took them both		Hey down a down	50
The Percy out of Northumberland			23
The rain rins doun through Merry Lincoln			6
There is a garden in her face	T. Campian	T. Campian	92
There is a lady sweet and kind		T. Ford	116
There is no rose of such virtue			14
There was a jovial tinker		Joan's ale is new	150
There was a shepherd's daughter			127
There were three ravens			19
The sweet pretty Jinny		Paddy Whack	104
This ender night			15
Though I am young and cannot tell	Ben Jonson	Nicholas Laniere	146
Three merry men			79
Thrice toss these oaken ashes	T. Campian	T. Campian	95
Thus Angels sang	G. Wither	O. Gibbons	161
'Tis true 'tis day	J. Donne	J. Dowland	155
"To a Lady Singing"	E. Waller	H. Lawes	180
"To Althea, from Prison"	R. Lovelace	J. Wilson	183
"To Chloris"	E. Waller	H. Lawes	179
To couple is a custom		Newcastle	83
"To Phillis"	E. Waller	H. Lawes	178
Toss the pot		"Melismata"	111
Trip and go			55
Trip it, gipsies, trip it fine	Rowley	Gipsies' Round	128
Triumph now with joy and mirth	T. Campian	T. Giles	62
Troll, troll, troll the bowl		"Pammelia"	109
"Tune of Packington's Pound"			150
Two friends that had a shock of corn	A. Munday	Spanish Pavan	58
Under the greenwood tree	Shakespeare		56
"Urchins' Dance, The"		T. Ravenscroft	132
We be three poor mariners		Branle of Poictu	56
Welcome be ye when ye go			21
Western wind, when wilt thou blow			33
What Booker can prognosticate	M. Parker		191

First Line or Title	Author	Composer, Tune, or Songbook	Page
What if my mistress now		T. Morley	113
What shall he have that killed the deer	Shakespeare	J. Hilton	111
What tidings bringest thou, messenger			16
When as I view your comely face		Calen o Casture Me	50
When Love, with unconfinèd wings	R. Lovelace	J. Wilson	183
When Samson was a tall young man		Spanish Pavan	58
When I survey the world around		The Leather Bottel	44
When the King enjoys his own again	M. Parker		191
When thou must home	T. Campian	T. Campian	92
When we did sit in Babylon		"Day's Psalter"	41
Where the bee sucks	Shakespeare	R. Johnson	120
While I listen to your voice	E. Waller	H. Lawes	180
While long I did with patient constancy	Sidney	"Huguenot Psalter"	72
"White Paternoster, The"			8
White though ye be, yet, Lilies, know	R. Herrick	N. Laniere	167
Who hath his fancy pleased	Sir P. Sidney	Wilhelmus van Nassauen	70
Who is at my window? Who, who?	J. Wedderburn		136
Whoop! Do me no harm!		Paddy Whack	104
Why live I muddling here	G. Wither	In sad and ashy weeds	158
Why should I not love my love		Newcastle	83
Why should we boast of Arthur and his knights			149
Why shouldst thou swear I am forsworn	R. Lovelace	N. Laniere	183
Why so pale and wan, fond lover?	J. Suckling		186
"Willow Song"			107
Will you hear a Spanish lady?	T. Deloney	Spanish Lady	48
Willy, prithee go to bed		Trenchmore	43
Wilt thou forgive the sins where I began	J. Donne	J. Hilton	156
Wilt thou, unkind, thus reave me?		J. Dowland	135
"Woods so Wild, The"			30
Ye noble minds and famous martial wights		Fortune My Foe	49
Yonder comes a courteous knight			54